Selective Serotonin Re-uptake Inhibitors

The Clinical Use of Citalopram, Fluoxetine, Fluvoxamine, Paroxetine, and Sertraline

J.P. Feighner and **W.F. Boyer**

D1647724

JOHN WILEY & SONS

Chichester · New York · Brisbane · Toronto · Singapore

Other Wiley Editorial Offices

John Wiley & Sons, Inc., 605 Third Avenue,
New York, NY 10158-0012, USA

Jacaranda Wiley Ltd, G.P.O. Box 859, Brisbane,
Queensland 4001, Australia

John Wiley & Sons (Canada) Ltd, 22 Worcester Road,
Rexdale, Ontario M9W 1L1, Canada

John Wiley & Sons (SEA) Pte Ltd, 37 Jalan Pemimpin 05-04,
Block B, Union Industrial Building, Singapore 2057

Library of Congress Cataloging-in-Publication Data
Feighner, John Preston. 1937–
    Selective serotonin re-uptake inhibitors / J.P. Feighner and W.F.-Boyer.
        p. cm.—(Perspectives in psychiatry : v. 1)
    Includes bibliographical references and index.
    ISBN 0-471-92890-9
    1. Antidepressants.   2. Serotonin—Agonists.   3. Serotoninergic
mechanisms.   I. Boyer, W. F.   II. Title.   III. Series: Perspectives in
psychiatry (Chichester, England) : v. 1.
    [DNLM: 1. Depression—drug therapy.   2. Depressive Disorders—drug
therapy.   3. Serotonin Antagonists—therapeutic use.   QV 126 F297s]
RM332.F45 1991
616.85'27061—dc20
DNLM/DLC
for Library of Congress   90-13134
                                                                      CIP

British Library Cataloguing in Publication Data
Selective serotonin re-uptake inhibitors.
    1. Man. Mental disorders. Drug therapy
    I. Feighner, J.P.   II. Boyer, W.F.   III. Series
    616.8918

    ISBN 0 471 92890 9

Typeset by P&P Photosetting, London
Printed and bound in Great Britain by
Biddles Ltd, Guildford and King's Lynn

Foreword

'Perspectives in Psychiatry' is an important new book series which will bring together the latest results in CNS research with clinical experience and expertise from around the world. Successive volumes will benefit practising psychiatrists and their patients by transferring as rapidly as possible advances made in worldwide academia to the wider medical community

Selective Serotonin Re-uptake Inhibitors: The Clinical Use of Citalopram, Fluoxetine, Fluvoxamine, Paroxetine, and Sertraline is the first book in the 'Perspectives in Psychiatry' series.

The aim of this book is to provide clinicians worldwide with an authoritative and common knowledge base on this exciting group of compounds, and also to provide the most comprehensive reference source on the selective serotonin re-uptake inhibitors.

We would like to thank Dr Stuart Montgomery for reading the text and for his many constructive comments. We would also like to thank Franklin Scientific Projects for co-ordinating the production of this book.

In appreciation of all my patients and their families who continue to teach me a great deal about psychiatric disorders

J.P. Feighner

To Kathy and the boys

W.F. Boyer

Contents

List of authors

W.F. Boyer — *Feighner Research Institute, San Diego, California, USA*

J.P. Feighner — *President and Director of Research, Feighner Research Institute, San Diego, California, USA*

A.M. Johnson — *Assistant Director, Technical Licensing Department, SmithKline Beecham Pharmaceuticals, The Frythe, Welwyn Garden City, Hertfordshire, UK*

C.A. Marsden — *Professor of Neuropharmacology, Department of Physiology and Pharmacology, Medical School, Queen's Medical Centre, The University of Nottingham, Nottingham, UK*

G.A. McFadden — *Founder and Medical Director, Anxiety and Depression Center, LaJolla, California, USA*
Director, Panic and Anxiety Research, Feighner Research Institute, San Diego, California, USA

Preface

Over the past ten years, we have had the opportunity to work with citalopram, fluoxetine, fluvoxamine, paroxetine, sertraline, and other selective serotonin re-uptake inhibitors. We are convinced that these drugs represent a significant addition in psychiatry because of their relative lack of side-effects, low toxicity in overdose, and broad range of potential clinical indications. Indeed, their widespread and increasing use in the United States and other countries underlines this importance. We therefore undertook the writing of this book to create a document that reflects the state of the art in terms of the clinical issues surrounding these medications.

The first chapter of the book reviews the evidence that points to the effects of these drugs on serotonergic function and the central role of serotonin in many psychiatric disorders, while the following chapter reviews the pharmacology of the selective serotonin re-uptake inhibitors. The remaining chapters contain reviews of clinical trials of the selective serotonin re-uptake inhibitors in many of the conditions previously mentioned, concluding with a chapter on important clinical issues in the use of these agents.

We have aimed this book at all those who take care of depressed patients, but especially at residents and clinicians in psychiatry and general medicine. Clinicians are confronted daily with human suffering and require knowledge of what is both safe and effective for their patients. This is a different stance from that of the pure scientist, who accepts nothing as fact until replicated experimental evidence is available. Hence the purpose of this book is to review the available evidence from a clinical standpoint. We have offered conclusions based on considerable data and conjectures based on more limited evidence and have tried to indicate which is which. We have made use of our own experience, controlled studies, case series, and case reports, as well as studies from the animal literature. We have also included an extensive bibliography to allow the reader to delve into subjects at greater depth. It is our sincere hope that the reader will find this book not only an introduction to an important and rapidly growing area but also a useful reference work.

John P. Feighner, M.D.

W. Boyer, M.D.

J.P. Feighner

W.F. Boyer

1

The neuropharmacology of serotonin in the central nervous system

C.A. Marsden

Introduction

Serotonin (5-hydroxytryptamine, 5-HT) is an indoleamine with a wide distribution in plants, animals, and man. In mammals it is found in blood platelets, mast cells, and the enterochromaffin cells of the gut. The peripheral actions of serotonin include vasoconstriction (and some vasodilatation) together with a role in the control of gut tone and motility due to smooth muscle contraction. Platelet serotonin has an important role in platelet aggregation involving 5-HT_2 receptor activation. Within the brain and spinal cord serotonin acts as an important neurotransmitter involved in a variety of physiological and behavioural functions ranging from the control of sleep and wakefulness, feeding, thermoregulation, cardiovascular function, emesis, sexual behaviour, spinal regulation of motor function, emotional and psychotic behaviour, and drug-induced hallucinatory states.

Our knowledge of the basic plan of the serotonin-containing pathways in the central nervous system (CNS) dates from the pioneering work of the Swedish school of histochemists established by Falck and Hillarp (Falck *et al*, 1962) who used the fluorescence histochemical method to visualize catechol and indoleamines *in situ* in the brain. These studies showed that serotonin was localized within specific neuronal pathways, the cell bodies being found in discrete brain nuclei — the midbrain and brain stem raphe nuclei (Dahlström and Fuxe, 1964). During the following 15-20 years, information about the role of serotonin pathways in the control of physiological and behavioural functions has expanded, largely based on a growing understanding of the control of serotonin metabolism in nerve endings and on the development of drugs that interfered with this process. One of the major events in this process was the development of compounds that prevented the enzymatic inactivation, or the re-uptake of serotonin released from nerve endings and the finding that such drugs possessed antidepressant effects.

It was not until the late 1970s and the early 1980s that the great explosion occurred in our understanding of the receptor systems involved in serotonergic function. It is now clear that there is not a single 5-HT receptor, but a family of receptors subserving specific functions at pre- and postsynaptic sites. The identification of these receptor subtypes and the development of relatively selective agonists and antagonists has and will continue to increase our understanding of the functional role of serotonin and our awareness of the large clinical potential of drugs that alter serotonergic function.

The aim of the present article is to provide a general overview of the current state of knowledge of the neuroanatomy, neurochemistry, and neuropharmacology of the serotonergic neurones in the CNS.

Serotonergic pathways in the CNS

Early studies demonstrated that serotonin was found in substantial amounts in cat and dog brain with regional variations occurring in the levels (Twarog and Page, 1953; Amin *et al*, 1954): the limbic regions showed especially high serotonin levels, indicating an involvement in emotional behaviour. It was the systematic studies of the Swedish group, using fluorescence histochemistry, that led to the detailed mapping of the serotonin-containing neurones in the raphe nuclei and their forebrain and spinal projections (Dahlström and Fuxe, 1964; Fuxe 1965; Fuxe *et al*, 1968). Later, Steinbusch and colleagues in Holland developed an antibody to serotonin and refined the earlier maps of the serotonergic pathways in the rat brain using immunohistochemistry (Steinbusch *et al*, 1978; Steinbusch, 1981). More recently, further immunocytochemical studies have revealed a structural heterogeneity in the axon terminals that arise from the dorsal and median raphe (Kosofsky and Molliver, 1987). Such morphological diversity, linked with the receptor diversity described later, may be important in understanding the role of serotonin in the control of emotional behaviour.

Serotonin pathways to the forebrain
Numerous studies have shown that the serotonergic projections to the forebrain arise from cell bodies within the raphe nuclei of the rostral brainstem: principally the dorsal and median raphe nuclei (Figure 1). The projections of these two nuclei do not fully overlap with a relatively specific innervation of some forebrain areas by one of the nuclei. While the projections to the hippocampus come mainly from the median raphe those to the striatum are from the dorsal raphe, but both nuclei send serotonergic projections to the cortex. Thus, the rostral part of the dorsal raphe projects to the striatum and cortex while the caudal portion, along with neurones in the median raphe, projects to the hippocampus (Jacobs *et al*, 1974). Furthermore, the cortical pathways from the different parts of the dorsal raphe may use separate routes (Tohyama *et al*, 1980). Hence the innervation of the forebrain by serotonergic fibres is widespread (cortex, hippocampus,

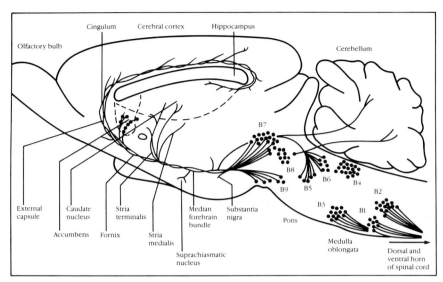

Figure 1. Schematic diagram illustrating the distribution of the main serotonin-containing pathways in the rat central nervous system. B4-B9 = midbrain raphe nuclei 5-HT neuronal cell bodies; B1-B3 = brain stem raphe 5-HT neuronal cell bodies. (Adapted from Cooper *et al*, 1982.)

striatum, amygdala, accumbens, substantia nigra, hypothalamus) and arises from neurones within two discrete raphe nuclei. However, within the various brain regions, the serotonergic innervation is organized so that identifiable cell groups within the two raphe nuclei send projections to multiple, but functionally related, cortical regions.

Further diversification occurs at the level of axons and their terminals, with regional specialization in the pattern of the cortical serotonergic innervation. There are differences within the various cortical areas in the morphology, density, and orientation of the serotonin terminals (Molliver, 1987). Their density is very high in the frontal cortex and decreases in more caudal areas, while in the cingulate cortex, outer areas of the parietal cortex, and the hippocampus there is a clear laminated arrangement of coarse beaded fibres. In other areas of the cortex the fibres are very fine.

Interestingly, this morphological heterogeneity of the fibres appears to be linked to their origins in the two raphe nuclei, the coarse beaded fibres being derived from serotonergic neurones in the median raphe and the fine fibres from the dorsal raphe (Kosofsky and Molliver, 1987).

The morphological diversity of the serotonergic innervation of the cortical and hippocampal (limbic) regions raises several intriguing questions:

1. Do the two types of fibres have different sensitivities to drugs that modify serotonin function?

2. Are the different fibre types associated with specific behaviours?

3. Are there mechanisms (receptors?) that allow selective activation or inhibition of specific serotonergic cell groups within the two raphe nuclei and thus allow differential control of the serotonergic innervation of the areas of the cortex?

Answers to such questions will undoubtedly help us to understand how a neurotransmitter that provides such diffuse innervation from two discrete cell body locations (dorsal and median raphe) is involved in a wide range of physiological and behavioural functions. More specifically, they may help to determine whether affective disorders involve a generalized change or constitute a localized disorder of serotonergic function.

Serotonergic innervation of the spinal cord
Both the dorsal and ventral horns and the intermediolateral column of the spinal cord receive a serotonergic innervation from cell bodies located within the raphe nuclei of the caudal brain stem (raphe magnus, pallidus, and obscurus, Figure 1). The innervation of the dorsal horn comes mainly from neurones situated in the raphe magnus and is principally concerned with modulation of sensory (pain) information. In contrast, the ventral horn innervation comes from serotonergic cells in the raphe pallidus and obscurus and plays an important role in the regulation of motor function, while the serotonergic fibres in the intermediolateral column come from the same raphe nuclei and are involved in the regulation of sympathetic activity.

An important feature of the spinal serotonergic system is the co-existence of various neuropeptides with serotonin. Specific examples of this are the co-existence of substance P, thyrotrophin-releasing hormone, a proctolin-like peptide, and galanin with serotonin in the neurones projecting to the ventral horn (Johanssen *et al*, 1981; Gilbert *et al*, 1982). The relationship between the indoleamine and the peptides is not simple. Firstly, not all the peptides are found in all serotonergic neurones: some contain only serotonin, while others contain serotonin plus one or more of the peptides (Hökfelt *et al*, 1989). Secondly, some peptides (e.g. substance P, thyrotrophin-releasing hormone) enhance the 5-HT$_2$ postsynaptic receptor-mediated responses (e.g. back muscle contractions, Fone *et al*, 1989), while proctolin has inhibitory effects on the same responses. In some cases, the peptide interaction may be via direct modulation of serotonergic receptor function at the postsynaptic level, while in others the peptide may act at a presynaptic site to modulate the release of serotonin. An improved understanding of these mechanisms will increase our knowledge of the control of spinal motor function and aid the treatment of motor disorders (e.g. amylolateral sclerosis).

It should be borne in mind that drugs that act on serotonergic systems, such as serotonin re-uptake inhibitors, will potentiate 5-HT receptor-mediated events in the spinal cord as well as in the brain; thus spinal effects may have a role in the clinical profile of these drugs. For example, re-uptake inhibitors are known to alter reproductive activity in female animals (Everitt, 1977), and such effects may involve a spinal serotonergic motor component. A final point for consideration with regard to spinal serotonergic innervation is the need carefully to assign the correct serotonergic system (forebrain or spinal) to the behavioural effects observed with serotonergic drugs. Thus, many components of the classical serotonin syndrome (e.g. hindlimb abduction and forepaw treading) that are produced by systemic administration of serotonin agonists (Green and Heal, 1985; Glennon and Lucki, 1988) also occur when the drugs are given intrathecally — i.e. directly into the lumbar region of the spinal cord, indicating that they are mediated by 5-HT receptors in the spinal cord and not in the brain (Fone *et al*, 1989).

Synthesis and metabolism of serotonin in the CNS

The levels of serotonin in the CNS only represent about 1-2% of the total amount found in the body (Bradley, 1989). The indoleamine cannot cross the blood-brain barrier, and hence all the neuronal serotonin in the CNS is synthesized locally. Serotonin is formed by a two-step process involving the hydroxylation of the essential amino acid L-tryptophan to 5-hydroxytryptophan (5-HTP), which is then decarboxylated to serotonin (Figure 2).

L-tryptophan crosses the blood-brain and neuronal barriers using a competitive, facilitated transported carrier for neutral amino acids. Tryptophan is hydroxylated by tryptophan hydroxylase; this is the rate-limiting step in the synthesis of serotonin and as under normal physiological conditions the enzyme is not saturated, situations that lead to an increase in brain tryptophan will enhance the synthesis of serotonin. Thus, increased dietary tryptophan and oral tryptophan stimulate synthesis and, on this basis, L-tryptophan preparations have been used in the treatment of depression. There is, however, still debate as to whether the increase in synthesis results in increased release; a controversy supported by the equivocal results obtained with L-tryptophan in depressed patients, although it has been established that tryptophan potentiates the antidepressant effects of monoamine oxidase inhibitors (Coppen and Swade, 1988). There are also several studies illustrating the successful use of L-tryptophan challenges to investigate neuroendocrine function (prolactin release) in normal and depressed patients (Siever *et al*, 1986; Cowen *et al*, 1988; Goodwin *et al*, 1987; Deakin *et al*, 1990). Various other factors have been shown to influence the availability of tryptophan to the CNS, including the state of the liver with respect to tryptophan metabolism (hepatic encephalopathy is characterized by very high levels of tryptophan in the brain) and the degree of plasma protein binding.

Serotonin is synthesized in both the nucleus and the terminals, though the latter site is probably more important in the short-term regulation of serotonin synthesis. Serotonin formed in the nucleus is transported to the terminals of the dendrites and axon, release taking place by a Ca^{++}-dependent process from the readily releasable pool of serotonin stored in vesicles. Within the vesicles, serotonin is protected from metabolism by mitochondrial monoamine oxidase

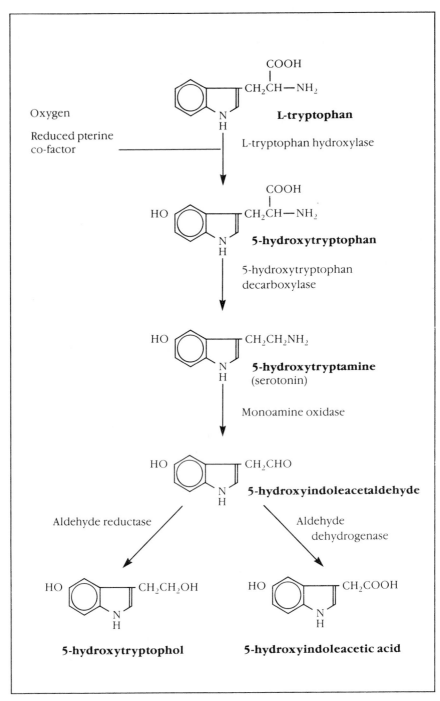

Figure 2. Production and metabolism of serotonin.

(MAO). There is evidence that newly synthesized serotonin is preferentially released (Kuhn *et al*, 1986), but it is not clear whether release takes place exclusively from the vesicles: there may be two pools of serotonin in the terminals, cytoplasmic and vesicular, which release serotonin under different physiological conditions (Grahame-Smith, 1974; Elks *et al*, 1979).

Following its release, serotonin is inactivated principally by re-uptake into serotonergic nerve terminals using a Na^+/K^+ ATPase-dependent carrier (Shaskan and Snyder, 1970). Once back inside the serotonergic neurone the transmitter is then either re-stored in the vesicles (Slotkin *et al*, 1978) or metabolized by MAO, an enzyme that is widely distributed throughout the body and is primarily located within the brain on the outer mitochondrial membrane. Not only does MAO metabolize serotonin, it also deaminates amines with the general formula R-CH_2-NH_2, where R is a substituted aryl or alkyl group. The amines that fall into this category include serotonin, dopamine, noradrenaline, adrenaline, tyramine, and tryptamine. It is now evident that there are two forms of MAO: A and B — the preferred substrates for A being noradrenaline and serotonin, while tyramine, tryptamine, and dopamine are the preferred substrates for type B although they can also be deaminated by type A. This recognition of the A and B isoenzymes has led to the development of MAO inhibitors with selectivity for either of the isoenzymes.

Sites of drug action

Within this scheme of the synthesis and metabolism of serotonin there are several steps at which drugs can either increase or decrease the neuronal function of serotonin (Figure 3, Fuller, 1985):

Changes in the availability of tryptophan due to tryptophan administration or a low-tryptophan diet will increase or decrease, respectively, the metabolism of serotonin although this will not necessarily alter the release of serotonin from the brain neurones.

Decreased synthesis of serotonin has been seen following the inhibition of tryptophan hydroxylase by parachlorophenylalanine. As tryptophan hydroxylase is the rate-limiting step in the production of serotonin, inhibition of this enzyme leads to a profound decrease in the levels of serotonin in the brain. There are other compounds that decrease tryptophan hydroxylase activity, including various tryptophan analogues (e.g. 6-fluorotryptophan) and halogenated analogues of amphetamine (e.g. p-chloroamphetamine and fenfluramine). The full mechanism of action of the latter group of compounds on serotonergic neurones is not fully understood but involves several actions apart from inhibition of tryptophan hydroxylase (Fuller, 1985), including non-Ca^{++}-dependent release of serotonin (see below), re-uptake inhibition, and a possible neurotoxic action on selected serotonergic neurones. Inhibitors of tryptophan hydroxylase have had considerable impact on experimental work to investigate the function of serotonin, but have no clinical value.

Inhibition of 5-HTP decarboxylase has little effect on serotonin levels as this

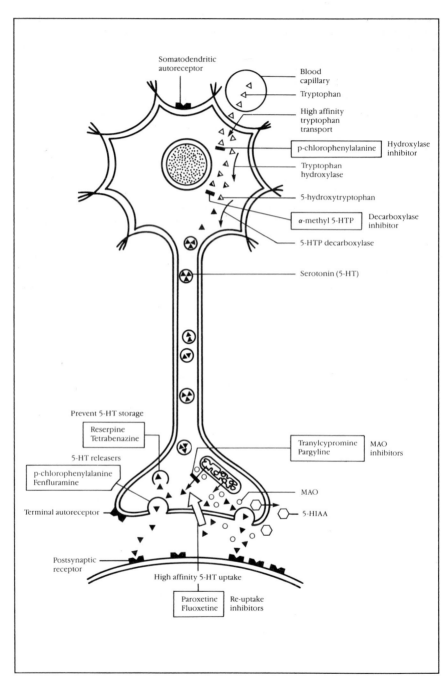

Figure 3. Diagram of a serotonin neurone showing the main steps in the life cycle of serotonin and the sites at which drugs act. For clarity, drugs acting at 5-HT receptors have been omitted (see Figure 4 for details of these). (Adapted from Cooper *et al*, 1982.)

enzyme is normally saturated. Furthermore, this enzyme also decarboxylates DOPA so that inhibitors will influence the synthesis of both serotonin and dopamine. The basal levels of 5-HTP (and DOPA) are normally too low to be measured by existing methodology. However, decarboxylase inhibition leads to a rapid accumulation of these precursors, and this can be used as an index of the rate of serotonin synthesis.

Reserpine — which produces long-term depletion of serotonin (and catecholamines) and tetrabenazine — which causes short-term depletion of serotonin, prevent the intraneuronal storage of serotonin. By preventing storage, these drugs expose newly synthesized serotonin to MAO, leading to amine depletion and increased tissue levels of the metabolites (5-HIAA in the case of serotonin). The behavioural effects of amine depletion by reserpine constituted a landmark in the early understanding of the possible involvement of serotonin and noradrenaline in depression, but the universal effect of the drug on intraneuronal amine storage systems and the consequent general depletion of all amines limit the use of reserpine in studies that specifically investigate the function of serotonin.

Drugs that increase serotonin release (p-chloroamphetamine, fenfluramine) act by causing Ca^{++} -independent release and have relatively specific effects because they enter serotonergic nerve terminals using the selective uptake system. A long established *in vivo* test for novel uptake inhibitors has been their ability to prevent the effects of serotonin released by p-chloroamphetamine. Both p-chloroamphetamine and fenfluramine increase serotonin release *in vitro* (Garattini *et al*, 1975) and *in vivo* (Marsden *et al*, 1979; Crespi *et al*, 1990), resulting acutely in behaviours induced by stimulation of the serotonin receptor (Trulson and Jacobs, 1976). The usefulness of these drugs for the investigation of serotonergic function has been limited by their long-term effects on tryptophan hydroxylase and by possible neurotoxicity towards serotonergic neurones, resulting in decreased neuronal serotonin.

The monoamine oxidase inhibitors such as tranylcypromine, parygline and, more recently the selective MAO A (clorgyline) and MAO B (selegiline) inhibitors, reduce serotonin metabolism. These drugs will principally increase intraneuronal cytoplasmic serotonin as it will not be metabolized following re-uptake from the synaptic cleft. This results in an increase in the amount of serotonin available for release, and consequently in an increase in extracellular serotonin and a decrease in 5-HIAA *in vivo* (Sleight *et al*, 1988a; Crespi *et al*, 1990).

The antidepressant properties of the non-selective (i.e. A and B) and the A, but not the, B, selective MAO inhibitors (for review see Murphy *et al*, 1986) have played an important role in the development of the amine theory of depression. The potential advantage of the selective MAO B inhibitors as antidepressants was that they would have the clinical effects of the non-selective inhibitors without the adverse effects caused by the inhibition of tyramine metabolism, as this amine is metabolized by MAO A.

Drugs that inhibit the neuronal re-uptake of serotonin range from compounds that inhibit both noradrenaline and serotonin re-uptake (amitriptyline, imipramine) to those that are selective for either noradrenaline (maprotiline) or serotonin (paroxetine, fluoxetine) re-uptake. Recent studies have shown that, after acute administration, these drugs increase the extracellular levels of either noradrenaline or serotonin or one of the amines in the rat *in vivo* depending on the selectivity of the drug under investigation. Over many years these drugs have been conspicuously the most successful antidepressants, although possessing certain disadvantages in the case of the non-selective tricyclics (notably antimuscarinic side-effects) and the common problem of a slow onset of antidepressant action (two to three weeks). The delay in onset of action provides a challenge to supporters of the amine theory in terms of explaining why the delay occurs when inhibition of re-uptake is immediate. This has led to the concept that adaptive changes are involved in the clinical effects of the re-uptake and MAO inhibitors as well as those of lithium. Thus the most relevant experimental work involves chronic treatment with antidepressants, combined with a detailed investigation of the functional status of serotonergic neurones. In recent years, this work has made considerable advances due to the marked increase in our understanding of the 5-HT receptor and, in particular, the emergence of a variety of 5-HT receptor subtypes and increased knowledge about their specific functional roles (see below).

In 1979, Raisman *et al* demonstrated that the tritiated form of the tricyclic antidepressant, imipramine, bound to a specific high-affinity site which has subsequently been shown to be a modulatory site on the serotonin uptake system located on serotonergic nerve terminals and platelets (Briley, 1985). This site is decreased in platelets obtained from patients with affective disorders and hence may act as a biological marker in depression (Raisman *et al*, 1982), although it is not clear whether successful treatment of the disorder results in a reversal of the deficit in the binding sites (i.e state dependent) (Briley, 1985; Langer *et al*, 1986). More recently, [^{3}H]-paroxetine has also been shown to bind to cortical membranes at a site similar, but not necessarily identical, to the imipramine site — again with properties similar to a pharmacological receptor. A central question with these studies is the identity of the endogenous ligand at this modulatory site on the serotonergic uptake system; evidence suggests that it may have a structure similar to methoxytryptoline, but the precise identity needs to be determined (Langer *et al*, 1984).

Serotonin receptors

As already mentioned, there has been a rapid increase in our understanding of the receptors associated with serotonergic function in the periphery and in central neurones. It is now well established that there are multiple 5-HT receptors (Bradley *et al*, 1986): currently the number is about nine and there has been a consequent development of numerous compounds with relative specificity for one or more of those receptor subtypes. The initial classification of 5-HT receptors was based on ligand binding studies, any functional identification being based largely on investigations using peripheral preparations (Bradley *et al*, 1986).

The question of physiological function in the brain is generally the least understood because of the lack of appropriate methodology with which to overcome the problems of studying CNS mechanisms. Despite these limitations, there is now substantial information to indicate the possible role of specific 5-HT receptors in the regulation of serotonergic function in the brain (Marsden *et al*, 1989). The present discussion will concentrate on the functional role of the 5-HT receptor subtypes and on their possible involvement in the antidepressant action of inhibitors of serotonin re-uptake (e.g. paroxetine).

The existing classification of 5-HT receptors and their subtypes is shown in Figure 4, together with the main examples of drugs that act as agonists, partial agonists, or antagonists at these subtypes. It should be noted that very few drugs are really selective for one subtype receptor. The exceptions are few and include 8-OH-DPAT, an agonist at the 5-HT_{1A} receptor, and some of the 5-HT_{1A} partial agonists, ketanserin as an antagonist of 5-HT_2 receptors, some of the 5-HT_3 antagonists (e.g. ondansetron). However, while ketanserin shows high selectivity for 5-HT_2 receptors, it also has high affinity for α_1-adrenoceptors. This lack of absolute selectivity for a specific receptor complicates investigations using these novel compounds to determine the functional role of the receptor subtypes but three approaches have been used:

Identification of the effector systems that link the receptor subtype with a physiological response such as release of Ca^{++}
The effector systems are either biochemical (coupled to adenylate cyclase or phosphoinositide hydrolysis) or involve direct linkage to a cation membrane channel (K^+) (Figure 5, Conn and Sanders-Bush, 1987).

Adenylate cyclase 5-HT receptors are either negatively or positively coupled to adenylate cyclase. It is important, when trying to understand the physiological relevance of the 5-HT receptor-linked changes in adenylate cyclase or phosphoinositide hydrolysis, also to understand how information is transduced from the membrane recognition site (the receptor) through the receptor-coupled mechanisms. The receptors are coupled to the biochemical effector system by one of several G protein systems. The effector system influences the physiology of the neurone (or other cell type) by altering ion conductance across membranes, either directly or by producing second messengers inside the cell (cyclic AMP from ATP or inositol phosphates and diacylglycerol from polyphosphoinositides). These second messengers can then mobilize intracellular Ca^{++} or activate protein kinases (Berridge, 1984).

The cyclic AMP/adenylate cyclase-linked receptors work through the protein kinases, which lead to the phosphorylation of phosphoproteins inside the cells, which in turn regulate various aspects of cell function (including carbohydrate metabolism, neurotransmitter release, and ion conductance) (Nestler and Greengard, 1983). Thus activation or inhibition of adenylate cyclase and the subsequent change in the conversion of ATP to cyclic AMP can have a variety of effects on cellular function but, in the case of neuronal 5-HT receptors, the most important are the effects on cation conductance and neurotransmitter release.

One further complication should be considered when assessing the importance of observed changes in the accumulation of cyclic AMP (the normal way of measuring changes in adenylate cyclase activity). There are examples of receptors that activate more than one type of effector pathway; hence, although one might establish that a particular 5-HT receptor subtype is linked to adenylate cyclase, the same receptor may also be linked to another effector system through a different G protein. With these points in mind, one can consider the relevance of the linkage of 5-HT receptor subtypes to adenylate cyclase (Figure 4).

All the existing 5-HT_1 subtypes, with the exception of 5-HT_{1C}, are negatively linked to adenylate cyclase. This effect is difficult to show experimentally as the reduction is small (20-30%), and the most effective studies have investigated the inhibition by 5-HT_1 agonists of the forskolin-induced increase in adenylate cyclase in cultured (Bockaert *et al*, 1987) and homogenate hippocampal preparations (De Vivo and Maayani, 1986). The pharmacological data indicate that such inhibition is associated with 5-HT_{1A} receptor activation (De Vivo and Maayani 1988; Sleight *et al*, 1988b). Similar studies have shown that the 5-HT_{1D} receptor in the substantia nigra of the guinea pig is also negatively linked to adenylate cyclase (Waeber *et al*, 1989) as is the 5-HT_{1B} receptor in cultures of hamster fibroblasts (Sevwen *et al*, 1988).

Although there are no published accounts that 5-HT_1 receptors are positively linked to adenylate cyclase in whole cells, there are several reports of such a linkage in membrane preparations of mouse primary cell cultures with a pharmacology similar to that of the 5-HT_{1A} receptor (for review see De Vivo and Maayani, 1988).

In summary, there is evidence that 5HT_{1A} and 5HT_{1B} receptors are negatively linked to adenylate cyclase, probably leading to increased K^+ conductance, thereby decreasing the entry of Ca^{++}. Whether 5-HT_{1A} receptors are positively linked to adenylate cyclase in neuronal preparations remains to be determined.

More recently, it has been demonstrated that another 5-HT receptor not

Figure 4. (opposite) Drugs and central 5-HT receptors. Abbreviations: 8-OH-DPAT=(±)-2-dipropylamino-8-hydroxy-1,2,3,4,-tetrahydronaphthylene; RU-24969 = 5-methoxy-3-(1,2,3,6-tetrahydropyridin-4-yl)-1H indol; TFMPP = 1-(m-trifluoromethylphenyl) piperazine; mCPP = 1-(3-chlorophenyl) piperazine; DOI = ±-1-(2,5-dimethoxy-1-iodophenyl)-2-aminopropane; DOM = 2,5-dimethoxy-*α*-4-dimethylbenzene ethamine; NAN 190 = 1-(2-methoxyphenyl)-4-[4-(2-phthalimido)entyl] piperazine; MDL 73005 EP = 8-2[2,3-dihydro-1,4-benzodioxin-2-yl] methylaminoethyl]-8-azaspiro[4,5] decan-7,9-dione; BMY 7378 = (8-[2-[4-(2-methoxyphenyl)-1-piperazinyl]ethyl]-8-azaspiro [4,5]-decane-7,9,-dione; ICI 169369 = (2-(2-dimethylamino-ethylthio-3-phenylquinoline; ICS205-930 = (3d-tropanyl)-1H-indole-3-carboxylic acid ester; BRL 46470 = ndo-N-(8-methyl-8-azabicyclo[3.2.1]xt-3-yl)2,3-dihydro-3,3,-dimethyl-indole-1-carbǔxamide; 2-methyl 5-HT= 3-(2-aminoethyl)-2-methyl-1-1H-indo-5-ol; 5-CT= 5-carboxamidotryptamine; LSD = (+) lysergic acid diethylamide; MDL 72222 = 1dH, 3d, 5d H tropan-3-yl)3,5-dichlorobenzoate. (Review references: Leysen, 1985; Fozard, 1987; Glennon, 1987; Lyon and Titeler, 1988; Fraser *et al*, 1990.)

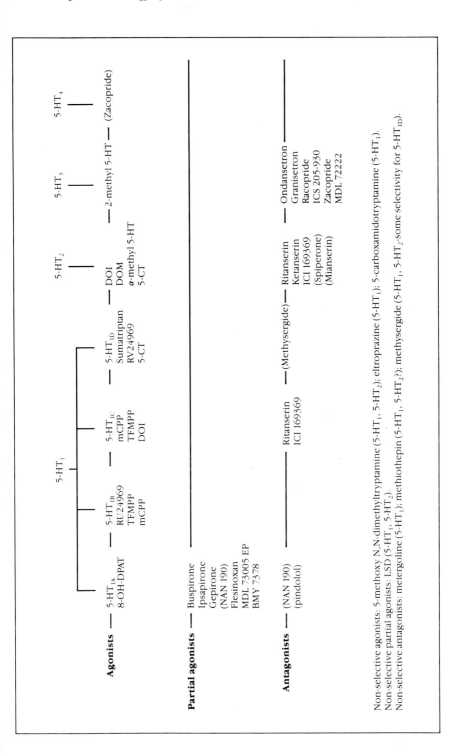

Non-selective agonists: 5-methoxy N,N-dimethyltryptamine (5-HT₁, 5-HT₂); eltroprazine (5-HT₁); 5-carboxamidotryptamine (5-HT₁).
Non-selective partial agonists: LSD (5-HT₁, 5-HT₂).
Non-selective antagonists: metergoline (5-HT₁); methiothepin (5-HT₁, 5-HT₂); methysergide (5-HT₁, 5-HT₂-some selectivity for 5-HT₁ᴅ).

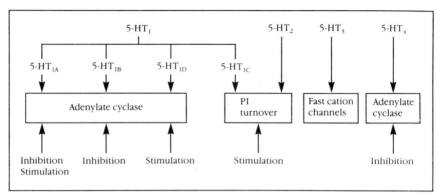

Figure 5. The main effector links between 5-HT binding sites and neuronal responses. (Review references: De Vivo and Maayani, 1988; Sanders-Bush, 1988.)

classified as $5\text{-}HT_1$, $5\text{-}HT_2$ or $5\text{-}HT_3$ is present in guinea pig and mouse hippocampal and colliculus neurones. This has been termed the $5\text{-}HT_4$ receptor, and is also positively linked to adenylate cyclase (Shenker *et al*, 1987; Dumuis *et al*, 1988). The functional role of the $5\text{-}HT_4$ receptor remains to be determined (Clarke *et al*, 1989).

Phosphoinositide hydrolysis The phosophoinositide second messenger can, through the major products of the reactions (diacylglycerol and inositol triphosphate), either increase intracellular Ca^{++} or activate specific protein kinases in a similar manner to the adenylate cyclase system. Extensive pharmacological studies have demonstrated that two 5-HT receptors ($5\text{-}HT_{1C}$ and $5\text{-}HT_2$) are linked to the phosphoinositide hydrolysis system (for review see Sanders-Bush, 1988). In blood platelets and the cerebral cortex, which are both rich in $5\text{-}HT_2$ binding sites, serotonin stimulates the formation of inositol phosphate with a good correlation between the increase and its inhibition by known $5\text{-}HT_2$ antagonists. This indicates that the response is mediated via the $5\text{-}HT_2$ receptor (Kendall and Nahorski 1985; Conn and Sanders-Bush, 1985).

Within the choroid plexus, which regulates both the formation and composition of cerebrospinal fluid, the only 5-HT receptor subtype identified using radioligand binding studies is the $5\text{-}HT_{1C}$ site (Pazos *et al*, 1985). This receptor, like the $5\text{-}HT_2$ site in the cortex, is also linked to phosophoinositide hydrolysis, based on antagonist studies (Conn *et al*, 1986). $5\text{-}HT_{1C}$ receptors are not exclusively located within the choroid plexus, and behavioural effects following activation of $5\text{-}HT_{1C}$ receptors (e.g. administration of m-CPP) have been reported which are not associated with choroid plexus function. However, the stimulation of phosphoinositol hydrolysis in the choroid plexus is the most potent 5-HT-mediated effect in this system, and should serve as an important tool to study the regulation of $5\text{-}HT_{1C}$ receptors in this area. Interestingly, the response is increased following serotonergic denervation with the neurotoxin 5,7-dihydroxytryptamine, indicating denervation supersensitivity and a postsynaptic location for the $5\text{-}HT_{1C}$ receptor (Conn *et al*, 1987, Figure 6).

However, similar denervation had no effect on the $5\text{-}HT_2$-mediated cortical response (Conn and Sanders-Bush, 1986).

Identification of serotonin receptors that regulate serotonin neuronal firing, release, and metabolism
It is now established that negative feedback, autoreceptor control of neuronal function is a common feature of amine neurones, the receptors being located on the dendrites and on the neuronal soma (somatodendritic autoreceptors), and on the nerve terminals (terminal autoreceptors). The interesting feature of the serotonergic system is that the somatodendritic and terminal autoreceptors are different subtypes, in contrast to the noradrenergic system where the function at both sites is served by the α_2-adrenoceptor.

Electrophysiological studies have shown that the $5\text{-}HT_{1A}$ agonist 8-OH-DPAT, whether applied systemically or iontophoretically, is a potent inhibitor of neuronal firing of raphé neurones. The $5\text{-}HT_{1A}$ agonists mimic the effects of 5-HT (de Montigny *et al*, 1984; Sprouse and Aghajanian, 1986, 1988). This inhibition of firing is associated with decreased release of cortical 5-HT *in vivo* (Crespi *et al*, 1990) and is not produced by $5\text{-}HT_{1B}$ agonists (Crespi *et al*, 1990). The $5\text{-}HT_{1A}$ partial agonists and potential anxiolytics (buspirone, gepirone, and ipsapirone) also inhibit the firing of raphé neurones and inhibit release as full agonists (Sharp *et al*, 1990), but they act as partial agonists on the postsynaptic $5\text{-}HT_{1A}$ receptor on hippocampal pyramidal cells (Martin and Mason, 1987; Sprouse and Aghajanian, 1988). Thus there is evidence that the $5\text{-}HT_{1A}$ receptor acts as the somatodendritic autoreceptor in the raphé nuclei as well as being a postsynaptic receptor in the hippocampus (Figure 6).

Extensive *in vitro* and *in vivo* studies in the rat have shown that the pharmacology of the terminal autoreceptor differs from that of the $5\text{-}HT_{1A}$ somatodendritic autoreceptor, having the profile of the $5\text{-}HT_{1B}$ receptor: activation of the receptor causes inhibition of serotonin release at the terminal (Brazell *et al*, 1985; for review see Middlemiss, 1988) (Figure 6). The story is complicated by the fact that the $5\text{-}HT_{1B}$ receptor is not present in man or in the guinea pig, where its role is replaced by a similar, but not identical, receptor — the $5\text{-}HT_{1D}$ subtype (Waeber *et al*, 1989). Hence the $5\text{-}HT_{1D}$ receptor is the terminal autoreceptor in man, but this is probably not the only location for this receptor. For example, the substantia nigra is relatively rich in $5\text{-}HT_{1D}$ receptors where they may be involved in the modulation of dopaminergic function.

Identification of serotonin receptors that regulate the release of other neurotransmitters
Serotonin has been shown to be involved in the pre-synaptic regulation of the release of other transmitters and the role of $5\text{-}HT_3$ receptors has attracted most attention in this respect. *In vitro* and *in vivo* studies have shown that $5\text{-}HT_3$ receptors inhibit the release of acetylcholine in the cortex but increase the release of dopamine in the striatal and mesolimbic systems (Barnes *et al*, 1989; Hagan *et al*, 1987, Figure 7). These effects may be relevant in terms of the improvement

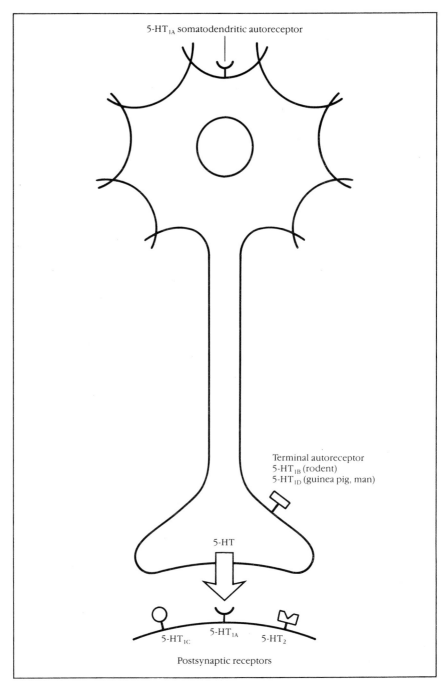

Figure 6. The suggested locations of the 5-HT receptor subtypes associated with pre- and postsynaptic sites of the serotonergic neurone.

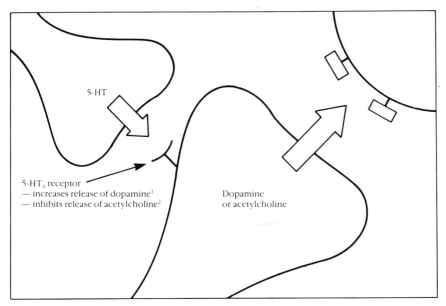

5-HT

5-HT₃ receptor
— increases release of dopamine[1]
— inhibits release of acetylcholine[2]

Dopamine
or acetylcholine

Figure 7. Diagram showing how 5-HT₃ receptors may modulate transmitter release presynaptically. (Adapted from Hagan *et al*,[1] 1987; Barnes *et al*,[2] 1989.)

in cognitive function and the anti-schizophrenic effects seen in animals after administration of 5-HT₃ antagonists (e.g. ondansetron, zacopride, granisetron). It remains to be determined whether a similar presynaptic action of 5-HT₃ receptors could be involved in the putative anxiolytic effect of these drugs.

Identification of serotonin receptors using behavioural tests
Since the original observation by Grahame-Smith of the serotonin behavioural syndrome observed in rats given L-tryptophan plus an MAOI (see Green and Heal, 1985 for review), considerable effort has been made to identify specific behaviours associated with the pharmacological activation of serotonin receptors. This short review cannot possibly cover the area in any detail, and in the absence of compounds that are fully selective for a particular receptor subtype, the findings are always subject to modification in the light of new data. Despite these limitations, certain responses can be used with some certainty to identify serotonin receptor subtypes (Glennon and Lucki, 1988):

5-HT₂ receptor function
1. Head twitch in mice.

2. Head shakes/wet dog shakes in the rat.

3. Back muscle contractions after intrathecal administration of 5-HT₂ agonists in the rat (Fone *et al*, 1989).

5-HT$_1$ receptor function

1. Behavioural syndrome (forepaw treading and hind limb abduction) produced by 5-HT$_{1A}$ agonists (e.g. 8-OH-DPAT) — a postsynaptic 5-HT$_{1A}$ response.

2. 8-OH-DPAT-induced hypothermia in mice — a presynaptic 5-HT$_{1A}$ response?

3. 5-HT$_{1A}$ receptor-induced hyperphagia in rats — a presynaptic 5-HT$_{1A}$ response.

4. 5-HT$_{1C}$ receptor-mediated hypophagia in the rat — a postsynaptic 5-HT$_{1A}$ response (also 5-HT$_{1B}$).

There are no pharmacologically induced behavioural effects that can be used to identify the responsiveness of 5-HT$_3$ or 5-HT$_4$ receptors. Thus, while 5-HT$_3$ antagonists produce an anxiolytic profile in several of the existing models used to identify anxiolytic drugs, similar profiles are shown by 5-HT$_{1A}$ partial agonists and some 5-HT$_2$ antagonists.

Testing of the responsiveness of 5-HT receptor subtypes in man is mainly limited to neuroendocrinological responses, as already mentioned (Siever *et al*, 1986; Goodwin *et al*, 1987; Cowen *et al*, 1988; Deakin, 1989; Deakin *et al*, 1990). An interesting new additional test is the increase in slow wave sleep produced by selective 5-HT$_2$ antagonists in man.

In summary, our knowledge of the functional role of the individual serotonin receptor subtypes is increasing as more selective compounds are used to establish biochemical, physiological, and behavioural measures (Table I and Figure 5). With the new tests now available, it becomes increasingly possible to determine the adaptive changes in serotonin neuronal function that may explain the clinical effects — not only of drugs acting directly on 5-HT receptors but also of well established antidepressants such as the monoamine uptake inhibitors.

Adaptive changes in serotonergic neuronal function and antidepressant drugs

Inhibitors of re-uptake initially increase the synaptic concentration of serotonin (and noradrenaline), probably by binding to the modulatory site identified using [^{3}H]-imipramine or paroxetine. From what has been described about the serotonin autoreceptors, one immediate consequence of the increased synaptic concentration of serotonin will be activation of the 5-HT$_{1A}$ and 5-HT$_{1B}$ receptors, leading to decreased neuronal firing and terminal release (for review see Aghajanian *et al*, 1988). This suggests that after chronic treatment, the net effect of the change in synaptic serotonin and the activation of the autoreceptors will determine the pharmacological actions that are important for the antidepressant properties of the re-uptake inhibitors. Such studies have utilized the various tests available to investigate the function of the serotonin receptor subtypes.

One of the most consistent changes observed after antidepressant treatment

Receptor	CNS localization	Function
5-HT₁		
5-HT$_{1A}$	Somatodendritic autoreceptor Postsynaptic in 5-HT terminal regions	Inhibits 5-HT neuronal firing Induction of specific behaviours, neuroendocrine responses in man, adaptive-protective response to aversive stimulation
5-HT$_{1B}$	Terminal autoreceptor (rat)	Inhibits 5-HT release
5-HT$_{1C}$	Choroid plexus and brain regions	Induction of specific behaviours, feeding, anxiety
5-HT$_{1D}$	Terminal autoreceptor (man) Heteroreceptors on nigral terminals Postsynaptic in the striatum	Inhibits 5-HT release
5-HT₂ Subtypes?	Postsynaptic in hippocampus, frontal cortex, spinal cord	Induction of specific behaviours Slow wave sleep in man
5-HT₃ Subtypes?	Area postrema, limbic regions Nucleus tractus solitarius	Control of emesis Modulation of transmitter release, e.g. dopamine, acetylcholine in limbic areas
5-HT₄ Subtypes?	Hippocampus (guinea pig) Colliculus (mouse)	?

Table I. Function of 5-HT receptors in the brain.

is down-regulation of 5-HT$_2$ receptors, both using measurement of [^{3}H]-ligand binding and functional tests. However, if the change in binding is used as a measure, not all selective serotonin re-uptake inhibitors appear to down-regulate the 5-HT$_2$ site (Fraser *et al*, 1988). Interestingly, 5-HT$_2$ agonists (ketanserin and ritanserin) as well as 5-HT$_2$ agonists (DOM, DOI), against conventional wisdom, also down-regulate the responsiveness of 5-HT$_2$ receptors. Neither 5-HT$_2$ antagonists nor agonists are established antidepressants, indicating that the down-regulation of 5-HT$_2$ receptors is not essential for an antidepressant effect. Indeed, electroconvulsive shock treatment increases the responsiveness of 5-HT$_2$ receptors in rats (Green and Heal, 1985, Table II).

The effects of antidepressant drugs on 5-HT$_1$ receptor binding are inconclusive — another example of the problems encountered with interpretation of such data. Functional studies on the 5-HT$_{1A}$ receptor indicate that chronic uptake inhibition decreases the functional state of the 5-HT$_{1A}$ somatodendritic autoreceptor, i.e. the ability of this receptor to reduce serotonin neuronal firing is attenuated (de Montigny *et al*, 1984; Grahame-Smith, 1988).

Receptor	Drugs	Lithium	Electroconvulsive shock
5-HT$_{1A}$ postsynaptic	Increased	Increased	Increased
5-HT$_{1A}$ somatodendritic autoreceptor	Attenuated	Attenuated	Attenuated
5-HT$_2$ postsynaptic	Decreased	Decreased	Increased

Table II. 5-HT receptor function and chronic antidepressant treatment.
(Review references: Grahame-Smith 1974, 1988; Green and Heal, 1985; Frazer *et al*, 1988.)

In contrast, there is no detectable change in the terminal autoreceptor (5-HT$_{1B}$) in the rat (Sleight *et al*, 1989). There may, however, be a relationship between the down-regulation of 5-HT$_2$ receptors and the attenuated responsiveness of the presynaptic 5-HT$_{1A}$ receptor, as we have recently shown that chronic treatment with either 5-HT$_2$ agonists or antagonists down-regulate 5-HT$_2$ receptors and reduce the effects of 8-OH-DPAT on the release of serotonin (Kidd *et al*, in preparation).

The final serotonin receptor that has been studied in any detail is the 5-HT$_{1A}$ postsynaptic site. In general, the results indicate that these sites, which are markedly localized within the hippocampus (Traber and Glaser, 1987), show enhanced responsiveness after chronic antidepressant treatment — particularly with respect to their electrophysiological properties (Aghajanian *et al*, 1988).

In summary, it appears that long-term antidepressant treatment with re-uptake inhibitors decreases 5-HT$_2$ receptor function, thereby decreasing the effects of the aversive stimuli mediated by 5-HT$_2$ receptors (Deakin, 1989) while increasing the responsiveness of the postsynaptic 5-HT$_1$ receptors. These receptors may be involved in the activation of systems that provide protection against aversive events. The enhancement of this protective action is increased by an attenuation of the receptor mechanisms (somatodendritic 5-HT$_{1A}$ autoreceptors) that inhibit serotonergic neuronal function (Table II). The role played by the other 5-HT receptor subtypes (5-HT$_{1C}$, 5-HT$_3$, and 5-HT$_4$) in this process remains to be determined. A final point is the need to determine the importance of the ß-adrenoceptor down-regulation observed with many, but not all (notably the selective serotonin re-uptake inhibitors), antidepressant drugs in the adaptive changes in serotonin receptors.

Conclusions

The serotonin systems in the brain show considerable diversity, in particular, a structural variety in terms of the morphological characteristics of the innervation of cortical structures and the diversity of serotonin receptors and their biochemical and functional linkages. This diversity will help examine how a transmitter system derived from discrete groups of nerve cells in the midbrain raphe nuclei, but providing wide innervation of forebrain areas, is involved in the control of behaviour such as mood, motor function, cognition, feeding, and sex. The emergence of this new information on serotonin will improve our understanding of the adaptive mechanisms involved in the beneficial clinical actions of such drugs as the well established and successful serotonin re-uptake inhibitors.

Acknowledgements

Work from the Nottingham laboratory described in this chapter was financially supported by the Wellcome Trust, MRC, and SERC.

References

Aghajanian GK, Sprouse JS and Rasmussen K (1988) Electrophysiology of central serotonin receptor subtypes. In: Sanders-Bush E (ed.) *The Serotonin Receptors*, pp.225-252. Humana Press: New Jersey.

Amin AH, Crawford TBB and Gaddum JH (1954) The distribution of substance P and 5-hydroxy-tryptamine in the central nervous system of the dog. *J Physiol* **126**, 596-618.

Barnes JM, Barnes NM, Costall B, *et al* (1989) 5-HT$_3$ receptors mediate inhibition of acetylcholine release in cortical tissue. *Nature* **338**, 762-763.

Berridge MJ (1984) Inositol triphosphate and diacylglycerol as second messengers. *Biochem J* **220**, 345-360.

Blackburn TP, Cox B, Thornber CW, *et al* (1990) Pharmacological studies *in vivo* with ICI 169, 369, a chemically novel 5-HT$_2$/5-HT$_{1C}$ receptor antagonist. *Eur J Pharmacol* **180**, 229-237.

Bockaert J, Dumuis A, Bonhelal R, *et al* (1987) Piperazine derivatives including the anxiolytic drugs, byspirone and buspirone are agonists at 5-HT$_{1A}$ receptors negatively coupled with adenylate cyclase in hippocampal neurons. *Naunyn Schmiedebergs Arch Pharmacol* **335**, 588-592.

Bradley PB (1989) *Introduction to Neuropharmacology*, p.351. Butterworth and Co.

Bradley PB, Engel G, Fennik W, *et al* (1986) Proposals for the classification and nomenclature of functional receptors for 5-hydroxytryptamine. *Neuropharmacology* **25**, 563-567.

Brazell MP, Marsden CA, Nisbet AP, *et al* (1985) The 5-HT$_1$ receptor agonist RU 24969 decreases 5-hydroxytryptamine (5-HT) release and metabolism in the rat frontal cortex *in vitro* and *in vivo*. *Br J Pharmacol* **86**, 209-216.

Briley M (1985) Imipramine binding — its relationship with serotonin uptake and depression. In: Green AR (ed.) *Neuropharmacology of Serotonin*, pp.50-78. Oxford University Press.

Clarke DE, Craig DA and Fozard JR (1989) The 5-HT$_4$ receptor naughty, but nice. *Trends Pharmacol Sci* **10**, 385-386.

Conn PJ and Sanders-Bush E (1985) Serotonin-stimulated phosphoinositide turnover. Mediated by the S2 binding site in rat cerebral cortex but not in subcortical regions. *J Pharmacol Exp Ther* **234**, 195-203.

Conn PJ and Sanders-Bush E (1986) Regulation of serotonin-stimulated phosphoinositide hydrolysis: Relation to serotonin 5-HT$_2$ binding site. *J Neurosci* **6**, 3669-3675.

Conn PJ and Sanders-Bush E (1987) Central serotonin receptors: effector systems, physiological roles and regulation. *Psychopharmacology* **92**, 267-277.

Conn PJ, Sanders-Bush E, Hoffman BJ, et al (1986) A unique serotonin receptor in choroid plexus is linked to phosphatidylinositol turnover. Proc Natl Acad Sci 83, 4086-4088.

Conn PJ, Janowsky A and Sanders-Bush E (1987) Denervation supersensitivity of 5-HT$_{1C}$ receptors in rat choroid plexus. Brain Res 400, 396-398.

Cooper JR, Bloom FE and Roth RH (1982) The biochemical basis of neuropharmacology, 4th edition. Oxford University Press.

Coppen A and Swade C (1988) 5-HT and depression: The present position. In: Briley M and Fillion G (eds.) New Concepts in Depression, pp.120-136. Macmillan Press: London.

Cowen PJ, Charig EM, McCance SL, et al (1988) The effect of amitriptyline and mianserin on the prolactin response to intravenous tryptophan. J Psychopharmacol 2, 2.

Crespi F, Garratt JC, Sleight AJ, et al (1990) In vivo evidence that 5-hydroxytryptamine (5-HT) neuronal firing and release are not necessarily correlated with 5-HT metabolism. Neuroscience 35, 139-144.

Dahlström A and Fuxe K (1964) Evidence for the existence of monoamine-containing neurons in the central nervous system. I. Demonstration of monoamines in cell bodies of brain neurons. Acta Physiol Scand 62 (Suppl 232), 1-55.

Deakin JFW (1989) 5-HT receptor subtypes in depression. In: Bevan P, Cools AR, Archer T (eds.) Behavioural Pharmacology of 5-HT, pp. 179-204. Lawrence Erlbaum: New Jersey.

Deakin JFW, Pennell I, Upadhyada AJ, et al (1990) A neuroendocrine study of 5-HT function in depression: evidence for biological mechanisms of endogenous and psychosocial causation. Psychopharmacology 101, 85-92.

De Vivo M and Maayani S (1986) Characterisation of the 5-HT$_{1A}$ receptor-mediated inhibition of forskolin-stimulated adenylate cyclase activity in guinea-pig and rat hippocampal membranes. J Pharmacol Exp Ther 238, 248-253.

De Vivo M and Maayani S (1988) 5-HT receptors coupled to adenylate cyclase. In: Sanders-Bush E (ed.) The Serotonin Receptors, pp.141-179. Humana Press: New Jersey.

Dumuis A, Bonhelal R, Sebben M, et al (1988) A 5-HT receptor in the central nervous system, positively coupled with adenylate cyclase antagonised by ICS 20593C. Eur J Pharmacol 146, 187-188.

Elks ML, Youngblood WW and Kizer JS (1979) Serotonin synthesis and release in brain slices, independence of tryptophan. Brain Res 172, 471-486.

Everitt BJ (1977) Effects of clomipramine and other inhibitors of monoamine uptake on the sexual behaviour of female rats and rhesus monkeys. Postgrad Med J 53 (Suppl 4), 202-210.

Falck B, Hillarp N-A, Thieme G, et al (1962) Fluorescence of catecholamines and related compounds condensed with formaldehyde. J Histochem Cytochem 10, 348-354.

Fone KCF, Johnson JV, Bennett GW, et al (1989) Involvement of 5-HT$_2$ receptors in the behaviours produced by intrathecal administration of selected 5-HT agonists and the TRH analogue (CG3509) to rats. Br J Pharmacol 96, 599-608.

Fozard JR (1987) 5-HT the enigma variations. Trends Pharmacol Sci 8, 501-508.

Fraser A, Offord SJ and Lucki I (1988) Regulation of serotonin receptors and responsiveness in the brain. In: Sanders-Bush E (ed.) The Serotonin Receptors, pp.319-362. Humana Press: New Jersey.

Fraser A, Maayani S and Wolfe BB (1990) Subtypes of receptors for serotonin. Pharmacol Toxicol 30, 307-348.

Fuller RW (1985) Drugs altering serotonin synthesis and metabolism. In: Green AR (ed.) Neuropharmacology of Serotonin, pp.1-20. Oxford University Press.

Fuxe K (1965) Evidence for the existence of monoamine neurons in the central nervous system. IV. Distribution of monoamine nerve terminals in the central nervous system. Acta Physiol Scand 64 (Suppl 247), 39-85.

Fuxe K, Hökfelt T and Ungerstedt U (1968) Localization of indolealkylamine in the CNS. Adv Pharmacol 6, 235-251.

Garattini S, Buczko W, Jori A, et al (1975) The mechanism of action of fenfluramine. Postgrad Med J 51 (Suppl 1), 27-35.

Gilbert RFT, Emson PC, Hunt SP, *et al* (1982) The effects of monoamine neurotoxins on peptides in rat spinal cord. *Neuroscience* **7**, 69-88.

Glennon RA (1987) Central serotonin receptors as targets for drug research. *J Med Chem* **30**, 1-12.

Glennon RA and Lucki I (1988) Behavioural models of serotonin receptor activation. In: Sanders-Bush E (ed.) *The Serotonin Receptors*, pp.253-293. Humana Press. New Jersey.

Goodwin GM, Fairburn CG and Cowen PJ (1987) The effects of dieting and weight loss on neuroendocrine responses to L-tryptophan, clonidine and apomorphine in volunteers: important implications for neuroendocrine investigation in depression. *Arch Gen Psychiatry* **44**, 952-955.

Grahame-Smith DG (1974) How important is the synthesis of brain 5-HT in the physiological control of its central function. *Adv Biochem Psychopharmacol* **10**, 83-91.

Grahame-Smith DG (1988) Neuropharmacological adaptive effects in the actions of antidepressant drugs, ECT and Lithium. In: Briley M and Fillion G (eds.) *New Concepts in Depression*, pp.1-14. Macmillan Press: London.

Green AR and Heal DJ (1985) The effect of drugs on serotonin-mediated behavioural models. In: Green AR (ed.) *Neuropharmacology of Serotonin*, pp.326-368. Oxford University Press.

Habert E, Graham D, Tahraoui L, *et al* (1985) Characterization of [^{3}H]-paroxetine binding to rat cortical membranes. *Eur J Pharmacol* **118**, 107-114.

Hagan RM, Butler A, Hill JM, *et al* (1987) Effect of the 5-HT$_3$ receptor antagonist GR 38032F on responses to injection of a neurokinin agonist into the ventral tegmental area of the rat brain. *Eur J Pharmacol* **138**, 303-305.

Hökfelt T, Tsuruo Y, Ulfhake B, *et al* (1989) Distribution of TRH-like immunoreactivity with special reference to coexistence with other neuroactive compounds. *Ann NY Acad Sci* **553**, 76-105.

Hoyer D (1988) Functional correlates of serotonin 5-HT$_1$ recognition sites. *J Recept Res* **8**, 59-81.

Jacobs BL, Wise WD and Taylor KM (1974) Differential behavioural and neurochemical effects following lesions of the dorsal or median raphe nuclei in rats. *Brain Res* **79**, 353-361.

Johanssen O, Hökfelt T, Pernow B, *et al* (1981) Immunohistochemical support for three putative transmitters in one neuron: Co-existence of 5-hydroxytryptamine substance P and thyrotropin releasing hormone-like immunoreactivity in medullary neurons projecting to the spinal cord. *Neuroscience* **6**, 1857-1881.

Kendall DA and Nahorski SR (1985) 5-Hydroxytryptamine-stimulated inositol phospholipid hydrolysis in rat cerebral cortex slices. Pharmacological characterization and effects of antidepressants. *J Pharmacol Exp Ther* **233**, 473-479.

Kilpatrick GJ, Jones BJ and Tyers MB (1988) Identification and distribution of 5-HT$_3$ receptors in rat brain using radioligand binding. *Nature* **330**, 746-748.

Kosofsky BE and Molliver ME (1987) The serotoninergic innervation of the cerebral cortex: Different classes of axon terminals arise from dorsal and median raphe nuclei. *Synapse* **1**, 153-168.

Kuhn DM, Wolf WA and Yondim MBN (1986) Serotonin neurochemistry revisited: A new look at some old axioms. *Neurochem Int* **8**, 141-154.

Langer SZ, Raisman R, Tahraoui Z, *et al* (1984) Substituted tetrahydro-ß-carbolines are possible candidates as endogenous ligands of the [^{3}H]-imipramine recognition site. *Eur J Pharmacol* **98**, 153-154.

Langer SZ, Galzin AM, Lee CR, *et al* (1986) Antidepressant binding sites in brain and platelets. In: Antidepressants and Receptor Function. *Ciba Found Symp* **123**, 3-29.

Leysen JE (1985) Characterization of serotonin receptor binding sites. In: Green AR (ed.) *Neuropharmacology of Serotonin*, pp.79-116. Oxford University Press.

Leysen JE, van Gompel P, Gommeren W, *et al* (1986) Down regulation of serotonin-S$_2$ receptor sites in rat brain by chronic treatment with the serotonin-S$_2$ antagonists: ritanserin and setoperol. *Psychopharmacology* **88**, 434-444.

Lyon RA and Titeler M (1988) Pharmacology and biochemistry of the 5-HT$_2$ receptors. In: Sanders-Bush E (ed.) *The Serotonin Receptors*, pp.59-88. Humana Press: New Jersey.

Marsden CA (1989) 5-hydroxytryptamine receptor subtypes and new anxiolytic drugs: an appraisal. In: Tyrer PJ (ed.) *Psychopharmacology of anxiety*, pp.3-27. Oxford University Press.

Marsden CA, Conti J, Strope E, *et al* (1979) Monitoring 5-hydroxytryptamine release in the brain of the freely moving unanaesthetised rat using *in vivo* voltammetry. *Brain Res* **171**, 85-99.

Marsden CA, Sleight AJ, Fone KCF, *et al* (1989) Functional identification of 5-HT receptor subtypes. *Comp Biochem Physiol* **93A**, 107-114.

Martin KF and Mason F (1987) Ipsapirone is a partial agonist at 5-hydroxytryptamine$_{1A}$ receptors in the rat hippocampus: electrophysiological evidence. *Eur J Pharmacol* **141**, 479-483.

Middlemiss DN (1988) Autoreceptors regulating serotonin release. In: Sanders-Bush E (ed.) *The Serotonin Receptors*, pp.201-224. Humana Press: New Jersey.

Molliver ME (1987) Serotonergic neuronal systems: What their anatomic organisation tells us about function. *J Clin Psychopharmacol* **7** (Suppl 6), 3S-23S.

de Montigny C, Blier P and Chaput Y (1984) Electrophysiologically identified serotonin receptors in the rat CNS. *Neuropharmacology* **23**, 1511-1520.

Murphy DL, Aulakh CS and Garrick NA (1986) How antidepressants work: cautionary conclusions based on clinical and laboratory studies of the longer term consequences of antidepressant drug treatment. In: Antidepressants and receptor function. *Ciba Found Symp* **123**, 106-125.

Nestler EJ and Greengard P (1983) Protein phosphorylation in the brain. *Nature* **305**, 583-588.

Newman ME and Lehrer B (1988) Chronic electroconvulsive shock and desipramine reduce the degree of inhibition by 5-HT and carbachol of forskolin-stimulated adenylate cyclase in rat hippocampal membranes. *Eur J Pharmacol* **148**, 257-260.

Palacios M and Dietl MM (1988) Autoradiographic studies of serotonin receptors. In: Sanders-Bush E (ed.) *The Serotonin Receptors*, pp.89-138. Humana Press: New Jersey.

Pazos A, Hoyer D and Palacios JM (1985) The binding of serotoninergic ligands to the choroid plexus: characterization of a new type of serotonin recognition site. *Eur J Pharmacol* **106**, 539-546.

Raisman R, Briley MS and Langer SZ (1979) Specific tricyclic antidepressant binding sites in rat brain. *Nature* **281**, 148-150.

Raisman R, Briley MS, Bonchami F, *et al* (1982) [^{3}H]-imipramine binding and serotonin uptake in platelets from untreated depressed patients and control volunteers. *Psychopharmacology* **77**, 332-335.

Sanders-Bush E (1988) 5-HT receptor coupled to phosphoinositide hydrolysis. In: Sanders-Bush E (ed.) *The Serotonin Receptors*, pp.181-198. Humana Press: New Jersey.

Sevwen K, Magnaldo I and Pouyssegur J (1988) Serotonin stimulates DNA synthesis in fibroblasts acting through 5-HT$_{1B}$ receptors coupled to a G$_1$-protein. *Nature* **335**, 254-256.

Sharp T, Buckus LI, Hjorth S, *et al* (1990) Further investigations of the *in vivo* pharmacological properties of the putative 5-HT$_{1A}$ antagonist, BMY 7378. *Eur J Pharmacol* **176**, 331-340.

Shaskan EG and Snyder SH (1970) Kinetics of serotonin accumulation into slices from rat brain: Relationship to catecholamine uptake. *J Pharmacol Exp Ther* **163**, 425.

Shenker A, Maayani S, Weinstein H (1987) Pharmacological characterization of two 5-hydroxytryptamine receptors coupled to adenylate cyclase in guinea pig hippocampal membranes. *Mol Pharmacol* **31**, 357-367.

Siever LJ, Coccaro EF, Benjamin E, *et al* (1986) Adrenergic and serotonergic receptor responsiveness in depression. In: Antidepressants and receptor function. *Ciba Found Symp* **123**, 148-163.

Sleight AJ, Marsden CA, Martin KF, *et al* (1988a) Relationship between extracellular 5-hydroxytryptamine and behaviour following monoamine oxidase inhibition and L-tryptophan. *Br J Pharmacol* **93**, 303-310.

Sleight AJ, Marsden CA, Palfreyman MG, *et al* (1988b) Chronic MAO A and MAO B inhibition decreases the 5-HT$_{1A}$ receptor-mediated inhibition of forskolin-stimulated adenylate cyclase. *Eur J Pharmacol* **154**, 225-261.

Sleight AJ, Smith RJ, Marsden CA, *et al* (1989) The effects of chronic treatment with amitriptyline and MDL 72394 on the control of 5-HT release *in vivo*. *Neuropharmacology* **28**, 477-480.

Slotkin TA, Seidler FJ, Withmore WL, *et al* (1978) Rat brain synaptic vesicles. Uptake and specification of [^{3}H] norepinephrine and [^{3}H] serotonin in preparations from the whole brain and brain regions. *J Neurochem* **31**, 961-962.

Sprouse JS and Aghajanian GK (1986) (-)-Propranolol blocks the inhibition of serotonergic dorsal raphe cell firing by 5-HT$_{1A}$ selective agonists. *Eur J Pharmacol* **128**, 295-298.

Sprouse JS and Aghajanian GK (1988) Responses of hippocampal pyramidal cells to putative serotonin 5HT$_{1A}$ and 5-HT$_{1B}$ agonists: A comparative study with dorsal raphe neurones. *Neuropharmacology* **27**, 707-715.

Steinbusch HWM (1981) Distribution of serotonin-immunoreactivity in the central nervous system of the rat: cell bodies and terminals. *Neuroscience* **6**, 557-618.

Steinbusch HWM, Verhofstad AAJ and Joosten HWJ (1978) Localization of serotonin in the central nervous system by immunohistochemistry: description of a specific and sensitive technique and some applications. *Neuroscience* **3**, 81.

Tohyama M, Shiosaka S, Sakanaka M, *et al* (1980) Detailed pathways of the raphe dorsalis neuron to the cerebral cortex with use of horseradish peroxidase-3,3',5,5' tetramethylbenzidine reaction as a tool for the fibre tracing technique. *Brain Res* **181**, 433-439.

Traber J and Glaser T (1987) 5-HT$_{1A}$ receptor-related anxiolytics. *Trends Pharmacol Sci* **8**, 432-437.

Trulson ME and Jacobs BL (1976) Behavioural evidence for the rapid release of CNS serotonin by PCA and fenfluramine. *Eur J Pharmacol* **36**, 149-154.

Twarog BM and Page IH (1953) Serotonin content of some mammalian tissues and urine and method for its determination. *Am J Physiol* **175**, 157-161.

Waeber C, Schoeffter P, Palacios JM, *et al* (1989) 5-HT$_{1D}$ receptors in guinea-pig and pigeon brain. *Naunyn Schmiedebergs Arch Pharmacol* **340**, 479-485.

2

The comparative pharmacological properties of selective serotonin re-uptake inhibitors in animals

A.M. Johnson

Introduction

The observation by Kühn in 1957 that imipramine improved the symptoms of depression in psychiatric patients stimulated investigations into its pharmacological actions that might explain the clinical effect of this new class of drug. Initial studies in animals by Sigg (1959) showed that, amongst other actions, imipramine potentiated the peripheral actions of noradrenaline. Subsequent studies demonstrated that imipramine was a potent inhibitor of neuronal catecholamine uptake in rat heart and other tissues including the brain (Dengler and Titus, 1961; Hertting *et al*, 1961; Glowinski and Axelrod, 1964). *In vivo* investigations on catecholamine uptake mechanisms were followed by studies that provided evidence of an active transport mechanism for serotonin in the cell membrane of central neurones (Aghajanian and Bloom, 1967; Blackburn *et al*, 1967; Fuxe and Ungerstedt, 1967; Palaic *et al*, 1967). Following these studies, Corrodi and Fuxe (1968) demonstrated that imipramine also influenced serotonergic re-uptake into neurones in rat brain.

Schildkraut (1965), Coppen (1967), and Lapin and Oxenkrug (1969) had earlier proposed monoamine hypotheses of depression which suggested that depression occurred as a result of the reduced availability of noradrenaline and/or serotonin in the central nervous system. Carlsson *et al* (1969a, b) and Ross and Renyi (1969) showed that the tricyclic antidepressants differed in their relative affinities for catecholaminergic and serotonergic uptake mechanisms, but the relative roles of the two monoamines in depression remained controversial and drugs with greater selectivity for one or other monoamine re-uptake mechanism were required to attempt to resolve these questions. These drugs also offered the promise of a possible increase in therapeutic response and an improvement in safety and tolerability compared with the tricyclic antidepressants and monoamine oxidase inhibitors (MAOIs).

Selective inhibitors of serotonin re-uptake

Among the tricyclic antidepressants that achieved early clinical use, clomipramine appeared to be one of the more selective inhibitors of serotonin compared with noradrenaline re-uptake (Ross and Renyi, 1969). However, clomipramine is metabolized *in vivo* by N-demethylation to desmethyl-chlorimipramine, a potent inhibitor of neuronal noradrenaline re-uptake (Benfield *et al*, 1980). Therefore, as the plasma levels of desmethyl-chlorimipramine exceed those of the parent compound in man (Jones and Luscombe, 1977), the therapeutic actions of clomipramine could not be attributed only to inhibition of serotonin re-uptake.

One of the earliest of the new generation of selective serotonin re-uptake inhibitors (SSRIs) to be subjected to worldwide clinical study was zimeldine (Ross and Renyi, 1975; Ross *et al*, 1976). Although not as potent as clomipramine at inhibiting re-uptake of serotonin, it was more selective for serotonin compared with noradrenaline uptake *in vitro* and *in vivo*. Zimeldine is metabolized to norzimeldine, which shows a reduced selectivity for serotonin uptake *in vitro* and is more potent than zimeldine at inhibiting re-uptake of both serotonin and noradrenaline (Ross and Renyi, 1977). As the plasma levels of norzimeldine exceed those of zimeldine in man, it is likely that the pharmacological properties of both parent and metabolite contribute to the overall therapeutic effect. Zimeldine was shown to be an effective antidepressant in man (Heel *et al*, 1982), but was withdrawn from worldwide use in 1982 on toxicity grounds.

The pharmacological properties of other SSRIs that have been subjected to extensive clinical investigation — namely citalopram, fluoxetine, fluvoxamine, paroxetine, and sertraline — were reported initially by Hyttel (1977a) and Christensen *et al* (1977), Wong *et al* (1974), Claassen *et al* (1977), Buus Lassen (1978 a, b), and Koe *et al* (1983), respectively.

The comparative pharmacology of these drugs is described in this overview. The overview focuses on the actions of these drugs on the central nervous system and, in particular, on the adaptive changes induced by these drugs in central neurotransmitter receptors following repeated administration. These latter effects are likely to be responsible for the therapeutic actions observed with these drugs in the clinic.

The structural formulae of paroxetine, citalopram, fluoxetine, fluvoxamine and sertraline are shown in Figure 1. It should be noted that paroxetine and sertraline are single stereoisomers, whereas citalopram and fluoxetine are racemic mixtures. Fluvoxamine does not have an asymmetric carbon atom and hence does not exist in optically active forms.

Initial and subsequent studies with these drugs have demonstrated that they

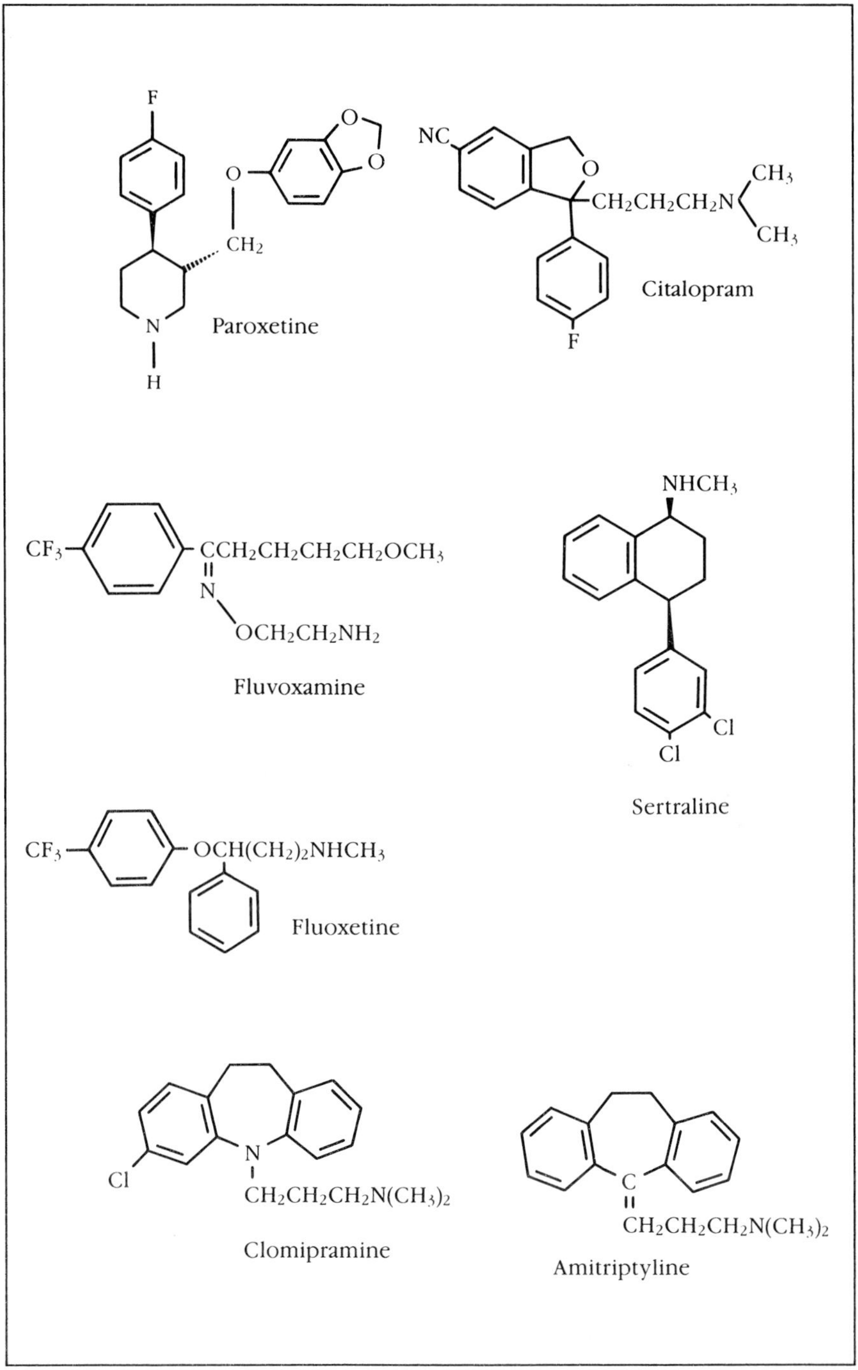

Figure 1. Structural formulae of the SSRIs and some tricyclic antidepressants.

are potent and competitive inhibitors of the high affinity neuronal re-uptake mechanism for serotonin, an action that can be readily demonstrated in synaptosome preparations from rodent brain *in vitro.* These drugs also inhibit the re-uptake of noradrenaline and, generally to a lesser extent, dopamine, at higher concentrations. The comparative inhibitory properties of these SSRIs on [^{3}H]-monoamine uptake in rat brain synaptosomes *in vitro* are shown in Table I. Considerable variation exists in the experimental conditions under which the inhibitory properties of these drugs on neuronal monoamine uptake have been investigated. However, as shown by Hyttel (1982), Maitre *et al* (1982), Koe *et al* (1983), and Thomas *et al* (1987), paroxetine is the most potent serotonin uptake inhibitor *in vitro* of the drugs investigated, and citalopram is the most selective inhibitor of serotonin re-uptake, with paroxetine being more selective than fluoxetine, fluvoxamine, and sertraline. Of the drugs investigated, only sertraline is a more potent inhibitor of dopamine compared with noradrenaline uptake.

Both stereoisomers of fluoxetine are inhibitors of serotonin uptake with the (+)-enantiomer being slightly more potent than the (−)-enantiomer *in vitro* (Wong *et al,* 1985a). The selective serotonin uptake inhibitory properties of citalopram are reported to reside almost exclusively in the (+)-enantiomer (Boegesoe and Perregaard, 1989).

Pharmacological activity of metabolites

As discussed earlier, the biochemical profile of a drug *in vitro* may be compromised *in vivo* by metabolism to products which also possess biological activity. Furthermore, a metabolite that possesses a similar pharmacological profile to that of the parent molecule may differ from it in its pharmacokinetic properties. Of the SSRIs, the principal metabolite of citalopram, desmethylcitalopram, is four times less potent at inhibiting uptake of serotonin than the parent compound and 11 times more potent at inhibiting uptake of noradrenaline *in vitro* (Hyttel, 1982). However, as citalopram is highly selective for serotonin uptake, these represent relatively minor changes in its pharmacological profile. Furthermore, as the plasma levels of the metabolites in man are about half those of the parent molecule and they are less likely to penetrate the central nervous system, the contribution of metabolites to the clinical activity of citalopram is likely to be negligible (Overo, 1989).

In contrast, fluoxetine is metabolized to norfluoxetine and other products, and the plasma levels of norfluoxetine exceed those of fluoxetine (Lemberger *et al,* 1985). *In vitro* studies in rat synaptosome preparations indicate that norfluoxetine is as potent as fluoxetine in inhibiting [^{3}H]-5-HT uptake and that it exhibits a similar degree of selectivity for serotonin compared with noradrenaline uptake (Wong *et al,* 1975). However, elimination of norfluoxetine from the body is slower (half life 7-15 days) than that of the parent compound (three to five days) (Lemberger *et al,* 1985). Norfluoxetine is therefore likely to

References	Inhibition of [³H]-serotonin uptake IC$_{50}$ (nM) except (1): K$_i$				Ratio[+]: NA/serotonin				Ratio[+]: DA/serotonin		
	(1)	(2)	(3)	(4)	(1)	(2)	(3)	(4)	(1)	(2)	(3)
Paroxetine	1.1	0.31	—	—	320	280	—	—	1800	19,000	—
Citalopram	2.6	1.8	—	6	1500	4900	—	730	3900	23,000	—
Fluoxetine	25	6.9	270	27	20	55	2.7	20	170	730	44
Fluvoxamine	6.2	—	540	—	180	—	3.5	—	>1600	—	83
Sertraline	7.3	—	58	—	190	—	21	—	32	—	19
Clomipramine	7.4	1.5	99	5	13	16	1.1	9.2	1200	2900	82
Imipramine	100	35	810	44	0.65	—	0.08	1	85	—	25
Amitriptyline	87	40	1200	44	0.91	0.6	0.11	1	54	140	11

Table I. Potency and relative selectivity of inhibitors of serotonin re-uptake *in vitro*: inhibition of [³H]-monoamine uptake in rodent brain synaptosomes. NA = noradrenaline; DA = dopamine. [+]:ratio of IC$_{50}$s except reference (1) = K$_i$s. References: 1. Thomas *et al* (1987) and unpublished observations. 2. Hyttel (1982). 3. Koe *et al* (1983). 4. Maitre *et al* (1982).

contribute to the pharmacological effects of fluoxetine in man.

Fluvoxamine is extensively metabolized in man, and evaluation of two of the metabolites indicates that they are not likely to contribute to the clinical actions of the parent (Claassen, 1983).

The principal metabolite of sertraline, norsertraline or desmethylsertraline, is eight times less potent than the parent as an inhibitor of serotonin uptake *in vitro*. It is 3.5 and 4 times less potent at inhibiting noradrenaline and dopamine uptake, respectively (Koe *et al*, 1983), and 5-10 times less potent than sertraline *in vivo*, based on measures of enhanced serotonergic neurotransmission (Heym and Koe, 1988). The metabolite thus retains selectivity for the inhibition of serotonin uptake compared with the parent molecule. The elimination half life of desmethylsertraline is 66 hours compared with 25 hours for the parent compound (Doogan and Caillard, 1988). Some contribution of the metabolite to the clinical effect of sertraline may therefore occur.

Paroxetine is metabolized in man by oxidative opening of the methylene-dioxyphenyl ring, followed by methylation and conjugation of the resulting catechol (Haddock *et al*, 1989). Haddock *et al* (1989) also demonstrated that the sulphate- and glucuronide-conjugated metabolites are 3000 and at least 9000 times, respectively, less potent than paroxetine in inhibiting uptake of serotonin into rat brain synaptosomes *in vitro*. These metabolites were also devoid of effects on serotonin or noradrenaline uptake in rat brain synaptosomes after intravenous administration of doses that were at least 40 times greater than those at which paroxetine markedly inhibits [^{3}H]-5-HT uptake *ex vivo*. Therefore, although plasma levels of the metabolites may exceed those of paroxetine (Kaye *et al*, 1989), the metabolites are not likely to contribute to the clinical effects of paroxetine.

Inhibition of monoamine uptake *in vivo*

The potency of these drugs as selective inhibitors of neuronal serotonin re-uptake *in vivo* has been investigated using a number of experimental methods. These methods include:

1. The determination of the inhibition of uptake of [^{3}H]-monoamines into brain synaptosome preparations obtained from animals which have previously received the drugs, i.e. *ex vivo* administration studies.

2. Inhibition of the pharmacological effects of compounds whose expression depends on the neuronal re-uptake carrier mechanism, e.g. inhibition of the depletion of brain serotonin and noradrenaline by H75/12 (α-ethyl-3-hydroxy-4-methylphenethylamine) and H77/77 (3-hydroxy-4-methyl-α-methylphenethylamine), respectively, as described by Carlsson *et al* (1969a, b).

3. The potentiation of the pharmacological effects of the serotonin precursor, 5-hydroxytryptophan.

The relative potencies of the SSRIs and tricyclic antidepressants in a number of these studies after oral administration to rodents are shown in Table II.

Paroxetine was the most potent inhibitor of serotonin re-uptake in all the

	Inhibition of serotonin uptake				Inhibition of NA uptake		
	Rat			Mouse		Rat	
	Inhibition of [^{3}H]-serotonin uptake *ex vivo*		Inhibition of H75/12-induced depletion of brain serotonin	Potentiation of 5-HTP-induced symptoms; Electroshock threshold	Serotonergic syndrome	Inhibition of [^{3}H]-NA uptake *ex vivo*		Inhibition of H77/77 induced depletion of brain NA
References	(1)	(2)	(2)	(3)	(4)	(5)	(1)	(2)	(2)
Paroxetine	1.9	—	0.4	0.4	—	—	>30	—	—
Citalopram	5.9	5	2	—	—	1.2	>30	> 10	>100
Fluoxetine	7.0	6	8	0.5	9.9	—	>30	>100	>100
Fluvoxamine	23	—	5	—	12.9	—	>30	—	> 30
Sertraline	—	—	—	—	1.0	—	—	—	—
Clomipramine	17	30	15	17	47.3	12	29	30	80
Imipramine	>30	70	50	>100	—	31	>30	7	17
Amitriptyline	>30	200	120	—	—	> 20	>50	50	100
Desipramine	>30	ca.100	180	—	>178	> 20	7	3	11

Table II. Relative potency (ED$_{50}$s, mg/kg) of SSRIs in tests for the inhibition of serotonin and noradrenaline uptake after oral administration to rodents. NA=noradrenaline. References: 1. Nelson *et al* (1989) and unpublished observations. 2. Maitre *et al* (1982). 3. Buus Lassen (1978a). 4. Koe *et al* (1983). 5. Christensen *et al* (1977).

studies in which direct comparisons were made, although again there was considerable variation in the experimental conditions used (Buus Lassen, 1978a; Maitre *et al,* 1982; Thomas *et al,* 1987). In general, fluoxetine, citalopram, and fluvoxamine appear to be of similar potency after oral administration and, in accord with the *in vitro* data, the (+)-enantiomer of fluoxetine is more potent than the (–)-isomer in inhibiting the depletion of brain serotonin by p-chloroamphetamine in rats, indicating that the (+)-enantiomer is a more potent inhibitor of serotonin re-uptake *in vivo* (Fuller and Snoddy, 1986). There is a lack of comparative data on the relative potency of sertraline as a serotonin re-uptake inhibitor after oral administration to rats. However, Koe *et al* (1983) have reported that sertraline was more potent than fluoxetine and fluvoxamine after oral administration to mice.

Of the tricyclic antidepressants, only clomipramine approaches the potency of the non-tricyclic SSRIs. Neither paroxetine, fluoxetine, citalopram nor fluvoxamine inhibits noradrenaline uptake in rat brain after oral administration at doses considerably higher than those required to inhibit serotonin re-uptake *in vivo* (Maitre *et al,* 1982; Thomas *et al,* 1987). Sertraline is reported not to inhibit noradrenaline uptake in rat brain *in vivo* after intraperitoneal administration to rats (Koe *et al,* 1983).

Magnussen *et al* (1982) and Thomas *et al* (1987) have confirmed the earlier studies of Buus Lassen *et al* (1980), which showed that the inhibitory effect of paroxetine on serotonin uptake in rodent brain synaptosomes is maintained on repeated administration . Similar data have been reported for fluoxetine (Hwang *et al,* 1980), fluvoxamine (Brunello *et al,* 1986), and citalopram (Hyttel *et al,* 1984). Specific studies on rodent brain synaptosomal uptake with sertraline after repeated administration have not been reported. However, long-term inhibition of platelet serotonin uptake, as evidenced by prolonged depletion of platelet serotonin in rat blood, has been reported after administration of sertraline for up to 11 days (Koe *et al,* 1983).

Effect on monoamine turnover

Monoamine re-uptake inhibitors probably reduce the levels of the metabolites of serotonin and noradrenaline in the brain as a consequence of the feedback inhibition of neuronal firing, and inhibition of neurotransmitter synthesis and release due to raised intrasynaptic levels of the monoamines following the inhibition of re-uptake (Schubert *et al,* 1970, Aghajanian, 1972).

Fuller *et al* (1974) reported that brain concentrations of the main metabolite of serotonin, 5-hydroxyindoleacetic acid (5-HIAA), were significantly reduced for up to 24 hours following administration of fluoxetine. This effect was not due to monoamine oxidase inhibition, and Hwang *et al* (1980) have confirmed that fluoxetine inhibits the synthesis of serotonin from [^{3}H]-tryptophan. The effect of fluoxetine on 5-HIAA was maintained after 14 daily administrations, and the reduction in serotonin synthesis was due in part to non-competitive inhibition of tryptophan uptake. Fluoxetine did not significantly reduce the levels of serotonin in the brain in this study, but Hrdina (1987) has shown that administration of fluoxetine for 21 days significantly reduced both serotonin and 5-HIAA levels in the rat brain. Furthermore, Wong *et al* (1985b) have shown that fluoxetine significantly reduced hippocampal levels of serotonin after a single dose, whereas levels in the cerebral cortex were unaffected. The levels of 5-HIAA were significantly reduced in both tissues. These data indicate that fluoxetine, presumably as a result of prolonged inhibition of serotonin re-uptake, may reduce the levels of serotonin as well as 5-HIAA in the rat brain.

The effect of citalopram on the turnover of serotonin has been reviewed by Hyttel (1982). As expected, after a single injection, citalopram reduces serotonin turnover, as evidenced by a reduction in the levels of 5-HIAA in the brain; levels of serotonin are unchanged (Hyttel, 1977b). The effect of citalopram on serotonin turnover in rodent brain has been confirmed by a number of investigators (Carlsson and Lindqvist, 1978; Keshavan *et al*, 1980; Baker and Goodwich, 1982). Carlsson and Lindqvist (1978) also demonstrated that the effect of citalopram was selective for serotonin metabolism, as the turnover of noradrenaline and dopamine in rat brain were unaffected.

Fluvoxamine has similarly been shown to reduce the turnover of serotonin in rat brain after a single dose (Claassen *et al*, 1977), and Lapierre *et al* (1983) showed that fluvoxamine reduced the turnover of serotonin in rat brain (a reduction in 5-HIAA with no change in levels of serotonin) in a number of regions after repeated administration for seven days. Fluvoxamine is reported not to influence the levels of noradrenaline or dopamine when administered daily for up to 35 days, and catecholamine turnover rates are also reported to remain unaltered following administration of fluvoxamine for 21 days (Benfield and Ward, 1986).

Sertraline reduced levels of 5-HIAA, but not serotonin, in rat brain after a single dose; noradrenaline and dopamine levels were unaffected (Koe *et al*, 1983). Further data on the levels of catecholamine metabolites are required to determine whether catecholamine turnover is influenced by sertraline.

Paroxetine reduces the levels of 5-HIAA in the brain when single doses are administered intraperitoneally (unpublished observations) or orally (Badawy and Morgan, 1990) to rats. At lower doses of paroxetine, a small increase was seen in the levels of serotonin in the brain, followed by a small decrease at higher doses (Badawy and Morgan, 1990). No marked effect on catecholamine metabolites has been observed after single oral doses of paroxetine to rodents (unpublished observations). It is concluded that the data available indicate that the effects of fluoxetine, fluvoxamine, sertraline, citalopram, and paroxetine on monoamine turnover reflect their selective effects on re-uptake of serotonin.

Interaction with neurotransmitter receptors *in vitro*

The tricyclic antidepressants are characterized by potent inhibitory properties at histaminergic, α_1-adrenergic, and muscarinic cholinergic receptors. The affinity of this class of drugs for these receptors can be readily demonstrated in radioligand binding studies (Hall and Ogren, 1981). Indeed, the ability of these drugs to inhibit the binding of radioligands to these receptors from rat brain membranes *in vitro* correlates with their propensity to induce drowsiness (Hall and Ogren, 1984), sedation, and hypotension (U'Prichard *et al*, 1978) as well as anticholinergic side-effects such as dry mouth, constipation, blurred vision, and urinary retention (Snyder and Yamamura, 1977).

The *in vitro* radioligand binding profiles of a number of SSRIs have been investigated by Wong *et al* (1983) and Thomas *et al* (1987). Hyttel (1977a) has also described the effect of citalopram on the binding of a range of receptor radioligands.

The data obtained by Thomas *et al* (1987) with paroxetine, citalopram, fluvoxamine, and fluoxetine compared with clomipramine, amitriptyline, and imipramine are shown in Table III. These data show that whereas the tricyclic antidepressants have high affinities (K_is<1μM) for ^{3}H-mepyramine (histamine, H_1), ^{3}H-prazosin (α_1-adrenoceptor) and ^{3}H-quinuclidinylbenzilate (QNB, muscarinic cholinergic receptors) binding sites, the SSRIs are much weaker in their affinities for histamine (H_1) receptors (K_is>1μM) and α_1-adrenoceptors (K_is 4.5->10μM). Some affinity of paroxetine, fluoxetine, and citalopram for muscarinic cholinergic receptors was observed (K_is 89, 1300 and 2900nM). However, these affinities are still less than those observed with the tricyclic antidepressants, and pharmacological studies with paroxetine (Johnson, 1989) indicate that the anticholinergic effects of paroxetine are not likely to be apparent at clinical doses. The data on fluoxetine, fluovoxamine, and citalopram obtained by Thomas *et al* (1987) and the *in vitro* radioligand binding studies were in accord with those described by Wong *et al* (1983), Claassen *et al* (1977), and Hyttel (1977a, b), respectively. Koe *et al* (1983) have reported that sertraline has a very weak affinity for muscarinic cholinergic receptors (IC_{50} =19μM) compared with amitriptyline (IC_{50} =0.32μM), as evidenced by the inhibition of [^{3}H]-QNB binding to rat brain membranes. Furthermore, Stockmeier *et al* (1987) have shown that sertraline (IC_{50} =245nM) also has some affinity for [^{3}H]-prazosin binding sites in rat frontal cortex membranes *in vitro*, being three to four times less potent than imipramine (IC_{50} =64nM) and desipramine (IC_{50} =88nM) in this respect. Sertraline also possesses a high affinity for sigma receptor binding sites in rat brain *in vitro*, whereas fluoxetine and paroxetine were much weaker in this respect (Schmidt *et al*, 1989).

In conclusion, *in vitro* radioligand binding studies indicate that the SSRIs have a considerably reduced affinity for the receptors associated with a propensity to induce the central and autonomic side-effects associated with the tricyclic antidepressants.

Kᵢ (nM)

Receptor [³H]-ligand	Catecholamine				Serotonin		Histamine	Cholinergic
	α_1 Prazosin	α_2 Clonidine / Rauwolscine		ß DHA	D_2 Spiperone	5-HT₁ 5-HT	5-HT₂ Ketanserin	H₁ Mepyramine	Muscarinic QNB
Paroxetine	>10,000	>10,000	>10,000	>5000	7700	>10,000	>1000	>1000	89
Citalopram	4500	>10,000	>10,000	>5000	>10,000	>10,000	>1000	>1000	2900
Fluvoxamine	>10,000	>10,000	>10,000	>5000	>10,000	>10,000	>1000	>1000	>10,000
Fluoxetine	>10,000	>10,000	>10,000	>5000	>10,000	>10,000	>1000	>1000	1300
Amitriptyline	170	540	410	>5000	1200	1000	8.3	3.3	5.1
Imipramine	440	1000	2500	>5000	2400	8900	120	35	37
Clomipramine	150	3300	2400	>5000	430	5200	63	47	34
Desipramine	1300	8600	5500	>5000	3800	2500	160	370	68

Table III. Inhibition of radioligand binding *in vitro* to rat brain membranes by SSRIs and tricyclic antidepressants. DHA=dihydroalprenolol; QNB=quinuclidinylbenzilate. Reference: Thomas *et al* (1987).

Effects of repeated administration of SSRIs on central neurotransmitter receptors

ß-adrenoceptors

Repeated administration of most tricyclic antidepressant drugs, MAOIs, and electroconvulsive shock decreases ß-adrenoceptor number and function as evidenced by a reduction in the number of [^{3}H]-dihydroalprenolol ([^{3}H]-DHA) binding sites and noradrenaline- or isoprenaline-stimulated production of cyclic adenosine monophosphate (AMP) in the rat brain (Vetulani *et al*, 1976, Banerjee *et al*, 1977; Wolfe *et al*, 1978; Bergstrom and Kellar, 1979a), and it has been suggested that this response is associated with antidepressant efficacy in man (Vetulani *et al*, 1976). However, the effects of the SSRIs on ß-adrenoceptors in the rodent brain are inconsistent. The data obtained from studies with citalopram, fluoxetine, fluvoxamine, paroxetine, and sertraline are summarized in Table IV.

Fluoxetine is the most extensively studied of the SSRIs. In four studies, no significant reduction in the number of ß-adrenoceptor binding sites in rat frontal cortex was observed after repeated administration of fluoxetine (Mishra *et al*, 1979; Maggi *et al*, 1980; Peroutka and Snyder, 1980; Wong *et al*, 1985b; Baron *et al*, 1988). Although no reduction has been reported in the ß-adrenoceptor-stimulated production of cyclic AMP in rat forebrain after this treatment by most investigators (Schmidt and Thornberry, 1977; Mishra *et al*, 1979; Kopanski *et al*, 1983), Baron *et al* (1988) have reported a significant reduction in the production

Effects on ß-adrenergic system		
Inhibition of specific [^{3}H]-radioligand binding		Inhibition of noradrenaline/ isoprenaline-stimulated adenyl cyclase
Membranes	Autoradiography	
Paroxetine 0^1	0^2	0^1
Citalopram $0^{3,4}$	NT	$0^{4,5}$
Fluvoxamine $0^6;{\downarrow}^7$	NT	$0^5;{\downarrow}^8$
Fluoxetine $0^{9,10,11,12}$	${\downarrow}^{13}$	$0^{5,10,14};{\downarrow}^{15}$
Sertraline ${\downarrow}^{16}$	${\downarrow}^{17}$	${\downarrow}^{16}$
Amitriptyline $0^{18};{\downarrow}^{2,12,19,20}$	0^2	$0^2;{\downarrow}^5$
Desipramine ${\downarrow}^{2,4,12,19,20}$	${\downarrow}^{2,21}$	${\downarrow}^{2,5,15,22}$

Table IV. Comparative effects of the SSRIs on ß-adrenoceptor number and function in rat brain. 0 and ↓ indicate no and statistically significant reductions, respectively, following chronic antidepressant treatment; NT= not tested.
References: 1. Nelson *et al* (1990a,b). 2. Pratt and Bowery (1990). 3. Hyttel *et al* (1984). 4. Garcha *et al* (1985). 5. Kopanski *et al* (1983). 6. Benfield and Ward (1986). 7. Brunello *et al* (1986). 8. Claassen (1983). 9. Wong *et al* (1985). 10. Mishra *et al* (1979). 11. Maggi *et al* (1980). 12. Peroutka and Snyder (1980). 13. Byerley *et al* (1988). 14. Schmidt and Thornberry (1977). 15. Baron *et al* (1988). 16. Koe *et al* (1983). 17. Byerley *et al* (1987). 18. Tang *et al* (1981). 19. Sulser (1982). 20. Sellinger-Barnette *et al* (1980). 21. Ordway *et al* (1988). 22. Schoffelmeer *et al* (1984).

of isoprenaline-stimulated cyclic AMP after 4 and 14 days of fluoxetine administration. Furthermore, Byerley *et al* (1988) have shown in autoradiographic studies that repeated administration of fluoxetine reduced the binding of [^{3}H]-DHA in specific laminae of rat frontal cortex. Baron *et al* (1988) also showed that the co-administration of fluoxetine and desipramine potentiated the reduction in ß-adrenoceptor number induced by desipramine alone, whereas the effect of the two drugs on isoprenaline-stimulated cyclic AMP production was additive. Asakura *et al* (1987) have also shown that the co-administration of fluoxetine with mianserin or maprotiline prolonged the short-lasting decrease in the number of cortical ß-adrenoceptors that was observed after seven days' administration of these antidepressants. These results lend support to the role of serotonin in the down-regulation of ß-adrenoceptors in the central nervous system by antidepressants as described by Bergstrom and Kellar (1979a), Janowsky *et al* (1982) and Manier *et al* (1984). However, the effect of fluoxetine on the pharmacokinetics of desipramine and other antidepressants in the rat has not been systematically investigated, and hence this cannot be discounted as a possible contributory mechanism to the observed effects.

In contrast to fluoxetine, sertraline reduces both the number of ß-adrenoceptors and stimulated cyclic AMP production in rat cerebral cortex and limbic forebrain, respectively (Koe *et al,* 1983, 1987). Down-regulation of ß-adrenoceptors by sertraline in laminae IV to VI of rat cerebral cortex was also observed in an autoradiographic study (Byerley *et al,* 1987). Racagni and Bradford (1984) report that fluvoxamine reduces the number of ß-adrenoceptors in rat brain after repeated administration, but this effect was not confirmed by Benfield and Ward (1986). Similarly, Claassen (1983) states that ß-adrenoceptor-stimulated cyclic AMP production in rat brain is reduced by repeated fluvoxamine administration, but Kopanski *et al* (1983) found no significant effect of fluvoxamine on this response. No autoradiographic studies have been carried out with fluvoxamine. Of the more potent and selective inhibitors of serotonin re-uptake, citalopram failed to down-regulate ß-adrenoceptors in membranes from rat cortex (Hyttel, 1977b; Garcha *et al,* 1985) or to reduce ß-adrenoceptor-stimulated cyclic AMP production in rat forebrain (Kopanski *et al,* 1983; Garcha *et al,* 1985).

Paroxetine did not reduce the number of ß$_1$- or ß$_2$-adrenoceptors or ß-adrenoceptor-stimulated cyclic AMP production in rat frontal cortex on repeated administration to rats (Nelson *et al,* 1989, 1990b), and no reduction in the number of ß-adrenoceptors in the laminae of rat frontal cortex was observed in a specific autoradiographic study (Pratt and Bowery, 1990).

It is hypothesized that the highly selective serotonin re-uptake inhibitors, e.g. paroxetine and citalopram, do not down-regulate ß-adrenoceptors, because of their relative lack of effect on the noradrenergic system. Further studies are required to substantiate this hypothesis, but the results obtained with paroxetine are in accord with the view that the down-regulation of central ß-adrenoceptors by antidepressants in animals does not correlate with their antidepressant properties in the clinic (Willner, 1984).

α-adrenoceptors

Repeated administration of paroxetine has no effect on the affinity (K_d) or number of binding sites for [^{3}H]-prazosin or [^{3}H]-idazoxan in rat cortical membranes (Nelson *et al*, 1989). Similarly, fluoxetine has no effect on these parameters of [^{3}H]-WB 4101 or [^{3}H]-clonidine binding under similar dosing regimes (Wong *et al*, 1985b). These data indicate that the number and affinity of $α_1$-and $α_2$-adrenoceptors in rat cortex are not altered by repeated administration of these drugs. Nowak (1989) has confirmed an earlier report (Maj *et al*, 1985) that citalopram—like imipramine, amitriptyline, mianserin, and electroconvulsive shock increases [^{3}H]-prazosin binding in rat cortex, although there is evidence that the changes induced by the antidepressants were dependent on the strain of rat tested (Stockmeier *et al*, 1987; Nowak and Przegalinski, 1988). Earlier, Arnt *et al* (1984a) reported that repeated administration of citalopram had no effect on [^{3}H]-prazosin binding (K_d or B_{max}) in a region of rat brain which comprised the brain stem less the pons. In contrast to desipramine, citalopram had no effect on the clonidine-induced reduction in [^{3}H]-dopamine release from the nucleus accumbens (Russell *et al*, 1987). Therefore, these data confirm repeated administration of citalopram does not induce any changes in $α_2$-adrenoceptors in the nucleus accumbens.

The effect of repeated administration of fluvoxamine and sertraline on central $α_1$- and $α_2$-adrenoceptors has not been investigated. Sertraline shows a weak affinity for $α_1$-adrenoceptors, being two to four times less potent than imipramine and desipramine, as evidenced by the inhibition of [^{3}H]-prazosin binding *in vitro* (Stockmeier *et al*, 1987).

In conclusion, the SSRIs as a class do not appear to influence $α_1$- or $α_2$-adrenoceptors on repeated administration. Further comparative studies are required to determine whether the changes induced by citalopram in $α_1$-adrenoceptors in the rat brain can be brought about by other SSRIs.

Dopamine receptors

When given repeatedly, neither fluoxetine (Peroutka and Snyder, 1980) nor citalopram (Hyttel *et al*, 1984) had any effect on the binding of [^{3}H]-spiperone to dopamine D_2-receptor binding sites in the rat striatum. However, citalopram, imipramine, amitriptyline, and other antidepressants reduced the binding of [^{3}H]-SCH-23390 to dopamine D_1-receptors in the rat striatum and limbic system after repeated administration, again without affecting [^{3}H]-spiperone binding to D_2 sites in these tissues (Klimek and Nielsen, 1987).

There is also evidence that behavioural responses to dopaminergic agents are altered after repeated administration of the SSRIs. In contrast to single doses of paroxetine, citalopram, and fluoxetine, which had no effect on the hypermotility response of rats to d-amphetamine, repeated administration of these drugs significantly potentiated the response to amphetamine when administered 2, and in some cases 24, hours after the last dose (Arnt *et al*, 1984a, b). Maj *et al* (1984) have also reported that citalopram, zimeldine, imipramine, and amitriptyline potentiate the hypermotility response to amphetamine 2 or 72 hours after repeated administration to mice. Fluvoxamine was not effective at either time point. The hypermotility responses to the indirect dopamine agonist methylphenidate and the direct dopamine agonist (+)-3-PPP were also potentiated after repeated administration of citalopram (Arnt *et al,* 1984a). Similarly, repeated but not single-dose administration of citalopram, imipramine, amitriptyline, and mianserin potentiated the hypermotility response of rats to quinpirole, a dopamine D_2-receptor agonist, when given 1.5 hours after the last dose (Maj *et al,* 1989). Furthermore, the hypermotility response to a subthreshold dose of dopamine or apomorphine injected into the nucleus accumbens was potentiated 24 hours after the cessation of repeated administration of citalopram, desipramine, or electroconvulsive shock (Plaznick and Kostowski, 1987).

The hypermotility response to apomorphine was also reduced after repeated administration of citalopram (Arnt *et al,* 1984b), indicating a possible decreased sensitivity of the dopamine autoreceptors that mediate sedation.

Pharmacological studies indicate that the SSRIs, like the tricyclic antidepressants and mianserin, generally increase the sensitivity of dopaminergic mechanisms in the mesolimbic system. In the case of citalopram, this has been shown to be associated with a reduction in the number of dopamine D_1- but not D_2-receptor binding sites in this tissue. It remains to be determined whether this effect is relevant to the therapeutic actions of these drugs.

Serotonin receptors

The observation by Peroutka and Snyder (1980) that the repeated administration of the tricyclic antidepressants amitriptyline, imipramine, and desipramine leads to a reduction in the number of $5-HT_2$ receptor binding sites in rat frontal cortex followed the neurophysiological study of de Montigny and Aghajanian (1978), which had shown that repeated administration of the tricyclic antidepressants amitriptyline, imipramine, desipramine, and clomipramine enhanced the responsiveness of rat forebrain neurones to the inhibitory effect of serotonin. This work stimulated further investigation of the adaptive changes that occur in central serotonergic mechanisms in response to repeated antidepressant administration. In these early studies, both de Montigny and Aghajanian (1978) and Peroutka and Snyder (1980) reported that fluoxetine did not induce the changes in serotonergic receptors that were typical of the tricyclic antidepressants, and this difference between the two classes of antidepressant has been substantiated by further investigations.

Following the initial neurophysiological studies of de Montigny and Aghajanian (1978), de Montigny and co-workers have comprehensively investigated the electrophysiological effects of repeated administration of a number of antidepressant treatments, i.e. the tricyclics, MAOIs, electroconvulsive shock, and the SSRIs including fluoxetine (Blier *et al,* 1988), citalopram (Chaput *et al,* 1986), and paroxetine (de Montigny *et al,* 1989). They have studied the effects of these drugs, after single and repeated administration, on serotonergic projections from the dorsal raphé nucleus to the postsynaptic receptors on the CA_3 pyramidal cells of the hippocampus. Citalopram (Chaput *et al,* 1986) and zimeldine (Blier and de Montigny, 1983), like other SSRIs, are potent inhibitors of the firing of 5-HT neurones in the dorsal raphé nucleus. Tolerance develops to this effect on repeated administration such that citalopram and zimeldine were no longer effective after daily dosing for 14 days. The suppression of firing of dorsal raphé neurones by fluvoxamine and sertraline has also been reported by Dresse and Scuvee-Moreau (1984) and by Heym and Koe (1988). Chaput *et al* (1986) further showed that inhibition of the firing of dorsal raphé neurones by the 5-HT autoreceptor agonist LSD, which was not influenced by a single dose of citalopram, was attenuated after repeated administration of citalopram. This suggests that citalopram reduces the sensitivity of the somatodendritic 5-HT autoreceptor after repeated administration.

Citalopram, zimeldine, fluoxetine, and paroxetine also enhanced the firing of hippocampal neurones in response to electrical stimulation of the ascending serotonergic pathway after repeated administration but not after single doses. However, the firing of hippocampal CA_3 pyramidal neurones in response to iontophoretically applied 5-HT—a response mediated by postsynaptic 5-HT_{1A} receptor activation (Andrade and Nicole, 1987) and enhanced by repeatedly administered imipramine, clomipramine, or electroconvulsive shock — was not affected by repeated administration of zimeldine or citalopram. Chaput *et al* (1986) concluded that long-term but not acute treatment with citalopram increases serotonergic synaptic neurotransmission in the rat hippocampus via decreased function of terminal 5-HT autoreceptors as methiothepin, a terminal 5-HT autoreceptor antagonist, failed to enhance the suppression of firing of the pyramidal cells produced by electrical stimulation of the ascending pathway as it did in untreated animals. Similar results have been obtained with fluoxetine (Blier *et al*, 1988) and paroxetine (de Montigny *et al*, 1989).

In summary, Blier *et al* (1990) have concluded from electrophysiological studies that repeated administration of tricyclic antidepressants and SSRIs enhances serotonergic neurotransmission in the hippocampus by different mechanisms. The enhancement by tricyclic antidepressants appears to be due to the development of supersensitivity of postsynaptic 5-HT (5-HT_{1A}) receptors whereas the SSRIs enhance serotonergic neurotransmission by reducing the responsiveness of the somatodendritic and terminal 5-HT autoreceptors.

Radioligand binding techniques, initially using [^{3}H]-5-HT and [^{3}H]-spiperone or [^{3}H]-ketanserin as ligands for 5-HT_1 and 5-HT_2 receptor binding sites, have used extensively in an attempt to characterize changes in serotonergic receptors in response to the repeated administration of antidepressants. However, recent advances in the identification and characterization of 5-HT receptor subtypes (see chapter 1) indicate that [^{3}H]-5-HT binds to a number of subtypes of the 5-HT_1 receptor, and hence observations on the effects of the SSRIs on the binding of this ligand cannot be interpreted in terms of changes in a type of single receptor. Although the majority of studies (Table V) indicate that fluoxetine has no effect on [^{3}H]-5-HT binding in the rat brain, two studies—Wong *et al* (1985b) and Dumbrille-Ross and Tang (1983)— reported significant reductions in the binding of this ligand. More recent studies with ligands for specific $5\text{-}HT_1$ receptor subtypes have confirmed that fluoxetine induces changes in certain receptors. Indeed, Welner *et al* (1989) have recently shown in an autoradiographic study that repeated administration of fluoxetine to rats results in a significant reduction in the number of binding sites for [^{3}H]-8-hydroxy-N,N-dipropyl-2-aminotetralin (8-OH-DPAT), a specific $5\text{-}HT_{1A}$ receptor agonist, in the dorsal raphé nucleus. No changes were observed in hippocampal binding. In contrast, amitriptyline did not affect binding in the dorsal raphé nucleus but increased [^{3}H]-8-OH-DPAT binding in the dorsal hippocampus. An increase in the number of binding sites was also observed in membranes prepared from the forebrain in rats that had received amitriptyline but not fluoxetine. These data are consistent with the electrophysiological studies summarized by Blier *et al* (1990).

Goodwin *et al* (1985) have reported that the hypothermia induced by 8-OH-DPAT administration in mice, a response believed to be mediated by presynaptic $5\text{-}HT_{1A}$ receptors, is reduced by repeated administration of the antidepressants desipramine, zimeldine, and mianserin, but no studies on this response with the more selective inhibitors of serotonin re-uptake have been reported.

Reynolds *et al* (1989) have reported that sertraline reduces the number of binding sites for [^{3}H]-8-OH-DPAT in the hippocampus after two weeks of administration, an effect that was accompanied by a reduction in the reciprocal forepaw treading response elicited by 8-OH-DPAT. These actions were attributed to a reduction in postsynaptic $5\text{-}HT_{1A}$ receptors subsequent to chronic administration of sertraline. Few other studies have been carried out on the effects of repeated administration of the SSRIs. Nelson *et al* (1989) showed that repeated administration of paroxetine was not associated with a reduction in [^{3}H]-8-OH-DPAT binding in rat cortex.

The initial study by Peroutka and Snyder (1980) on changes in $5\text{-}HT_2$ receptor binding sites after antidepressant administration was followed by further studies. Review of the studies of the effects of repeated administration of the SSRIs on the binding of radioligands for the $5\text{-}HT_2$ receptor in rat brain (Table V) indicates that although the observation that the tricyclic antidepressants, including desipramine, down-regulate $5\text{-}HT_2$ receptor binding sites in rat frontal cortex is a robust one, the effects of the more potent and selective inhibitors of serotonin re-uptake are less consistent.

Nelson *et al* (1989), Kubota *et al* (1989), Stolz *et al* (1983), and Claassen (1983) have reported that repeated administration of paroxetine, citalopram, fluoxetine, and fluvoxamine, respectively, reduces $5\text{-}HT_2$ receptor binding sites in rat frontal cortex, but other authors (Table V) have reported no changes with any of these drugs, except paroxetine. Recently, Sanders-Bush *et al* (1989) reported that sertraline and amitriptyline reduced 5-HT-stimulated ($5\text{-}HT_2$-mediated) phosphoinositide hydrolysis in the rat cortex when administered repeatedly for 28 days. The effect of amitriptyline, but not sertraline, was associated with a reduction in $5\text{-}HT_2$ receptor binding sites in this tissue. These results indicate that functional desensitization of $5\text{-}HT_2$ receptor mechanisms by drugs may not be associated with changes in the number of $5\text{-}HT_2$ receptors.

	Inhibition of radioligand binding (reduction in B_{max}) in frontal cortex	
	[3H]-ketanserin or [3H]-spiperone (5-HT$_2$)	[3H]-5-HT (5-HT$_1$-like)
Paroxetine	↓[1]	0[1]
Citalopram	0[2,3];↓[4]	
Fluoxetine	0[5];↓[6]	0[5,6,7,8,9]; ↓[10,11]
Fluvoxamine	0[12]; ↓[13]	0[12]
Sertraline	0[14]; ↓*	
Amitriptyline	↓[5,11,14,15]	0[6,8,16]
Clomipramine	↓[6]	0[6,8,16,17]
Desipramine	↓[5,6,11,13,15]	↓[7]
Electroconvulsive shock	↑[18,19,20]	

Table V. Effect of repeated administration of SSRIs on the binding of radioligands to serotonergic receptor sites in the rat brain.

0, ↓, and ↑ indicate no, statistically significant reductions, and statistically significant increases, respectively, following repeated SSRI administration. *reduction in 5-HT-stimulated phosphotidylinositide turnover (Sanders-Bush *et al*, 1989).

References: 1. Nelson *et al* (1989). 2. Hyttel *et al* (1984). 3. Buckett *et al* (1983). 4. Kubota *et al* (1989). 5. Peroutka and Snyder (1980). 6. Stolz *et al* (1983). 7. Maggi *et al* (1980). 8. Savage *et al* (1980). 9. Hwang *et al* (1980). 10. Wong *et al* (1985). 11. Dumbrille-Ross and Tang (1983). 12. Claassen (1983). 13. Bradford *et al* (1985). 14. Armstrong *et al* (1985). 15. Dumbrille-Ross *et al* (1982). 16. Lucki and Fraser (1982). 17. Wirz-Justice *et al* (1978). 18. Kellar *et al* (1981). 19. Vetulani *et al* (1981). 20. Green *et al* (1983).

Behavioural studies with 5-HT agonists give some support to the hypothesis that paroxetine, citalopram, and fluoxetine reduce the sensitivity of 5-HT$_2$ receptors in the rodent brain. For example, the potentiated head twitch response of mice to 5-hydroxytryptophan (5-HTP) administration that has been observed after a single dose of paroxetine is reduced after repeated administration (Marshall *et al*, 1988). Similarly the 'wet dog shake' response induced by 5-HTP in rats is reduced after repeated administration of citalopram (Arnt *et al*, 1984b). These data suggest that the function of 5-HT$_2$ receptors may be reduced after repeated administration of paroxetine and citalopram, although Pawlowski and Melzacka (1986) have reported that the head twitch response to the 5-HT agonist quipazine in rats was reduced after repeated administration of amitriptyline but not fluvoxamine or citalopram. A reduced serotonergic syndrome in response to the direct 5-HT agonist 5-methoxy-N,N-dimethyltryptamine (5-MDMT) has also been observed after repeated administration of citalopram (Arnt *et al*, 1984a) and fluoxetine (Stolz *et al*, 1983). Similarly, the serotonergic syndrome induced in rats by tryptophan and tranylcypromine after a single dose of paroxetine or fluoxetine is márkedly reduced after repeated administration of these drugs (Hwang and van Woert, 1980). As the behavioural response to 5-MDMT probably involves activation of both 5-HT_2 and 5-HT_1 receptor subtypes (Tricklebank *et al*, 1985), and the combination of tryptophan and tranylcypromine will non-specifically increase the availability of serotonin at central receptors, it is not possible to identify which 5-HT receptor subtypes have been influenced by the SSRIs in these studies.

In conclusion, electrophysiological studies on the serotonergic projection from the dorsal raphé nucleus to the CA_3 pyramidal cells in the rat hippocampus indicate that the SSRIs desensitize somatodendritic 5-HT autoreceptors and the terminal 5-HT autoreceptors in this pathway. The somatodendritic 5-HT autoreceptors have been classified as the 5-HT_{1A} subtype (Vergé *et al*, 1985, Weissman-Nanopoulous *et al*, 1985; Blier and de Montigny, 1987; Sprouse and Aghajanian, 1987) and the terminal 5-HT autoreceptors as the 5-HT_{1B} subtype in the rat (Engel *et al*, 1986; Maura *et al*, 1986). In man, pig, and guinea-pig, terminal 5-HT autoreceptors have been classified as the 5-HT_{1D} subtype (Hoyer *et al*, 1988; Waeber *et al*, 1988). In contrast to the tricyclic antidepressants, which sensitize postsynaptic 5-HT_{1A}-receptors in the hippocampus, the SSRIs had no effect on these postsynaptic receptors. The SSRIs and tricyclic antidepressants therefore facilitate serotonergic neurotransmission in the central nervous system by actions at different 5-HT receptors.

Biochemical and pharmacological studies indicate that both the SSRIs and the tricyclic antidepressants down-regulate 5-HT_2 receptor-mediated mechanisms in the rat brain. The relevance of this antidepressant effect on 5-HT_2 receptor-mediated function remains controversial as these receptors are up-regulated by electroconvulsive shock treatment in animals. However, whereas facilitation of serotonergic function at, for example, 5-HT_{1A} receptors, may be important for efficacy in depression, a reduction in 5-HT_2 receptor-mediated function may be important for efficacy in other conditions, such as anxiety states (Deakin, 1988).

Further comparative neurochemical, electrophysiological, and pharmacological studies with antidepressants of various selective and non-selective mechanisms are required to clarify these issues, but adaptive changes in 5-HT-receptor-mediated events appear to be central to the therapeutic action of antidepressants.

GABAergic receptors
Lloyd *et al* (1985) reported that the repeated administration to rats of antidepressants of different classes (including the SSRIs zimeldine, fluoxetine, and citalopram) and electroconvulsive shock resulted in an increase in the number of $GABA_B$ binding sites in the frontal cortex. The effects of zimeldine and desipramine on $GABA_B$ binding in rat cortex were not confirmed by Cross and Horton (1988), but Gray *et al* (1987) have shown that the hypothermic response to the $GABA_B$ agonist baclofen was enhanced by repeated administration of zimeldine, desipramine and ECS. Pratt and Bowery (1989) were unable to demonstrate any change in $GABA_B$ binding to individual laminae of the rat frontal cortex after repeated administration of paroxetine or desipramine

in an autoradiographic study.

According to Sudzak and Gianutsos (1985), imipramine and nomifensine cause a reduction in ^{3}H-GABA binding in the rat cerebral cortex and hippocampus on repeated administration. Zimeldine, like desipramine and bupropion, is reported to reduce the density of benzodiazepine binding sites after repeated administration (Suranyi-Cadotte et al, 1984). However, no studies have been carried out with the more selective inhibitors of serotonin re-uptake. The role of GABA in the action of antidepressant drugs in general and the SSRIs in particular therefore remains to be clarified.

Effects on behaviour

Despite their potent effects on serotonin re-uptake, there are few reports that the SSRIs induce overt changes in behaviour, even when administered at high pharmacological doses to laboratory animals. For example, Johnson (1989) reported that paroxetine caused no marked effects on the spontaneous behaviour of mice in doses of up to 30mg/kg p.o. in a general observation test, a weak locomotor stimulation being observed only after subcutaneous administration of 10 to 50mg/kg to rats. Fluoxetine does not induce hypermotility or behavioural stimulation in animals (Keshavan et al, 1981; Stark et al, 1985). Similarly, sertraline does not stimulate locomotor activity in rats over a wide dosage range (Koe et al, 1983). As reported earlier, the SSRIs do induce symptoms of central serotonergic activation in rodents—the so-called serotonergic syndrome—when administered in combination with serotonin precursors such as L-tryptophan, L-5-hydroxytryptophan, and tryptamine. Such interactions have been used as the basis of in vivo assays for inhibition of serotonin re-uptake and will not be discussed in detail here. Paroxetine and clomipramine also induce the serotonin syndrome when administered in combination with MAOIs (Marley and Wozniak, 1983). As would be predicted, the rank order of potency of paroxetine, fluoxetine, fluvoxamine, and clomipramine in inducing the serotonin syndrome in rats treated with tranylcypromine was the same as that for the inhibition of serotonin re-uptake ex vivo in this species (unpublished observations).

Electroencephalogram and sleep studies

Kleinlogel and Bürki (1987) have shown that oral administration of low doses of paroxetine increased dozing, assessed by electroencephalogram (EEG) recordings, in conscious rats with chronically implanted electrodes, but as the dosage was increased there was a dose-dependent increase in wakening, decreased slow-wave sleep, and suppressed rapid eye movement (REM) sleep. Similarly, Watanabe et al (1988) have shown that intravenous administration of paroxetine caused an EEG arousal pattern in conscious rabbits with chronically implanted electrodes. Fluoxetine has been shown to increase the latencies to slow-wave and REM sleep in rats (Forval and Radulovacki, 1980). The duration of REM sleep was also reduced in a dose-dependent manner in cats after administration of fluoxetine (Slater *et al,* 1978). Citalopram also decreased REM sleep and increased deep slow-wave sleep in conscious cats with chronically implanted electrodes (Hilakivi *et al,* 1987), and fluvoxamine shortened REM sleep in this species (Scherschlicht *et al,* 1982).

These studies therefore indicate that the SSRIs, like other antidepressants, suppress REM sleep in laboratory animals.

Possible interaction with the extrapyramidal dopaminergic system

Evidence from studies in rodents indicates that the serotonergic system exerts tonic inhibition of the dopaminergic system in the central nervous system (Costall *et al,* 1975, Carter and Pycock 1977), although a co-operative interaction of serotonin and dopamine has also been observed (Waddington and Crow, 1979). It might therefore be predicted that inhibitors of serotonin re-uptake would reduce dopaminergic neurotransmission in the central nervous system. However, as discussed earlier, animal studies suggest that this class of drugs sensitizes dopaminergic mechanisms in the mesolimbic system. These data contrast with recent clinical observations that fluoxetine may exacerbate extrapyramidal symptoms in susceptible patients (Bouchard *et al,* 1989). The interaction of the SSRIs with the extrapyramidal dopaminergic system in animals has therefore been addressed specifically.

In pharmacological studies, paroxetine failed to induce catalepsy in the rat and also failed to inhibit apomorphine-induced catalepsy in this species (unpublished observations) indicating a lack of inhibitory action on central dopaminergic mechanisms. However, Balsara *et al* (1979) have reported that clomipramine exerts a dose-dependent potentiation of haloperidol-induced catalepsy in rats, and Waldmeier and Delini-Stula (1979) showed that clomipramine, citalopram, fluoxetine, and the SSRI CGP 6085A potentiated the increase seen in the striatal deaminated dopamine metabolites homovanillic acid and dihydroxyphenylacetic acid after haloperidol treatment whilst having no effect when given alone. The cataleptic response to haloperidol and the inhibitory effect of haloperidol on apomorphine-induced stereotypy were also potentiated by citalopram and CGP 6085A. However, Waldmeier (1979) has shown that CGP 6085A potentiates the effects of haloperidol only after acute treatment, not in chronically treated animals. Furthermore, Sugrue (1980) demonstrated that the potentiation of the haloperidol-induced increase in rat striatal dihydroxyphenyl-acetic acid and homovanillic acid observed after a single dose of fluoxetine was markedly reduced when fluoxetine was repeatedly administered.

A few studies have investigated the interaction of the SSRIs with extrapyramidal dopaminergic mechanisms in non-human primates. Paroxetine, like CGP 6085A, has been reported by Korsgaard *et al* (1985) to induce oral hyperkinesia in the monkey *(Cercopithecus aethiops).* Both drugs also produced a weak potentiation of the haloperidol-induced symptoms of Parkinsonism and dystonia in this species, whereas amphetamine-induced repetitive movements of the head, limbs, and trunk were decreased. In another study, citalopram was shown to have no effect on the dystonia induced by chronic haloperidol in the cebus monkey (Juul Povlsen *et al*, 1986).

As mentioned earlier, Carlsson and Lindqvist (1978) have investigated the action of single doses of a number of antidepressants on brain monoamine synthesis, including dopamine, in the rat. Of the drugs investigated that exhibited a predominant action on serotonin re-uptake, clomipramine and zimeldine increased dopamine turnover as evidenced by dopa (3,4-dihydroxyphenyl-alanine) accumulation in the striatum and limbic forebrain after dopa decarboxylase inhibition; citalopram caused occasional decreases or increases without any obvious dose dependence. The tricyclic antidepressants protriptyline and maprotiline caused a decrease in the turnover of dopamine, whereas an increase was observed after trimipramine and mianserin.

Baldessarini and Marsh (1990) have recently reported that fluoxetine causes a significant inhibition of dopa accumulation in the corpus striatum, nucleus accumbens, and frontal cortex of rats treated with the dopa decarboxylase inhibitor NSD-1015. On repeated administration of fluoxetine, the levels of dopa were also significantly reduced in the hippocampus, whereas those in the accumbens were no longer significantly different from control levels. The changes persisted in the striatum, whilst those in the frontal cortex were less although the levels were still significantly different from controls. The authors suggest that the fluoxetine-induced reduction in the turnover of dopamine in the striatum is particularly relevant to the clinical observations of Bouchard *et al* (1989).

The effects of paroxetine, fluvoxamine or sertraline on dopamine turnover in the rodent brain have not been extensively investigated, but the limited studies to date indicate no marked effects (unpublished observations; Koe *et al*, 1983; Benfield and Ward, 1986).

In conclusion, despite the evidence of a close association between the serotonergic and dopaminergic systems, particularly in the extrapyramidal system, the SSRIs do not appear to exert marked effects on the extrapyramidal dopaminergic system *per se*. However, these drugs do appear to potentiate the effects of neuroleptic drugs in rodents after single doses although tolerance develops to this effect on repeated administration. Further studies are required to determine whether the reduction in dopamine turnover in the extrapyramidal system observed after acute and chronic fluoxetine administration to rats which, as concluded by Baldessarini and Marsh (1990) could explain the apparent exacerbation of extrapyramidal symptoms observed with this drug in the clinic, is observed with other members of this class.

Few studies have been conducted in species other than rodents, and further studies are required — particularly in non-human primates. The possible pharmacokinetic interaction between antidepressants and neuroleptics or dopaminergic agonists in animals also requires further study.

Effect on food intake

Of the SSRIs, the effects of fluoxetine on food intake have been most extensively investigated, and the data on this compound have been reviewed by Fuller and Wong (1989). Goudie *et al* (1976) first reported that fluoxetine had a potent inhibitory effect of short duration on food intake and that it potentiated the anorectic effects of 5-HTP. The effects of fluoxetine were confirmed by Wong and Reid (1986) in meal-fed rats and these authors also showed that it suppressed the induction of feeding induced by 2-desoxyglucose, an action reported earlier by Carruba *et al* (1985). Leander (1987) has also demonstrated that fluoxetine reduces the intake of water sweetened with saccharin in non-water deprived rats.

Wurtman and Wurtman (1977, 1979) have shown that fluoxetine, fenfluramine, tryptophan, and the serotonin agonist MK-212 all selectively inhibited carbohydrate but not protein intake in rats given a choice between the two diets, whereas amphetamine reduced the intake of both carbohydrate and protein. A number of studies (Rowland *et al*, 1982; Wong *et al*, 1985b; Yen *et al*, 1987) have shown that the effect of fluoxetine on food intake in rodents is maintained on repeated administration. The inhibitory effect of fluoxetine on food intake in rats was not blocked by the non-specific serotonin antagonist, metergoline, the $5\text{-}HT_2$ antagonists ritanserin and LY 53857, or the peripheral $5\text{-}HT_2$ antagonists xylamidine and BS 501C57 (Wong *et al*, 1988).

An inhibitory effect of sertraline on food intake in rodents has been described by Lucki *et al* (1988). The intake of solid pellets by rats was significantly inhibited by sertraline, which also reduced milk consumption in food-deprived rats. The effect of sertraline on dry food intake was blocked by the non-selective serotonin antagonists metergoline and methysergide, but not by the selective $5\text{-}HT_2$ receptor antagonists ketanserin or xylamidine, indicating an action of sertraline on food intake via $5\text{-}HT_1$ rather than $5\text{-}HT_2$ receptors.

Paroxetine inhibits the intake of food pellets in rats after oral administration, being approximately equipotent to fluoxetine in this respect (Rasmussen *et al*, 1990). The relatively weak effect of paroxetine is surprising as the role of serotonin in the control of appetite and body weight in animals is well established (Blundell, 1984), and paroxetine is 3.5 to 20 times more potent than fluoxetine in inhibiting serotonin re-uptake after oral administration in the rat (Maitre *et al*, 1982; Thomas *et al*, 1987). The data contradict those of Angel *et al* (1988), who suggested that the potency of a number of SSRIs (which did not include paroxetine) correlated with their potency as SSRIs *in vivo*. The potency of the fluoxetine enantiomers parallels their potency as SSRIs *in vivo* (Wong *et al*, 1988), but Garattini *et al* (1986) have suggested that inhibition of serotonin re-uptake may not be a very effective mechanism of causing a depression of food intake.

The effects of fluvoxamine and citalopram on food intake have not been systematically evaluated, although fluvoxamine has been stated to reduce the consumption of food in rats (Benfield and Ward, 1986).

Events at pre- and postsynaptic 5-HT receptors can lead to a modification in feeding behaviour in rodents (Garattini *et al*, 1986). Further comparative studies with the SSRIs are required to elucidate the mechanisms involved in the anorectic and anti-obesity properties of these drugs.

Summary and conclusion

The SSRIs paroxetine, citalopram, fluvoxamine, fluoxetine, and sertraline constitute a structurally diverse group of drugs which vary in their relative potency and selectivity for the neuronal serotonin re-uptake mechanism.

Paroxetine is the most potent drug of this class *in vitro* and after oral administration, whereas citalopram exhibits the greatest selectivity for inhibition of serotonin re-uptake relative to that for catecholamine re-uptake. All the SSRIs show a greater selectivity for inhibition of serotonin re-uptake compared with that for noradrenaline in comparison to the tricyclic antidepressants, including clomipramine.

In contrast to paroxetine and fluvoxamine, citalopram, fluoxetine, and sertraline are metabolized *in vivo* to products that possess similar pharmacological properties to those of the parent molecule. In the case of fluoxetine, this results in a metabolite with a considerably longer elimination half-life than the parent molecule and which achieves clinically significant plasma levels.

The potency and selectivity of these drugs for inhibition of serotonin re-uptake is maintained on repeated administration. Furthermore, the prolonged inhibition of serotonin re-uptake causes adaptive changes in synaptic serotonergic receptors. Electrophysiological studies indicate that the drugs of this class desensitize somatodendritic and axonal serotonin autoreceptors without desensitizing postsynaptic 5-HT (5-HT$_{1A}$) receptors in the pyramidal cells of the rat hippocampus. In this respect, the SSRIs differ from the tricyclic antidepressants, which do not desensitize serotonergic autoreceptors but facilitate serotonergic neurotransmission by sensitizing postsynaptic 5-HT$_{1A}$ receptors in these structures. Biochemical and behavioural studies also suggest that 5-HT$_2$-receptor-mediated function may be down-regulated by the SSRIs. Further studies are required to establish which 5-HT receptor subtypes are desensitized, which are sensitized, and which remain unaffected by this class of drugs. The relatively different effects on serotonergic mechanisms involving different 5-HT receptor subtypes compared with the effects of the tricyclic antidepressants may explain the efficacy of the SSRIs in depression, anxiety disorders, panic disorder, and obsessive-compulsive disorder.

Interestingly, although sertraline, fluoxetine, and fluvoxamine all—to some extent—down-regulate central ß-adrenoceptors, no effects have been observed with the more potent and selective representatives of this class: paroxetine and citalopram. This provides further support for the hypothesis that the down-regulation of central ß-adrenoceptors in animals is not predictive of antidepressant properties in man.

No consistent changes in central α-adrenoceptors have been observed in rodents after repeated administration of the SSRIs, although citalopram has been reported to increase the number of α_1-adrenoceptors, in rat cerebral cortex.

However, more consistent effects are observed with these drugs on the dopaminergic system. Paroxetine, fluoxetine and, particularly, citalopram have been reported to increase the sensitivity of mesolimbic dopaminergic mechanisms after repeated administration, an effect that has also been demonstrated by the tricyclic antidepressants. Citalopram also reduces the binding of a specific ligand to dopamine D_1 sites on repeated administration. It remains to be demonstrated whether this property is shared with other drugs of this class and whether it is relevant to the potentiation of the effects mediated by the dopaminergic mesolimbic system.

No marked effects of these drugs on dopaminergic function *per se* have been observed, although fluoxetine has been shown to reduce the turnover of dopamine in several areas of the rat brain, including the extrapyramidal system, after both single and repeated administration. Further comparative studies with several members of this class are required to determine whether this effect is due to inhibition of serotonin re-uptake and whether it is associated with the suggested propensity of fluoxetine to exacerbate extrapyramidal effects in susceptible patients.

The SSRIs do not induce marked changes in animal behaviour, although activation of the EEG and suppression of REM sleep are also consistent findings in animals. In accord with the action of these drugs on serotonergic mechanisms, inhibition of feeding is observed after their administration. However, their potency in suppressing feeding does not appear to correlate with their potency as inhibitors of serotonin re-uptake, and further studies on the mechanisms involved are required.

In conclusion, the SSRIs offer exciting potential in the treatment of depression and anxiety, and in the investigation of the role of serotonin in other psychiatric disorders. Adaptive changes in neurotransmitter receptors take place in the central nervous system in animals in response to repeated administration of the drugs, probably as a result of persistent inhibition of serotonin re-uptake and the understanding of their mechanisms of action in the affective disorders is dependent upon the state of knowledge of the neuronal mechanisms in the central nervous system.

Acknowledgements

I am grateful to Dr Brian Jones for his comments and to Miss Helen Robey for her patience and care in preparing this manuscript.

References

Aghajanian GK (1972) Influence of drugs on the firing rate of serotonin containing neurones in brain. *Fed Proc* **31**, 91-96.

Aghajanian GK and Bloom FE (1967) Localisation of tritiated serotonin in rat brain by electron microscopic autoradiography. *J Pharmacol Exp Ther* **156**, 23-30.

Andrade R and Nicole RA (1987) Pharmacologically distinct actions of serotonin on single pyramidal neurones of the rat hippocampus recorded *in vitro. J Physiol* (Lond) **394**, 99-124.

Angel I, Taranger MA, Claustre Y, *et al* (1988) Anorectic activities of serotonin uptake inhibitors: Correlation with their potencies at inhibiting serotonin uptake *in vivo* and ³H-mazindol binding *in vitro. Life Sci* **43**, 651-658.

Armstrong NA, Stockmeier CA and Kellar KJ (1985) Neurochemical effects of repeated administration of sertraline. *Fed Proc* **44**, 887.

Arnt J, Hyttel J and Overo FK (1984a) Prolonged treatment with the specific 5-HT uptake inhibitor citalopram. Effect on dopaminergic and serotonergic functions. *Pol J Pharmacol Pharm* **36**, 221-230.

Arnt J, Overo KF, Hyttel J, *et al* (1984b) Changes in rat dopamine- and serotonin function *in vivo* after prolonged administration of the specific 5-HT uptake inhibitor citalopram. *Psychopharmacology* **84**, 457-465.

Asakura M, Tsukamoto T, Kubota H, *et al* (1987) Role of serotonin in regulation of ß-adrenoceptors by antidepressants. *Eur J Pharmacol* **141**, 95-100.

Badawy AA-B and Morgan C (1990) Effects of acute paroxetine administration on tryptophan metabolism and disposition in the rat. (Submitted for publication).

Baker PC and Goodwich CA (1982) The effect of the specific uptake inhibitor Lu 10-171 (citalopram) upon brain indoleamine stores in the maturing mouse. *Gen Pharmacol* **13**, 59-61.

Baldessarini RJ and Marsh E (1990) Fluoxetine and side effects. *Arch Gen Psychiatry* **47**, 191-192.

Balsara JJ, Jadhav JH and Chandorkar AG (1979) Effect of drugs influencing central serotonergic mechanisms on haloperidol-induced catalepsy. *Psychopharmacology* **62**, 67-69.

Banerjee SP, King LS, Riggi SJ, *et al* (1977) Development of ß-adrenoceptor subsensitivity by antidepressants. *Nature* **268**, 455-456.

Baron BM, Ogden AM, Siegel BW, *et al* (1988) Rapid down-regulation of ß-adrenoceptors by co-administration of desipramine and fluoxetine. *Eur J Pharmacol* **154**, 125-134.

Benfield DP, Harries CM and Luscombe DK (1980) Some pharmacological aspects of desmethyl-clomipramine. *Postgrad Med J* **56** (Suppl 1), 13-18.

Benfield P and Ward A (1986) Fluvoxamine. A review of its pharmacodynamic and pharmacokinetic properties and therapeutic efficacy in depressive illness. *Drugs* **32**, 313-334.

Bergstrom DA and Kellar JK (1979a) Adrenergic and serotonergic receptor binding in rat brain after chronic desmethylimipramine treatment. *J Pharmacol Exp Ther* **209**, 256-261.

Bergstrom DA and Kellar KJ (1979b) Effect of electroconvulsive shock on monoaminergic receptor binding sites in rat brain. *Nature* **278**, 464-466.

Blackburn KJ, French PC and Merrills RJ (1967) 5-hydroxytryptamine uptake by rat brain *in vitro. Life Sci* **6**, 1653-1663.

Blier P, Chaput Y and de Montigny C (1988) Long-term 5-HT reuptake blockade but not monoamine oxidase inhibition, decreases the function. of terminal 5-HT autoreceptors; an electrophysiological study in the rat brain. *Naunyn Schmiedebergs Arch Pharmacol* **337**, 246-254.

Blier P and de Montigny C (1983) Electrophysiological investigations on the effect of repeated zimelidine administration on serotonergic neurotransmission in the rat. *J Neurosci* **3**, 1270-1278.

Blier P and de Montigny C (1987) Modification of 5-HT neuron properties by sustained administration of the 5-HT₁ₐ agonist, gepirone: an electrophysiological study in rat brain. *Synapse* **1**, 470-480.

Blier P, de Montigny C and Chaput Y (1990) A role for the serotonin system in the mechanism of action of antidepressants. *J Clin Psychiatry* **51** (Suppl 4), 14-20.

Blundell JE (1984) Serotonin and appetite. *Neuropharmacology* **23**, 1537-1551.

Boegesoe KP and Perregaard J (1989) New enantiomers of citalopram and their isolation. *European Patent Application* No. 347 006.

Bouchard RH, Pourcher E and Vincent P (1989) Fluoxetine and extrapyramidal side effects. *Am J Psychiatry* **146**, 1352-1353.

Bradford LD, Tulp M Th M and Schipper J (1985) Biochemical effects in rats after long term treatment with fluvoxamine and clovoxamine: post-synaptic changes. *Soc Neurosci Abstracts* **11**, 774.

Brunello N, Riva M, Voltera A, *et al* (1986) Biochemical changes in rat brain after acute and chronic administration of fluvoxamine, a selective 5-HT uptake blocker: Comparison with desmethylimipramine. *Adv Pharmacother* **2**, 186-196.

Buckett WR, Strange PC, Stuart EM, *et al* (1983) Chronic antidepressant treatment, hormonal manipulation and cortical serotonin S_2 receptors. *Br J Pharmacol* **79**, 297P.

Buus Lassen J (1978a) Potent and long lasting potentiation of two 5-hydroxytryptophan-induced effects in mice by three selective 5-HT uptake inhibitors. *Eur J Pharmacol* **47**, 351-358.

Buus Lassen J (1978b) Influence of the new 5-HT uptake inhibitor paroxetine on hypermotility in rats produced by p-chloroamphetamine (PCA) and 4,α-dimethyl-m-tyramine (H77/77). *Psychopharmacology* **57**, 151-153.

Buus Lassen J, Lund J and Sondergaard I (1980) Central and peripheral 5-HT uptake in rats treated chronically with femoxetine, paroxetine and chlorimipramine. *Psychopharmacology* **68**, 229-233.

Byerley WF, McConnell EJ, McCabe RT, *et al* (1987) Chronic administration of sertraline, a selective serotonin uptake inhibitor, decreased the density of beta-adrenoceptors in rat frontoparietal cortex. *Brain Res* **421**, 377-381.

Byerley WF, McConnell EJ, McCabe RT, *et al* (1988) Decreased beta-adrenergic receptors in rat brain after chronic administration of the selective serotonin uptake inhibitor fluoxetine. *Psychopharmacology* **94**, 141-143.

Carlsson A, Corrodi H, Fuxe K, *et al* (1969a) Effect of antidepressant drugs on the depletion of intraneuronal 5-hydroxytryptamine stores caused by 4-methyl-α-ethyl-meta-tyramine. *Eur J Pharmacol* **5**, 357-366.

Carlsson A, Corrodi H, Fuxe K, *et al* (1969b) Effect of some antidepressant drugs on the depletion of intraneuronal brain catecholamine stores caused by 4,α-ethyl-meta-tyramine. *Eur J Pharmacol* **5**, 367-373.

Carlsson A and Lindqvist M (1978) Effects of antidepressant agents on the synthesis of brain monoamines. *J Neural Transm* **43**, 73-91.

Carruba MO, Ricciardi S, Spano P, *et al* (1985) Dopaminergic and serotonergic anorectics differentially antagonise insulin and 2-DG-induced hyperphagia. *Life Sci* **36**, 1739-1749.

Carter CJ and Pycock CJ (1977) Possible importance of 5-hydroxytryptamine in neuroleptic induced catalepsy in rats. *Br J Pharmacol* **60**, 267P-268P.

Chaput Y, de Montigny C and Blier P (1986) Effects of a selective 5-HT reuptake blocker citalopram on the sensitivity of 5-HT autoreceptors; electrophysiological studies in the rat. *Naunyn Schmiedebergs Arch Pharmacol* **333**, 342-348.

Christensen AV, Fjalland B, Pedersen V, *et al* (1977) Pharmacology of a new phthalane (Lu 10-171), with specific 5-HT uptake inhibitory properties. *Eur J Pharmacol* **41**, 153-162.

Claassen V (1983) Review of the animal pharmacology and pharmacokinetics of fluvoxamine. *Br J Clin Pharmacol* **15**, 349S-355S.

Claassen V, Davies JE, Hertting G, *et al* (1977) Fluvoxamine, a specific 5-hydroxytryptamine uptake inhibitor. *Br J Pharmacol* **60**, 505-516.

Coppen A (1967) The biochemistry of affective disorders. *Br J Psychiatry* **113**, 1237-1264.

Corrodi H and Fuxe K (1968) The effects of imipramine on central monoamine neurones. *J Pharm Pharmacol* **20**, 230-231.

Costall B, Fortune DH, Naylor RJ, *et al* (1975) Serotonergic involvement in neuroleptic catalepsy. *Neuropharmacology* **14**, 859-868.

Cross JA and Horton RW (1988) Effects of chronic oral administration of the antidepressants desmethylimipramine and zimeldine on rat cortical $GABA_B$ binding sites: a comparison with 5-HT_2 binding site changes. *Br J Pharmacol* **93**, 331-336.

Deakin JFW (1988) 5-HT_2 receptors, depression and anxiety. *Pharmacol Biochem Behav* **29**, 819-820.

de Montigny C and Aghajanian GK (1978) Tricyclic antidepressants: Long-term treatments increase responsiveness of rat forebrain neurones to serotonin. *Science* **202**, 1303-1306.

de Montigny C, Chaput Y and Blier P (1989) Long term tricyclic and electroconvulsive treatment increases responsiveness of dorsal hippocampus 5-HT_{1A} receptors; an electrophysiological study. *Soc Neuroscience Abstracts* **15**, 854.

Dengler HJ and Titus EO (1961) The effect of drugs on the uptake of isotopic norepinephrine in various tissues. *Biochem Pharmacol* **8**, 64.

Doogan DP and Caillard V (1988) Sertraline: A new antidepressant. *J Clin Psychiatry* **49** (Suppl), 46-51.

Dresse A and Scuvee-Moreau J (1984) The effects of various antidepressants on the spontaneous firing rates of noradrenergic and serotonergic neurones. *Clin Neuropharmacol* **7** (Suppl 1), 572-573.

Dumbrille-Ross A and Tang SW (1983) Manipulations of synaptic serotonin; discrepancy of effects on serotonin S and S_2 sites. *Life Sci* **32**, 2677-2684.

Dumbrille-Ross A, Tang SW and Cescina DV (1982) Lack of effect of raphe lesions on the serotonin S_2 receptor changes induced by amitriptyline and desmethylimipramine. *Psychiatry Res* **7**, 145-151.

Engel G, Göthert M, Hoyer D, *et al* (1986) Identity of inhibitory presynaptic 5-hydroxytryptamine (5-HT) autoreceptors in the rat brain cortex with 5-HT_{1B} binding sites. *Naunyn Schmiedebergs Arch Pharmacol* **322**, 1-7.

Freidman E, Cooper TB and Dallob A (1983) Effects of chronic antidepressant administration on serotonin receptor activity in mice. *Eur J Pharmacol* **89**, 69-76.

Forval C and Radulovacki M (1980) Fenfluramine, fluoxetine and quipazine suppress sleep in rats. *Soc Neuroscience Abstracts* **6**, 57.

Fuller RW, Perry KW and Molloy BA (1974) Effect of an uptake inhibitor on serotonin metabolism in rat brain: studies with 3-(p-trifluoromethylphenoxy)-N-methyl-3-phenylpropylamine (Lilly 110140). *Life Sci* **51**, 1161-1171.

Fuller RW and Snoddy HD (1986) Fluoxetine enantiomers as antagonists of p-chloroamphetamine effects in rats. *Pharmacol Biochem Behav* **24**, 281-284.

Fuller RW and Wong DT (1989) Fluoxetine: A serotonergic appetite suppressant drug. *Drug Dev Res* **17**, 1-15.

Fuxe K and Ungerstedt U (1967) Localisation of 5-hydroxytryptamine uptake in rat brain after intraventricular injection. *J Pharm Phamacol* **19**, 335-337.

Garattini S, Mennini T, Bendotti C, *et al* (1986) Neurochemical mechanism of action of drugs which modify feeding via the serotonergic system. *Appetite* **7** (Suppl), 15-38.

Garcha G, Smokum RWJ, Stephenson JD, *et al* (1985) Effects of some atypical antidepressants on ß-adrenoceptor binding and adenylate cyclase activity in the rat forebrain. *Eur J Pharmacol* **108**, 1-7.

Glowinski J and Axelrod J (1964) Inhibition of uptake of tritiated-noradrenaline in the intact rat brain by imipramine and structurally related compounds. *Nature* **204**, 1318-1319.

Goodwin GM, De Sousa RJ and Green AR (1985) Presynaptic serotonin receptor mediated response in mice attenuated by antidepressant drugs and electroconvulsive shock. *Nature* **317**, 531-533.

Goudie AJ, Thornton EW and Wheeler TJ (1976) Effects of Lilly 110140, a selective inhibitor of 5-hydroxytryptamine intake on food intake and on 5-hydroxytryptophan-induced anorexia. Evidence for serotonergic inhibition of feeding. *J Pharm Pharmacol* **28**, 318-320.

Gray JA, Goodwin GM, Heal DJ, *et al* (1987) Hypothermia induced by baclofen, a possible index of $GABA_B$ receptor function in mice, is enhanced by antidepressant drugs and ECS. *Br J Pharmacol* **92**, 863-870.

Green AR, Johnson P and Nimgaonkar VL (1983) Increased 5-HT$_2$ receptor number in rat brain as a probable explanation for the enhanced 5-hydroxytryptamine mediated behaviour following repeated electroconvulsive shock administration to rats. *Br J Pharmacol* **80**, 173-177.

Haddock RE, Johnson AM, Langley PE, *et al* (1989) Metabolic pathway of paroxetine in animals and man and the comparative pharmacological properties of its metabolites. *Acta Psychiatr Scand* **80** (Suppl 350), 24-26.

Hall H and Ogren SO (1981) Effects of antidepressant drugs on different receptors in rat brain. *Eur J Pharmacol* **70**, 393-407.

Hall H and Ogren SO (1984) Effects of antidepressant drugs on histamine-H$_1$ receptors in the brain. *Life Sci* **34**, 597-605.

Heel RC, Morley PA, Brogden RN, *et al* (1982) Zimeldine: a review of its pharmacological properties and therapeutic efficacy in depressive illness. *Drugs* **24**, 169-206.

Hertting, G, Axelrod J and Whitby LG (1961) Effect of drugs on the uptake and metabolism of ^{3}H-norepinephrine. *J Pharmacol Exp Ther* **134**, 146-153.

Heym J and Koe BK (1988) Pharmacology of sertraline: a review. *J Clin Psychiatry* **49** (Suppl), 40-45.

Hilakivi I, Kovala T, Leppavuori, *et al* (1987) Effects of serotonin and noradrenaline uptake blockers on wakefulness and sleep in cats. *Pharmacol Toxicol* **60**, 161-166.

Hoyer D, Waeber C, Pazos A, *et al* (1988) Identification of a 5-HT$_1$ recognition site in human brain membranes different from 5-HT$_{1A}$, 5-HT$_{1B}$ and 5-HT$_{1C}$ sites. *Neurosci Lett* **85**, 357-362.

Hrdina PD (1987) Regulation of high and low-affinity [^{3}H]-imipramine recognition sites in rat brain by chronic treatment with antidepressants. *Eur J Pharmacol* **138**, 159-168.

Hwang EC, Magnussen I and van Woert MH (1980) Effect of chronic fluoxetine administration on serotonin metabolism. *Res Commun Chem Pathol Pharmacol* **29**, 79-98.

Hwang EC and van Woert MH (1980) Acute versus chronic effects of serotonin uptake blockers on the potentiation of the 'serotonin syndrome'. *Commun Psychopharmacology* **4**, 161-167.

Hyttel J (1977a) Neurochemical characterization of a new potent and selective serotonin uptake inhibitor, Lu 10-171. *Psychopharmacology* **51**, 225-233.

Hyttel J (1977b) Effect of a specific serotonin uptake inhibitor, Lu 10-171, on rat brain serotonin turnover. *Acta Pharmacol Toxicol* **40**, 439-446.

Hyttel J (1982) Citalopram — pharmacological profile of a specific serotonin uptake inhibitor with antidepressant activity. *Prog Neuropsychopharmacol Biol Psychiatry* **6**, 277-295.

Hyttel J, Overo KF and Arnt J (1984) Biochemical effects and drug levels in rats after long-term treatment with the specific 5-HT uptake inhibitor, citalopram. *Psychopharmacology* **83**, 20-27.

Janowsky A, Okada F, Manier DH, *et al* (1982) Role of serotonergic input in the regulation of the ß-adrenergic receptor coupled adenylate cyclase system. *Science* **218**, 900-901.

Johnson AM (1989) An overview of the animal pharmacology of paroxetine. *Acta Psychiatr Scand* **80** (Suppl 350), 14-20.

Jones RB and Luscombe DK (1977) Plasma concentrations of clomipramine and its N-desmethyl metabolite in depressive patients following treatment with various dosage regimes of clomipramine. *Postgrad Med J* **53** (Suppl 4), 63-76.

Juul Povlsen U, Noring U, Lund Laursen A, *et al* (1986) Effects of serotonergic and anticholinergic drugs in haloperidol-induced dystonia in cebus monkeys. *Clin Neuropharmacol* **9**, 84-90.

Kaye CM, Haddock RE, Langley PF, *et al* (1989) A review of the metabolism and pharmacokinetics of paroxetine in man. *Acta Psychiatr Scand* **80** (Suppl 350), 60-75.

Kellar KJ, Cascio CS, Butler JA, *et al* (1981) Differential effects of electroconvulsive shock and antidepressant drugs on serotonin-2 receptors in rat brain. *Eur J Pharmacol* **69**, 515-518.

Keshavan HJH, Gurbani NK and Dandiya PC (1980) Effect of citalopram (Lu 10-171) on tranyl-cypramine and tryptophan-induced wet dog shakes in rats. *Psychopharmacology* **70**, 209-212.

Keshavan HJH, Gurbani NK and Dandiya PC (1981) Effects of fluoxetine on a specific serotonergic syndrome in rats. *Indian J Med Res* **73** 653-657.

Kleinlogel H and Bürki HR (1987) Effects of the selective 5-hydroxytryptamine uptake inhibitors, paroxetine and zimeldine, on EEG sleep and waking changes in the rat. *Neuropsychobiology* **17**, 206-212.

Klimek V and Nielsen M (1987) Chronic treatment with antidepressants decreases the number of [^{3}H]-SCH 23390 binding sites in rat striatum and limbic system. *Eur J Pharmacol* **139**, 163-169.

Koe BK, Koch SW, Lebel LA, *et al* (1987) Sertraline, a selective inhibitor of serotonin uptake, induces subsensitivity of ß-adrenoceptor of rat brain. *Eur J Pharmacol* **141**, 187-194.

Koe BK, Weissman A, Welch WM, *et al* (1983) Sertraline, IS,4S-N-methyl-4-(3,4-dichlorophenyl) -1,2,3,4-tetrahydro-1- naphthylamine, a new uptake inhibitor with selectivity for serotonin. *J Pharmacol Exp Ther* **226**, 686-700.

Kopanski C, Türck M and Schultz JE (1983) Effects of long-term treatment of rats with antidepressants on adrenergic receptor sensitivity in cerebral cortex; structure activity study. *Neurochem Int* **5**, 649-659

Korsgaard S, Gerlach J and Christensson E (1985) Behavioural aspects of serotonin-dopamine interaction in the monkey. *Eur J Pharmacol* **118**, 245-252.

Kubota M, Ueno K, Yamano M, *et al* (1989) Changes of 5-HT$_2$ receptor density induced by repeated administration with 5-HT uptake inhibitor or 5-HT agonist. *Jap J Psychopharmacol* **9**, 289-292.

Kühn R (1957) Über die Behandlung depressiver Zustände mit einem Iminodibenzyl Derivat (G 22355). *Schweiz Med Wochenschr* **87**, 1135-1140.

Lapierre YD, Rastogi RB and Singhal RL (1983) Fluvoxamine influences serotonergic systems in the brain; neurochemical evidence. *Neuropsychobiology* **10**, 213-216.

Lapin IP and Oxenkrug GF (1969) Intensification of the central serotonergic processes as a possible determinant of the thymoleptic effect. *Lancet* **I**, 132-136.

Leander JD (1987) Fluoxetine suppresses palatability-induced ingestion. *Psychopharmacology* **91**, 285-287.

Lemberger L, Bergstrom RF, Wolen RL, *et al* (1985) Fluoxetine: Clinical pharmacology and physiological disposition. *J Clin Psychiatry* **46**, 14-19 .

Lloyd KG, Thuret F and Pilc A (1985) Upregulation of γ-aminobutyric acid (GABA)B binding sites in rat frontal cortex: a common action of repeated administration of different classes of antidepressant and electroshock. *J Pharmacol Exp Ther* **235**, 191-199.

Lucki I and Frazer A (1982) Prevention of the serotonin syndrome in rats by repeated administration of monoamine uptake inhibitors but not tricyclic antidepressants. *Psychopharmacology* **77**, 205-211.

Lucki I, Kreider MS and Simansky KJ (1988) Reduction of feeding behaviour by the serotonin uptake inhibitor sertraline. *Psychopharmacology* **96**, 289-295.

Maggi A, U'Prichard DC and Enna SJ (1980) Differential effects of antidepessant treatment on brain monoaminergic receptors. *Eur J Pharmocol* **61**, 91-98.

Magnussen I, Tonder K and Engbaek F (1982) Paroxetine, a potent selective long-acting inhibitor of synaptosomal 5-HT uptake in mice. *J Neural Transm* **55**, 217-226.

Maitre L, Baumann PA, Jaekel J, *et al* (1982) 5-HT uptake inhibitors; psychopharmacological and neurochemical criteria of selectivity. In: Ho BT *et al* (eds.) *Serotonin in Biological Psychiatry,* pp229-246. Raven Press: New York.

Maj J, Klimek V and Nowak G (1985) Antidepressant drugs given repeatedly increase binding to α_1-adrenoceptors in the rat cortex. *Eur J Pharmacol* **119**, 113-116.

Maj J, Rogoz Z, Skuza G, *et al* (1984) Repeated treatment with antidepressant drugs potentiates the locomotor response to (+)-amphetamine. *J Pharm Pharmacol* **36**, 127-130.

Maj J, Rogoz Z, Skuza G, *et al* (1989) Antidepressants given repeatedly increase the behavioural effect of D$_2$ agonists. *J Neural Transm* **78**, 1-8.

Manier DH, Gillespie DD, Steranka LR, *et al* (1984) A pivotal role for serotonin (5-HT) in the regulation of beta-adrenoceptors: reversibility of an action of para-chlorophenylamine by 5-hydroxytryptophan. *Experientia* **40**, 1223-1226.

Marley E and Wozniak KM (1983) Clinical and experimental aspects of interactions between amine oxidase inhibitors and amine reuptake inhibitors. *Psychol Med* **13**, 735-749.

Marshall EF, Nelson DR, Johnson AM, *et al* (1988) Desensitisation of central 5-HT$_2$ receptor mechanisms after repeated administration of the antidepressant paroxetine. *J Psychopharmacol* **2**, 194.

Maura G, Roccatagliata E and Raiteri M (1986) Serotonin autoreceptor in rat hippocampus: pharmacological characterisation as a sub-type of the 5-HT$_1$ receptor. *Naunyn Schmeidebergs Arch Pharmacol* **334**, 323-326.

Mishra R, Janowsky A and Sulser F (1979) Subsensitivity of the norepinephrine receptor-coupled adenylate cyclase system in brain: Effects of nisoxetine or fluoxetine. *Eur J Pharmacol* **60**, 379-382.

Mogilinicka E and Klimek V (1979) Mianserin, danitracen and amitriptyline withdrawal increases the behavioural response of rats to l-5-HTP. *J Pharm Pharmacol* **31**, 704-705.

Nelson DR, Palmer KJ and Johnson AM (1990a) Effect of prolonged 5-hydroxytryptamine uptake inhibition by paroxetine on cortical ß$_1$- and ß$_2$-adrenoceptors in rat brain. (Submitted for publication).

Nelson DR, Palmer KJ and Johnson AM (1990b) Chronic administration of paroxetine and desipramine on ß-adrenoceptor number and function in rat brain. Presented at the *British Association for Psychopharmacology,* Cambridge, July.

Nelson DR, Thomas DR and Johnson AM (1989) Pharmacological effects of paroxetine after repeated administration to animals. *Acta Psychiatr Scand* **80** (Suppl 350), 21-23.

Nowak G (1989) Long term effect of antidepressant drugs and electroconvulsive shock (ECS) on cortical α_1-adrenoceptors following destruction of dopaminergic nerve terminals. *Pharmacol and Toxicol* **64**, 469-470.

Nowak G and Przegalinski E (1988) Effect of repeated treatment with antidepressant drugs and electroconvulsive shock (ECS) on ^{3}H-prazosin binding to different rat brain structures. *J Neural Transm* **71**, 57-64.

Ordway GA, Gambarana C and Frazer A (1988) Quantitative autoradiography of central beta-adrenoceptor subtypes: comparison of the effects of chronic treatment with desipramine or centrally administered l-isoproterenol. *J Pharmacol Exp Ther* **247**, 379-389.

Overo KF (1989) The pharmacokinetic and safety evaluation of citalopram from preclinical and clinical data. In: Montgomery SA (ed.) *Citalopram — the New Antidepressant from Lundbeck Research,* pp.22-30. Amersterdam: Excerpta Medica.

Palaic D, Page IH and Khairallah PA (1967) Uptake and metabolism of [^{14}C]-serotonin in rat brain. *J Neurochem* **14**, 63-69.

Pawlowski L and Melzacka M (1986) Inhibition of head twitch response to quipazine in rats by chronic amitriptyline but not fluvoxamine and citalopram. *Psychopharmacology* **88**, 279-284.

Peroutka SJ and Snyder SH (1980) Long-term antidepressant treatment decreases spiroperidol-labelled serotonin receptor binding. *Science* **210**, 88-90.

Plaznik A and Kostowski W (1987) The effects of antidepressants and electroconvulsive shocks on the functioning of the mesolimbic dopaminergic system: a behavioural study. *Eur J Pharmacol* **135**, 389-396.

Pratt GD and Bowery NG (1989) Autoradiographical analysis of GABA$_B$ sites in rat frontal cortex following chronic antidepressant treatment. Presented at the *1st International GABA$_B$ Symposium,* Cambridge, September.

Pratt GD and Bowery NG (1990) Chronic administration of the antidepressant paroxetine failed to decrease ß-adrenoceptor number in rat cerebral cortex sections. Presentation at the *British Association for Psychopharmacology,* Cambridge, July.

Racagni G and Bradford D (1984) Biochemical and behavioural changes on chronic fluvoxamine administration. *Clin Neuropharmacol* **7**, 733.

Rasmussen JGC, Johnson AM, Stewart BR, *et al* (1990) Comparative effects of the selective serotonin uptake inhibitors paroxetine and fluoxetine on food intake in rats and effect of paroxetine on body weight in depressed patients. Presented at the *British Association for Psychopharmacology,* Cambridge, July.

Reynolds LS, Connolly MH, McLean S, et al (1989) Behavioural and biochemical evidence for down-regulation of 5-HT$_{1A}$ receptors by sertraline. Soc Neuroscience Abstracts 15, 854.

Ross SB, Ogren SO and Renyi AL (1976) (Z)-Dimethylamino-1-(4-bromophenyl)-1-(3-pyridyl)propene (H102/09), a new selective inhibitor of neuronal 5-hydroxytryptamine uptake. Acta Pharmacol Toxicol 39, 152-166.

Ross SB and Renyi AL (1969) Inhibition of the uptake of tritiated 5-hydroxytryptamine in brain tissue. Eur J Pharmacol 7, 270-277.

Ross SB and Renyi AL (1975) Tricyclic antidepressant agents. Comparison of the inhibition of the uptake of ^{3}H-noradrenaline and ^{14}C-5-hydroxytryptamine in slices and crude synaptosome preparations of the midbrain hypothalamus regions of the rat brain. Acta Pharmacol Toxicol 36, 382-394.

Ross SB and Renyi AL (1977) Inhibition of the neuronal uptake of 5-hydroxytryptamine and noradrenaline by (Z) and (E)-3-(4-bromophenyl)-N,N-dimethyl-3-(3-pyridyl) alkylamines and their secondary analogues. Neuropharmacology 16, 57-63.

Rowland NE, Antelman SM and Kocan D (1982) Differences among serotonergic anorectics in a cross tolerance paradigm. Do they all act on serotonin systems? Eur J Pharmacol 81, 57-66.

Russell VA, Nurse B, Lamm MCL, et al (1987) Effect of chronic antidepressant treatment on noradrenergic modulation of [^{3}H]-dopamine release from rat nucleus accumbens and striatal slices. Brain Res 410, 78-82.

Sanders-Bush E, Breeding M, Knoth K, et al (1989) Sertraline-induced desensitisation of the serotonin 5-HT$_2$ receptor transmembrane signalling system. Psychopharmacology 99, 64-69.

Savage DD, Mendels J and Frazer A (1980) Monoamine oxidase inhibitors and serotonin reuptake inhibitors; differential effects on [^{3}H]-serotonin receptor binding in rat brain. J Pharmacol Exp Ther 212, 259-263.

Scherschlicht R, Polc P, Schneeberger J, et al (1982) Selective suppression of rapid eye movement sleep in cats by typical and atypical antidepressants. Adv Biochem Psychopharmacol 31, 359-364.

Schildkraut JJ (1965) The catecholamine hypothesis of affective disorders, a review of supporting evidence. Am J Psychiatry 122, 413-418.

Schmidt A, Lebel L, Koe BK, et al (1989) Sertraline patently displaces (+)-[^{3}H]-3-PPP binding to σ sites in rat brain. Eur J Pharmacol 165, 335-336.

Schmidt MJ and Thornberry JF (1977) Norepinephrine-stimulated cyclic AMP accumulation in brain slices in vitro after serotonin depletion or chronic administration of selective amine reuptake inhibitors. Arch Int Pharmacodyn Ther 229, 42-51.

Schoffelmeer ANM, Hoorneman EMD, Sminia P, et al (1984) Presynaptic α_2 and postsynaptic ß-adrenoceptor sensitivity in slices of rat neocortex after chronic treatment with various antidepressant drugs. Neuropharmacology 23, 115-119.

Schubert J, Nybäck H and Sedvall G (1970) Effect of antidepressant drugs on accumulation and disappearance of monoamines formed in vivo from labelled precursors in mouse brain. J Pharm Pharmacol 22, 136-139.

Sellinger-Barnette MM, Mendels J and Frazer A (1980) The effect of psychoactive drugs on beta-adrenergic receptor binding sites in rat brain. Neuropharmacology 19, 447-454.

Sigg EB (1959) Pharmacological studies with tofranil. Can J Psychiatry 4, S75-S85.

Slater IH, Jones GT and Moore RA (1978) Inhibition of REM sleep by fluoxetine, a specific inhibitor of serotonin uptake. Neuropharmacology 17, 383-389.

Snyder SH and Yamamura HI (1977) Antidepressants and the muscarinic acetylcholine receptor. Arch Gen Psychiatry 34, 236-239.

Sprouse JS and Aghajanian GK (1987) Electrophysiological responses of serotonergic dorsal raphé neurons to 5-HT$_{1A}$ and 5-HT$_{1B}$ agonists. Synapse 1, 3-9.

Stark P, Fuller RW and Wong DT (1985) The pharmacologic profile of fluoxetine. J Clin Psychiatry 46, 7-13.

Stockmeier CA, McLeskey SW, Blendy JA, *et al* (1987) Electroconvulsive shock but not antidepressant drugs increase α_1-adrenoceptor binding sites in rat brain. *Eur J Pharmacol* **139**, 259-266.

Stolz JF, Marsden CA and Middlemiss DN (1983) Effect of chronic antidepressant treatment and subsequent withdrawal on [^{3}H]-5-hydroxytryptamine and [^{3}H]-spiperone binding in rat frontal cortex and serotonin receptor mediated behaviour. *Psychopharmacology* **80**, 150-155.

Sudzak PD and Gianutsos G (1985) Parallel changes in the sensitivity of γ-amino butyric acid and noradrenergic receptors following chronic administration of antidepressants and GABAergic drugs: A possible role in affective disorders. *Neuropharmacology* **24**, 217-222.

Sugrue MF (1980) Inability of chronic fluoxetine to potentiate a serotonin mediated effect. *Commun Psychopharmacology* **4**, 131-134.

Sulser F (1982) Typical and Atypical Antidepressants: Molecular Mechanisms. *Adv Biochem Psychopharmacol* **31**, 1-20.

Suranyi-Cadotte BE, Dam TV and Quirion R (1984) Antidepressant-anxiolytic interaction: decreased density of benzodiazepine receptors in rat brain following chronic administration of antidepressants. *Eur J Pharmacol* **106**, 673-675.

Tang SW, Seeman P and Kwan S (1981) Differential effect of chronic desipramine and amitriptyline treatment on rat brain adrenergic and serotonergic receptors. *Psychiatry Res* **4**, 129-138.

Thomas DR, Nelson DR and Johnson AM (1987) Biochemical effects of the antidepressant paroxetine, a specific 5-hydroxytryptamine uptake inhibitor. *Psychopharmacology* **93**, 193-200.

Tricklebank MD, Forler C, Middlemiss DN, *et al* (1985) Subtypes of the 5-HT receptor mediating the behavioural response to 5-methoxy-N, N-dimethyltryptamine in the rat. *Eur J Pharmacol* **117**, 15-24.

U'Prichard DC, Greenberg DA, Sheehan PB, *et al* (1978) Tricyclic antidepressants; therapeutic properties and affinity for α-noradrenergic receptor binding sites in the brain. *Science* **199**, 197-198.

Vergé D, Daval G, Patey A, *et al* (1985) Presynaptic 5-HT autoreceptors on serotonergic cell bodies and/or dendrites but not terminals are of the 5-HT$_{1A}$ sub-type. *Eur J Pharmacol* **113**, 463-464.

Vetulani J, Lebrecht U and Pilc A (1981) Enhancement of responsiveness of the central serotonergic system and serotonin-2 receptor density in rat frontal cortex by electroconvulsive treatment. *Eur J Pharmacol* **76**, 81-85.

Vetulani J, Schwartz RJ, Dingell JV, *et al* (1976) A possible common mechanism of action of antidepressant treatments: reduction in the sensitivity of the noradrenergic cyclic AMP generating system in rat limbic forebrain. *Naunyn Schmiedebergs Arch Pharmacol* **293**, 109-114.

Waeber C, Schoeffter P, Palacios JM, *et al* (1988) Molecular pharmacology of 5-HT$_{1D}$ recognition sites: radioligand binding studies in human, pig and calf brain membranes. *Naunyn Schmiedebergs Arch Pharmacol* **337**, 595-601.

Waddington JL and Crow TJ (1979) Rotational responses to serotonergic and dopaminergic agonists after unilateral dihydroxy-tryptamine lesions of the medial forebrain bundle: co-operative interactions of serotonin and dopamine in neostriatum. *Life Sci* **25**, 1307-1314.

Waldmeier PC (1979) Analysis of the activation of dopamine metabolism by a serotonin uptake inhibitor. *Eur J Pharmacol* **60**, 315-322.

Waldmeier PC and Delini-Stula AA (1979) Serotonin-dopamine interactions in the nigrostriatal system. *Eur J Pharmacol* **55**, 363-373.

Watanabe S, Ohta H and Ohno M (1988) Elecroencephalographic effects of the new antidepressant paroxetine in the rabbit. *Arzneimittelforschung* **38**, 332-340.

Weissman-Nanopoulous D, Mach E, Magre J, *et al* (1985) Evidence for the localisation of 5-HT$_{1A}$ binding sites on serotonin-containing neurones in the raphé dorralis and raphé centralis nuclei of the rat brain. *Neuroscience* **17**, 1061-1072.

Welner SA, de Montigny C, Desroches J, *et al* (1989) Autoradiographic quantification of serotonin$_{1A}$ receptors in rat brain following antidepressant drug treatment. *Synapse* **4**, 347-352.

Willner P (1984) The ability of drugs to desensitise ß-adrenergic receptors is not correlated with their clinical potency. *J Affective Disord* **83**, 53-58.

Wirz-Justice A, Krauchi K, Lichtsteiner M, *et al* (1978) Is it possible to modify serotonin-receptor sensitivity? *Life Sci* **23**, 1249-1254.

Wolfe BB, Harden TK, Sporn JR, *et al* (1978) Presynaptic modulation of ß-adrenoceptors in rat cerebral cortex after treatment with antidepressants. *J Pharmacol Exp Ther* **207**, 446-457.

Wong DT, Bymaster FP, Horng JS, *et al* (1975) A new selective inhibitor for uptake of serotonin into synaptosomes of rat brain: 3-(p-trifluoromethylphenoxy)-N-methyl-3-phenyl propylamine. *J Pharmacol Exp Ther* **193**, 804-811.

Wong DT, Bymaster FP, Reid LR, *et al* (1983) Fluoxetine and two other serotonin uptake inhibitors without affinity for neuronal receptors. *Biochem Pharmacol* **32**, 1287-1293.

Wong DT, Bymaster FP, Reid LR, *et al* (1985a) Inhibition of serotonin uptake by optical isomers of fluoxetine. *Drug Dev Res* **6**, 397-403.

Wong DT, Horng JS, Bymaster FT, *et al* (1974) A selective inhibitor of serotonin uptake Lilly 110140, 3-(p-trifluoromethylphenoxy)-N-methyl-3-phenylpropylamine. *Life Sci* **15**, 471-479.

Wong DT and Reid LR (1986) Suppression of food intake in meal-fed and 2-desoxyglucose-treated rats by enantiomers of fluoxetine and other inhibitors of monoamine uptake. *Fed Proc* **45**, 609.

Wong DT, Reid LR, Bymaster FP, *et al* (1985b) Chronic effects of fluoxetine, a selective inhibitor of serotonin uptake, on neurotransmitter receptors. *J Neural Transm* **64**, 251-269.

Wong DT, Reid LR and Threlkeld PG (1988) Suppression of food intake in rats by fluoxetine: comparison with enantiomers and effects of serotonin antagonists. *Pharmacol Biochem Behav* **31**, 475-479.

Wurtman JJ and Wurtman RJ (1977) Fenfluramine and fluoxetine spare protein consumption while suppressing caloric intake by rats. *Science* **198**, 1178-1180.

Wurtman JJ and Wurtman RJ (1979) Fenfluramine and other serotonergic drugs depress food intake and carbohydrate consumption while sparing protein consumption. *Curr Med Res Opin* **6** (Supp 1), 28-33.

Yen TT, Wong DT and Bemis KG (1987) Reduction of food consumption and body weight of normal and obese mice by chronic treatment with fluoxetine. *Drug Dev Res* **10**, 37-47.

3

The serotonin hypothesis: necessary but not sufficient

W. F. Boyer and J. P. Feighner

A number of lines of evidence suggest that dysfunction of the serotonin system is involved in depression. In this chapter, we will briefly review some of the findings that support the importance of serotonin in psychiatric and other disorders. We will then outline why serotonin dysfunction, by itself, is not a sufficient explanation for these conditions.

Changes in measures of serotonin function

Five-hydroxyindoleacetic acid (5-HIAA) is the final product of serotonin (5-HT) metabolism in the brain, and its concentration in cerebrospinal fluid is considered to be a reflection of the metabolism of serotonin in the brain. Several studies have reported that levels of 5-HIAA in the cerebrospinal fluid are altered in depression (Asberg *et al*, 1984; van Praag, 1986). For example, Asberg and associates (1984) measured the neurotransmitter metabolites 5-HIAA, homovanillic acid, and 4-hydroxy-3-methoxyphenyl glycol in the cerebrospinal fluid of 83 patients suffering from melancholia and in 66 healthy subjects. After adjustment for differences between the groups in height, age, and sex distribution, significantly lower concentrations of 5-HIAA and homovanillic acid were found in the patients with melancholia than in the control subjects, while levels of 4-hydroxy-3-methoxyphenyl glycol did not differ between the groups. The differences could not be accounted for by variations in timing or examination techniques, or by previously administered drugs.

Levels of 5-HIAA may also normalize upon clinical recovery. Traskman-Bendz and colleagues (1984) reported that concentrations of 5-HIAA in the cerebrospinal fluid, but not homovanillic acid, were higher after recovery than during the depression in 11 patients. This increase in 5-HIAA after recovery was confined to patients whose initial serotonin metabolite levels were low.

In a similar study, Gjerris and colleagues (1987a) measured the levels of serotonin in the cerebrospinal fluid of endogenously depressed patients and controls, the distribution of sex, age, and height being similar in the two groups. In depressed patients, the concentration of serotonin in the cerebrospinal fluid was found to be significantly higher than in control patients. Further classification of the depressed patients using the Newcastle Scale showed that the highest values of serotonin were found in patients with endogenous depression than in those with non-endogenous depression.

Platelets are considered to be a model of both neuronal serotonin uptake and of receptor activity, platelet imipramine binding sites being related to the serotonin transport mechanism. A number of abnormalities of this platelet binding and transport complex have been reported in depression — for example, the number of imipramine binding sites, serotonin receptor activity, and serotonin uptake are generally lower in the platelets of patients with endogenous depression (Aberg-Wistedt et al, 1981; Kaplan and Mann, 1982; Healy et al, 1982-83, 1984, 1985; Wood et al, 1983; Modal et al, 1984; Rausch et al, 1986; Coppen and Doogan, 1988; Langer and Galzin, 1988; Langer and Schoemaker, 1988; Quintana, 1989; Slotkin et al, 1989) and normalize with antidepressant treatment (Quintana, 1989; Szadoczky et al, 1989).

Other findings implicating the serotonin system have been reported — for example, the prolactin response to the serotonergic agonists tryptophan and fenfluramine is blunted in depression (Soininen et al, 1981; Heninger et al, 1984), and this measure has also been reported to normalize with antidepressant treatment (Shapira et al, 1989). Depressed patients also tend to have reduced plasma, whole blood, and platelet levels of serotonin (Kim et al, 1982; Le-Quan-Bul et al, 1984; Rogeness et al, 1985; Sarrias et al, 1987).

Miller and colleagues (1986) measured the pretreatment ratios of tryptophan and tyrosine to those of other large neutral amino acids in the plasma. Amino acid ratios are important because the various amino acids in the plasma compete for uptake into the brain; and the higher the ratio the more likely a particular amino acid is to be absorbed by the brain. The subjects investigated were 27 depressed patients who completed a double-blind trial of citalopram (a selective serotonin re-uptake inhibitor (SSRI)) or maprotiline (a selective noradrenaline uptake inhibitor). The results showed that the tryptophan and tyrosine ratios were decreased in the total patient sample compared with healthy control subjects.

Measures of serotonin function vary throughout the day and with the seasons (Arora et al, 1984; Losonczy et al, 1984; Egrise et al, 1986; Healy et al, 1986; Brewerton, 1989), and the normal circadian rhythm of platelet serotonin uptake is disturbed in depressive illness (Healy et al, 1986). Some of the seasonal changes may also be disrupted in patients with major depression or with seasonal affective disorder (Malmgren et al, 1989; Nemeth et al, 1989b; Szadoczky et al, 1989).

Treatment with 5-hydroxytryptophan, the immediate precursor of serotonin, has been shown to be therapeutic in some depressed patients (Lopez-

Ibor *et al*, 1976; Zmilacher *et al*, 1988). For example Lopez-Ibor and colleagues (1976) reported that 5-hydroxytryptophan was as effective as the monoamine oxidase inhibitor nialamide in treating depression in a double-blind trial.

Complicating a simple model

Although the above studies underscore the importance of serotonin in depression, it would be wrong to conclude that a simple serotonergic model of over- or underactivity is sufficient. Indeed, there are several problems with such an approach.

One major problem with a simple serotonergic explanation is the sheer number of conditions in which serotonin-related abnormalities have been reported: a large number of studies implicate the dysfunction of serotonin in obsessive-compulsive disorder (Thoren *et al*, 1980; Zohar and Insel, 1987; Zohar *et al*, 1987; Charney *et al*, 1988; Hollander *et al*, 1989), panic disorder (Nemeth *et al*, 1989a; Targum and Marshall, 1989), eating disorders (Kaye *et al*, 1984, 1988; Marazziti *et al*, 1988; Jimerson *et al*, 1989), alcoholism (Borg *et al*, 1985), premenstrual syndrome (Poeldinger, 1984), and schizophrenia (Kaplan and Mann, 1982; Wood *et al*, 1983; Le-Quan-Bul *et al*, 1984). Decreased serotonergic activity may also occur in Parkinson's and Alzheimer's disease, and in other dementing disorders (Argentiero and Tavolato, 1980; Soininen *et al*, 1981; Palmer *et al*, 1984; Volicer *et al*, 1985; D'Amato *et al*, 1987; Mayeux *et al*, 1988).

Disorders with low levels of 5-HIAA in the cerebrospinal fluid include idiopathic pain, Tourette's syndrome, multiple sclerosis, progressive myoclonus epilepsy (Leino *et al*, 1980), infantile spasms (Silverstein and Johnston, 1984), and the psychiatric symptoms that accompany hyperparathyroidism (Butler *et al*, 1979; Andersen *et al*, 1981; Almay *et al*, 1987; Joborn *et al*, 1988). Conditions associated with high levels of 5-HIAA in the cerebrospinal fluid include hepatic coma (Sourkes, 1978), subarachnoid haemorrhage (Suzuki *et al*, 1987), seizure disorders (Verma *et al*, 1984), and hypertension (Sharma *et al*, 1985). Autistic subjects demonstrate a blunted prolactin response to fenfluramine, decreased numbers of platelet $5\text{-}HT_2$ receptors, decreased uptake of serotonin into platelets, and blunted serotonin-mediated platelet aggregation (MacBride *et al*, 1989; Rolf *et al*, 1989) as well as increased levels of serotonin in the blood (Launay *et al*, 1988). Hence, it is difficult to explain how a simple under- or overactivity of only one neurotransmitter system can be responsible for so many diverse conditions.

Another difficulty is that the serotonin system is anatomically and functionally linked to other neurotransmitter systems, so that alterations in serotonin activity often produce changes in measures of dopaminergic and noradrenergic function (Roccatagliata *et al*, 1979; Waldmeier and Delini-Stula, 1979; Arnt *et al*, 1984a,b; Agren *et al*, 1986; Sulser, 1987; Bijak and Smialowski, 1988; Potter *et al*, 1988). For example, treatment with an SSRI decreases the level of 5-HIAA in the cerebrospinal fluid, but may also decrease the level of

4-hydroxy-3-methoxyphenyl glycol, the primary metabolite of noradrenaline (Potter *et al*, 1988), and increase the level of homovanillic acid, the primary metabolite of dopamine (Bjerkenstedt *et al*, 1985). An intact serotonergic neuronal input is required for the proper functioning of beta-adrenoceptors and for the down-regulation of the density of these receptors by antidepressant treatments (Sulser, 1987). Animal data also suggest that serotonin activity may influence the function of acetylcholine (Jackson *et al*, 1988).

A third difficulty is the lack of association between serotonin markers and the response to treatment. Somatic treatments such as tricyclic antidepressants, bromocriptine, trazodone, and electroconvulsive therapy produce different changes in measures of serotonin activity in the cerebrospinal fluid, although all are clinically effective (Loeb *et al*, 1980). For example, antidepressant treatment may decrease an already low level of 5-HIAA (Mendlewicz *et al*, 1982; Bjerkenstedt *et al*, 1985) or may decrease the uptake of serotonin into platelets (Schlake, 1989). The SSRIs, which have highly specific effects on serotonergic activity, may be therapeutic in conditions which apparently exert opposite alterations in the function of serotonin. For example, the SSRIs may be helpful in both obsessive-compulsive disorder (Goodman *et al*, 1989a,b) and in impulsive-aggressive personality disorders (van Praag, 1986; Coccaro *et al*, 1989; Cornelius *et al*, 1989), although 5-HIAA concentrations in cerebrospinal fluid are elevated in the former (Thoren *et al*, 1980; Zohar and Insel, 1987; Zohar *et al*, 1987; Charney *et al*, 1988; Hollander *et al*, 1989) and decreased in the latter condition (Brown *et al*, 1982; Insel *et al*, 1985).

Several other problems are worth noting. Although most investigators find lower levels of 5-HIAA in the cerebrospinal fluid of patients who attempt to commit suicide, autopsy data suggest that concentrations of 5-HIAA are elevated immediately after a completed suicide (Arato *et al*, 1989). For example, Arato and colleagues (1989) found low levels of 5-HIAA in the cerebrospinal fluid of suicide attempters across various subgroups, but found increased levels of 5-HIAA in the cerebrospinal fluid of 22 suicide victims in whom fluid samples were taken within the first 10 hours of death. These increases were not found to be due to age, sex, post-mortem interval, or clock time of death, and the authors reported a replication of these findings in 35 further suicide victims. Such findings are difficult to reconcile with a simple view of serotonin deficiency and suicide.

There is also a problem of non-replication. A significant number of studies have not found any alterations in cerebrospinal fluid measures of serotonin or in platelet serotonin binding sites in depression (Korf *et al*, 1983; Braddock *et al*, 1986; Gjerris *et al*, 1987b; Cheetham *et al*, 1988; Dhaenen *et al*, 1988; Lykouras *et al*, 1988).

The validity of some of the serotonin research strategies also remains to be clarified. The relationship between concentrations of 5-HIAA in lumbar cerebrospinal fluid and in the brain has been seriously questioned (Gjerris *et al*, 1987b; Gjerris, 1988). For example, Gjerris (1988) found no correlation between lumbar and ventricular measures of monoamine metabolites in the cerebrospinal fluid, including 5-HIAA.

The role of SSRIs

However, despite uncertainties about the precise role of serotonin in psychiatric disorders, it is clear that the SSRIs, including citalopram, fluoxetine, fluvoxamine, paroxetine, and sertraline represent an important new class of compounds. Trazodone is sometimes included in the above list, but its metabolites have significant effects on other neurotransmitters and receptors (Cioli *et al*, 1984).

The SSRIs, and their major metabolites, are termed selective because their initial metabolic effects are limited to inhibition of serotonin re-uptake into the neurone (Hyttel, 1982, 1989; Koe *et al*, 1983; Wong *et al*, 1983; Tanigaki *et al*, 1987; Potter *et al*, 1988). This contrasts with first- and second-generation antidepressants, which inhibit re-uptake of several neurotransmitters and interact with a variety of receptors.

It is necessary to specify *initial* effects, since alteration of serotonergic activity can induce other neurochemical changes. Chronic administration of an SSRI may affect the number and sensitivity of various receptor groups, but this remains controversial (Wong *et al*, 1985; Chaput *et al*, 1986; Koe *et al*, 1987; Baron *et al*, 1988; Doogan and Caillard, 1988), and the net effect of chronic administration is to facilitate serotonergic neurotransmission (Chaput *et al*, 1988).

Conclusions

It may seem almost contradictory to argue that a serotonergic hypothesis of depression is incomplete, and then to state that drugs which inhibit serotonin re-uptake are very important antidepressants. However we will argue in the following chapters that their importance at present lies in clinical rather than in biochemical properties. Such clinical properties include efficacy in depression, obsessive-compulsive disorder, panic disorder, and other conditions, coupled with a relative lack of side-effects and toxicity in overdose.

References

Aberg-Wistedt A, Jostell KG, Ross SB, *et al* (1981) Effects of zimelidine and desipramine on serotonin and noradrenaline uptake mechanisms in relation to plasma concentrations and to therapeutic effects during treatment of depression. *Psychopharmacology* 74, 297-305.

Agren H, Mefford IN, Rudorfer MV, *et al* (1986) Interacting neurotransmitter systems. A non-experimental approach to the 5HIAA-HVA correlation in human CSF. *J Psychiatr Res* 20, 175-193.

Almay BG, Haggendal J, von-Knorring L, *et al* (1987) 5-HIAA and HVA in CSF in patients with idiopathic pain disorders. *Biol Psychiatry* 22, 403-412.

Andersen O, Johansson BB and Svennerholm L (1981) Monoamine metabolites in successive samples of spinal fluid. A comparison between healthy volunteers and patients with multiple sclerosis. *Acta Neurol Scand* 63, 247-254.

Arato M, Tothfaiusi L and Banki CM (1989) Serotonin and suicide. *Biol Psychiatry* 25 (Suppl 7A), 196A-197A.

Argentiero V and Tavolato B (1980) Dopamine (DA) and serotonin metabolic levels in the cerebrospinal fluid (CSF) in Alzheimer's presenile dementia under basic conditions and after stimulation with cerebral cortex phospholipids (BC-PL). _J Neurol_ **224**, 53-58.

Arnt J, Hyttel J and Overo KF (1984a) Prolonged treatment with the specific 5-HT-uptake inhibitor citalopram: effect on dopaminergic and serotonergic functions. _Pol J Pharmacol Pharm_ **36**, 221-230.

Arnt J, Overo KF, Hyttel J, _et al_ (1984b) Changes in rat dopamine — and serotonin function in vivo after prolonged administration of the specific 5-HT uptake inhibitor, citalopram. _Psychopharmacology_ **84**, 457-465.

Arora RC, Kregel L and Meltzer HY (1984) Seasonal variation of serotonin uptake in normal controls and depressed patients. _Biol Psychiatry_ **19**, 795-804.

Asberg M, Bertilsson L, Martensson B, _et al_ (1984) CSF monoamine metabolites in melancholia. _Acta Psychiatr Scand_ **69**, 201-219.

Baron BM, Ogden AM, Siegel BW, _et al_ (1988) Rapid down regulation of beta-adrenoceptors by co-administration of desipramine and fluoxetine. _Eur J Pharmacol_ **154**, 125-134.

Bijak M and Smialowski A (1988) The effect of acute and prolonged treatment with citalopram on the action of dopamine and SKF 38393 in rat hippocampal slices. _Eur J Pharmacol_ **149**, 41-47.

Bjerkenstedt L, Edman G, Flyckt L, _et al_ (1985) Clinical and biochemical effects of citalopram, a selective 5-HT reuptake inhibitor — a dose-response study in depressed patients. _Psychopharmacology_ **87**, 253-259.

Borg S, Kvande H, Liljeberg P, _et al_ (1985) 5-Hydroxyindoleacetic acid in cerebrospinal fluid in alcoholic patients under different clinical conditions. _Alcohol_ **2**, 415-418.

Braddock L, Cowen PJ, Elliott JM, _et al_ (1986) Binding of yohimbine and imipramine to platelets in depressive illness. _Psychol Med_ **16**, 765-773.

Brewerton T (1989) Seasonal variation of serotonin function: An overview. _Biol Psychiatry_ **25** (Suppl 7A), 82A.

Brown GL, Goodwin FK and Bunney WE (1982) Human aggression and suicide: Their relationship to neuropsychiatric diagnoses and serotonin metabolism. In: Ho BT, Schoolar JC and Usdin E (eds.) _Serotonin in Biological Psychiatry_, pp.287-307. New York: Raven Press.

Butler IJ, Koslow SH, Seifert WE Jr, _et al_ (1979) Biogenic amine metabolism in Tourette's syndrome. _Ann Neurol_ **6**, 37-39.

Chaput Y, Blier P and de Montigny C (1988) Acute and long-term effects of antidepressant serotonin (5-HT) reuptake blockers on the efficacy of 5-HT neurotransmission: Electrophysiological studies on the rat central nervous system. In: Gastpar M and Wakelin JS (eds.) _Selective 5-HT reuptake inhibitors: Novel or Commonplace agents?_, pp.1-17. Basel: Karger.

Chaput Y, de Montigny C and Blier P (1986) Effects of a selective 5-HT reuptake blocker, citalopram, on the sensitivity of 5-HT autoreceptors: electrophysiological studies in the rat brain. _Naunyn Schmiedebergs Arch Pharmacol_ **333**, 342-348.

Charney DS, Goodman WK, Price LH, _et al_ (1988) Serotonin function in obsessive-compulsive disorder. A comparison of the effects of tryptophan and m-chlorophenylpiperazine in patients and healthy subjects. _Arch Gen Psychiatry_ **45**, 177-185.

Cheetham SC, Crompton MR, Katona CL, _et al_ (1988) Brain 5-HT2 receptor binding sites in depressed suicide victims. _Brain Res_ **443**, 272-280.

Cioli V, Corradino C, Piccinelli D, _et al_ (1984) A comparative pharmacological study of trazodone, etoperidone and 1-(m-chlorophenyl)piperazine. _Pharmacol Res Commun_ **16**, 85-100.

Coccaro EF, Siever LJ, Klar HM, _et al_ (1989) Serotonergic studies in patients with affective and personality disorders: Correlates with suicidal and impulsive aggressive behavior. _Arch Gen Psychiatry_ **46**, 587-599.

Coppen AJ and Doogan DP (1988) Serotonin and its place in the pathogenesis of depression. _J Clin Psychiatry_ **49**, 4-11.

Cornelius JR, Soloff PH, Perel JM, _et al_ (1989) Fluoxetine trial in borderline personality. _New Research Program and Abstracts, American Psychiatric Association 142nd Annual Meeting_, p.192.

D'Amato RJ, Zweig RM, Whitehouse PJ, _et al_ (1987) Aminergic systems in Alzheimer's disease and Parkinson's disease. _Ann Neurol_ **22**, 229-236.

Dhaenen H, De-Waele M and Leysen JE (1988) Platelet 3H-paroxetine binding in depressed patients. *Psychiatry Res* **26**, 11-17.

Doogan DP and Caillard V (1988) Sertraline: A new antidepressant. *J Clin Psychiatry* **49** (8), 46-51.

Egrise D, Rubinstein M, Schoutens A, *et al* (1986) Seasonal variation of platelet serotonin uptake and 3H-imipramine binding in normal and depressed subjects. *Biol Psychiatry* **21**, 283-292.

Gjerris A (1988) Do concentrations of neurotransmitters in lumbar CSF reflect cerebral dysfunction in depression? *Acta Psychiatr Scand* **345**, 21-24.

Gjerris A, Srensen AS, Rafaelsen OJ, *et al* (1987a) 5-HT and 5-HIAA in cerebrospinal fluid in depression. *J Affective Disord* **12**, 13-22.

Gjerris A, Werdelin L, Gjerris F, *et al* (1987b) CSF-amine metabolites in depression, dementia and in controls. *Acta Psychiatr Scand* **75**, 619-628.

Goodman WK, Delgado PL, Price LH, *et al* (1989a) Fluvoxamine versus desipramine in OCD. *New Research Program and Abstracts, American Psychiatric Association 142nd Annual Meeting*, p.186.

Goodman WK, Price LH, Rasmussen SA, *et al* (1989b) Efficacy of fluvoxamine in obsessive-compulsive disorder. A double-blind comparison with placebo. *Arch Gen Psychiatry* **46**, 36-44.

Healy D, Carney PA and Leonard BE (1982-83) Monoamine-related markers of depression: changes following treatment. *J Psychiatr Res* **17**, 251-260.

Healy D, Carney PA and Leonard BE (1984) Biochemical correlates of antidepressant response. Results of a trazodone versus amitriptyline trial. *Psychopathology* **17** (Suppl 2), 82-87.

Healy D, Carney PA, O'Halloran A, *et al* (1985) Peripheral adrenoceptors and serotonin receptors in depression. Changes associated with response to treatment with trazodone or amitriptyline. *J Affective Disord* **9**, 285-296.

Healy D, O'Halloran A, Carney PA, *et al* (1986) Platelet 5-HT uptake in delusional and nondelusional depressions. *J Affective Disord* **10**, 233-239.

Heninger GR, Charney DS and Sternberg DE (1984) Serotonergic function in depression. Prolactin response to intravenous tryptophan in depressed patients and healthy subjects. *Arch Gen Psychiatry* **41**, 398-402.

Hollander E, Decaria C, Schneier F, *et al* (1989) Neuroendocrine sensitivity in obsessive compulsive disorder. *New Research Program and Abstracts, American Psychiatric Association 142nd Annual Meeting*, p.187.

Hyttel J (1982) Citalopram — pharmacological profile of a specific serotonin uptake inhibitor with antidepressant activity. *Prog Neuropsychopharmacol Biol Psychiatry* **6**, 277-295.

Hyttel J (1989) Citalopram: the pharmacological characteristics of the most selective inhibitor of serotonin uptake. In: Montgomery SA (ed.) *Citalopram: the New Antidepressant from Lundbeck Research*, pp.11-21. Amsterdam: Excerpta Medica.

Insel TR, Mueller EA, Alterman I, *et al* (1985) Obsessive-compulsive disorder and serotonin: is there a connection? *Biol Psychiatry* **20**, 1174-1188.

Jackson D, Stachowiak MK, Bruno JP, *et al* (1988) Inhibition of striatal acetylcholine release by endogenous serotonin. *Brain Res* **457**, 259-266.

Jimerson DC, Lesem MD, Kaye WH, *et al* (1989) Serotonin and symptom severity in eating disorders. *Biol Psychiatry* **25** (Suppl 7A), 143A.

Joborn C, Hetta J, Rastad J, *et al* (1988) Psychiatric symptoms and cerebrospinal fluid monoamine metabolites in primary hyperparathyroidism. *Biol Psychiatry* **23**, 149-158.

Kaplan RD and Mann JJ (1982) Altered platelet serotonin uptake kinetics in schizophrenia and depression. *Life Sci* **31**, 583-588.

Kaye WH, Ebert MH, Gwirtsman HE, *et al* (1984) Differences in brain serotonergic metabolism between nonbulimic and bulimic patients with anorexia nervosa. *Am J Psychiatry* **141**, 1598-1601.

Kaye WH, Gwirtsman HE, Brewerton TD, *et al* (1988) Bingeing behavior and plasma amino acids: a possible involvement of brain serotonin in bulimia nervosa. *Psychiatry Res* **23**, 31-43.

Kim HL, Plaisant O, Leboyer M, *et al* (1982) Reduction of platelet serotonin in major depression (endogenous depression). *C R Acad Sci [III]* **295**, 619-622.

Koe BK, Koch SW, Lebel LA, et al (1987) Sertraline, a selective inhibitor of serotonin uptake, induces subsensitivity of beta-adrenoceptor system of rat brain. Eur J Pharmacol 141, 187-194.

Koe BK, Weissman A, Welch WM, et al (1983) Sertraline, 1S,4S-N-methyl-4-(3,4-dichlorophenyl)-1,2,3,4-tetrahydro-1-naphthylamine, a new uptake inhibitor with selectivity for serotonin. J Pharmacol Exp Ther 226, 686-700.

Korf J, van-den-Burg W and van-den-Hoofdakker RH (1983) Acid metabolites and precursor amino acids of 5-hydroxytryptamine and dopamine in affective and other psychiatric disorders. Psychiatr Clin (Basel) 16, 1-16.

Langer SZ and Galzin AM (1988) Studies on the serotonin transporter in platelets. Experientia 44, 127-130.

Langer SZ and Schoemaker H (1988) Effects of antidepressants on monoamine transporters. Prog Neuropsychopharmacol Biol Psychiatry 12, 193-216.

Launay JM, Ferrari P, Haimart M, et al (1988) Serotonin metabolism and other biochemical parameters in infantile autism. Biol Psychiatry 20, 1-11.

Leino E, MacDonald E, Airaksinen MM, et al (1980) Homovanillic acid and 5-hydroxyindoleacetic acid levels in cerebrospinal fluid of patients with progressive myoclonus epilepsy. Acta Neurol Scand 62, 41-54.

Le-Quan-Bul KH, Plaisant O, Leboyer M, et al (1984) Reduced platelet serotonin in depression. Psychiatry Res 13, 129-139.

Loeb DC, Roccatagliata G, Albano C, et al (1980) Cerebrospinal HVA and 5-HIAA in patients with endogenous depression in the course of treatment. Endogena in corso di trattamento. Schweiz Arch Neurol Neurochir Psychiatr 126, 27-32.

Lopez-Ibor A, Guttierez JLA and Montejo-Iglesias ML (1976) 5-hydroxytryptophan (5-HTP) and IMAO (Nialimid) in the treatment of depression: A double-blind controlled study. Int J Pharmacopsychiat 11, 8-15.

Losonczy MF, Mohs RC and Davis KL (1984) Seasonal variations of human lumbar CSF neurotransmitter metabolite concentrations. Psychiatry Res 12, 79-87.

Lykouras E, Markianos M, Malliaras D, et al (1988) Neurochemical variables in delusional depression. Am J Psychiatry 145, 214-217.

MacBride PA, Anderson GM, Hertzig ME, et al (1989) Serotonin mediated responses in autistic disorder. New Research Program and Abstracts, American Psychiatric Association 142nd Annual Meeting, p.178.

Malmgren R, Aberg-Wistedt A and Martensson B (1989) Aberrant seasonal variations of platelet serotonin uptake in endogenous depression. Biol Psychiatry 25, 393-402.

Marazziti D, Macchi E, Rotondo A, et al (1988) Involvement of serotonin system in bulimia. Life Sci 43, 2123-2126.

Mayeux R, Stern Y, Sano M, et al (1988) The relationship of serotonin to depression in Parkinson's disease. Mov Disord 3, 237-244.

Mendlewicz J, Pinder RM, Stulemeijer SM, et al (1982) Monoamine metabolites in cerebrospinal fluid of depressed patients during treatment with mianserin or amitriptyline. J Affective Disord 4, 219-226.

Miller SE, de-Beurs P, Timmerman L, et al (1986) Plasma tryptophan and tyrosine ratios to competing amino acids in relation to antidepressant response to citalopram and maprotiline. A preliminary study. Psychopharmacology 88, 96-100.

Modal I, Zemishlany Z and Jerushalmy Z (1984) 5-Hydroxytryptamine uptake by blood platelets of unipolar and bipolar depressed patients. Neuropsychobiology 12, 93-95.

Nemeth A, Falus A, Szadoczky E, et al (1989a) Decreased platelet IMI-binding in panic disorder and major depression. In: Stefanis CN, Soldatos CR and Rabavilas AD (eds.) Psychiatry Today: VIII World Congress of Psychiatry Abstracts, p.115. New York: Elsevier.

Nemeth A, Szadoczky E, Falus A, et al (1989b) Winter depression, light therapy and platelet 3H-imipramine binding. In: Stefanis CN, Soldatos CR and Rabavilas AD (eds.) Psychiatry Today: VIII World Congress of Psychiatry Abstracts, p.119. New York: Elsevier.

Palmer AM, Sims NR, Bowen DM, *et al* (1984) Monoamine metabolite concentrations in lumbar cerebrospinal fluid of patients with histologically verified Alzheimer's dementia. *J Neurol Neurosurg Psychiatry* **47**, 481-484.

Poeldinger W (1984) Experiences with doxepin and trazodone in the therapy with outpatients suffering from depression. *Psychopathology* **17** (Suppl 2), 30-36.

Potter WZ, Rudorfer MV, Lesieur P, *et al* (1988) Biochemical effects of selective serotonin reuptake inhibitors in man. In: Gastpar M and Wakelin JS (eds.) *Selective 5-HT reuptake inhibitors: Novel or Commonplace agents?*, pp.18-30. Basel: Karger.

van Praag HM (1986) Affective disorders and aggression disorders: evidence for a common biological mechanism. *Suicide Life Threat Behav* **16**, 103-132.

Quintana J (1989) Platelet serotonin uptake dynamic changes in depression: effects of long-term imipramine treatment and clinical recovery. *J Affective Disord* **16**, 233-242.

Rausch JL, Janowsky DS, Risch SC, *et al* (1986) A kinetic analysis and replication of decreased platelet serotonin uptake in depressed patients. *Psychiatry Res* **19**, 105-112.

Roccatagliata G, Albano C, Cocito L, *et al* (1979) Interactions between central monoaminergic systems: dopamine-serotonin. *J Neurol Neurosurg Psychiatry* **42**, 1159-1162.

Rogeness GA, Mitchell, EL, Custer GJ, *et al* (1985) Comparison of whole blood serotonin and platelet MAO in children with schizophrenia and major depressive disorder. *Biol Psychiatry* **20**, 270-275.

Rolf LH, Haarman FY, Brune GG, *et al* (1989) Serotonin and amino acid content in platelets of autistic children. In: Stefanis CN, Soldatos CR and Rabavilas AD (eds.) *Psychiatry Today: VIII World Congress of Psychiatry Abstracts*, p.690. New York: Elsevier.

Sarrias MJ Artigas F, Martinez E, *et al* (1987) Decreased plasma serotonin in melancholic patients: a study with clomipramine. *Biol Psychiatry* **22**, 1429-1438.

Schlake HP, Kuhs H, Rolf LH, *et al* (1989) Platelet 5-HT transport in depressed patients under double-blind treatment with paroxetine versus amitriptyline. *Acta Psychiatr Scand* **80**, 149-151.

Shapira B, Reiss A, Kaiser N, *et al* (1989) Effect of imipramine treatment on the prolactin response to fenfluramine and placebo challenge in depressed patients. *J Affective Disord* **16**, 1-4.

Sharma A, Chandra M, Gujrati VR, *et al* (1985) Involvement of catecholamines and serotonin in human hypertension. *Pharmacol Res Commun* **17**, 565-574.

Siever LJ, Murphy DL, Slater S, *et al* (1984) Plasma prolactin changes following fenfluramine in depressed patients compared to controls: an evaluation of central serotonergic responsivity in depression. *Life Sci* **34**, 1029-1039.

Silverstein F and Johnston MV (1984) Cerebrospinal fluid monoamine metabolites in patients with infantile spasms. *Neurology* **34**, 102-105.

Slotkin TA, Whitmore WL, Barnes GA, *et al* (1989) Reduced inhibitory effect of imipramine on radiolabeled serotonin uptake into platelets in geriatric depression. *Biol Psychiatry* **25**, 687-691.

Soininen H, MacDonald E, Rekonen M, *et al* (1981) Homovanillic acid and 5-hydroxyindoleacetic acid levels in cerebrospinal fluid of patients with senile dementia of Alzheimer type. *Acta Neurol Scand* **64**, 101-107.

Sourkes TL (1978) Tryptophan in hepatic coma. *J Neural Transm* (Suppl) **14**, 79-86.

Sulser F (1987) Serotonin-norepinephrine receptor interactions in the brain: implications for the pharmacology and pathophysiology of affective disorders. *J Clin Psychiatry* (Suppl) **48**, 12-18.

Suzuki Y, Ogura K, Shibuya M, *et al* (1987) Alterations of monoamine metabolites and of tryptophan in the basal cisternal CSF of patients after subarachnoid haemorrhage. *Acta Neurochir* (Wien) **87**, 58-62.

Szadoczky E, Falus A, Arato M, *et al* (1989) Phototherapy increases platelet 3H imipramine binding in patients with winter depression. *J Affective Disord* **16**, 121-125.

Tanigaki N, Manno K, Sugihara K, *et al* (1987) Specific inhibitory action of a novel antidepressant paroxetine on 5-HT uptake. *Nippon Yakurigaku Zasshi* **89**, 175-180.

Targum SD and Marshall LE (1989) Fenfluramine provocation of anxiety in patients with panic disorder. *Psychiatry Res* **28**, 295-306.

Thoren P, Asberg M, Bertilsson L, *et al* (1980) Clomipramine treatment of obsessive-compulsive disorder. II. Biochemical aspects. *Arch Gen Psychiatry* **37**, 1289-1294.

Traskman-Bendz L, Asberg M, Bertilsson L, *et al* (1984) CSF monoamine metabolites of depressed patients during illness and after recovery. *Acta Psychiatr Scand* **69**, 333-342.

Verma AK, Gupta SK and Maheshwari MC (1984) 5-HIAA in cerebrospinal fluid of patients with status epilepticus. *Epilepsia* **25**, 499-501.

Volicer L, Langlais PJ, Matson WR, *et al* (1985) Serotoninergic system in dementia of the Alzheimer type. Abnormal forms of 5-hydroxytryptophan and serotonin in cerebrospinal fluid. *Arch Neurol* **42**, 1158-1161.

Waldmeier PC and Delini-Stula AA (1979) Serotonin-dopamine interactions in the nigrostriatal system. *Eur J Pharmacol* **55**, 363-373.

Wong DT, Bymaster FP, Reid LR, *et al* (1983) Fluoxetine and two other serotonin uptake inhibitors without affinity for neuronal receptors. *Biochem Pharmacol* **32**, 1287-1293.

Wong DT, Reid LR, Bymaster FP, *et al* (1985) Chronic effects of fluoxetine, a selective inhibitor of serotonin uptake, on neurotransmitter receptors. *J Neural Transm* **64**, 251-269.

Wood PL, Suranyi-Cadotte BE, Nair NP, *et al* (1983) Lack of association between [3H]imipramine binding sites and uptake of serotonin in control, depressed and schizophrenic patients. *Neuropharmacology* **22**, 1211-1214.

Zmilacher K, Battegay R and Gastpar M (1988) L-5-hydroxytryptophan alone and in combination with a peripheral decarboxylase inhibitor in the treatment of depression. *Neuropsychobiology* **20**, 28-35.

Zohar J and Insel TR (1987) Obsessive-compulsive disorder: psychobiological approaches to diagnosis, treatment, and pathophysiology. *Biol Psychiatry* **22**, 667-687.

Zohar J, Mueller EA, Insel TR, *et al* (1987) Serotonergic responsivity in obsessive-compulsive disorder. Comparison of patients and healthy controls. *Arch Gen Psychiatry* **44**, 946-951.

4

Pharmacokinetics and drug interactions

W. F. Boyer and J. P. Feighner

Pharmacokinetics

If the structures of the selective serotonin re-uptake inhibitors (SSRIs) are compared with those of the conventional tricyclic antidepressants (see chapter 2) it may be seen that while the tricyclic drugs possess a basic similarity of structure, the SSRIs are structurally distinct from each other. This is reflected in the differing pharmacokinetic profiles and potential for drug-drug interactions observed with this class of compounds.

Fluoxetine
Fluoxetine is well absorbed after oral administration and develops peak plasma concentrations after six to eight hours; food slows, but does not reduce, its absorption. Fluoxetine is approximately 94% bound to plasma proteins and its half-life is one to three days. Its major metabolite, norfluoxetine, is also serotonin-specific and has an exceptionally long half-life of 7-15 days. These pharmacokinetics are not significantly altered in healthy elderly subjects or in patients with renal impairment, but they may be prolonged in patients with hepatic insufficiency.

The EEG changes seen with fluoxetine are similar to those observed with activating antidepressants such as desipramine, except after relatively high doses, when the EEG profile of fluoxetine resembles that of the more sedating drugs such as amitriptyline (Saletu and Grunberger, 1985). The latter profile is sometimes seen clinically, when patients prescribed doses greater than 20mg per day may complain of sedation. Fluoxetine's long half-life may lead to rising plasma levels over several weeks, and this may account for the occasional complaints of sedation documented after three to six weeks of treatment at a steady dose.

81

Fluvoxamine
Fluvoxamine is completely absorbed from the gastrointestinal tract and develops peak plasma levels within two to eight hours. Food does not significantly affect absorption (Wheeler *et al*, 1985) and the drug is approximately 77% bound to plasma proteins (Benfield *et al*, 1986). The plasma half-life of fluvoxamine is about 15 hours and approximately 94% is recovered in the urine (De-Bree *et al*, 1983); metabolic studies suggest that its metabolites do not possess significant psychotropic activity (Overmars *et al*, 1983). Its pharmacokinetics are unaltered in healthy elderly subjects (Benfield *et al*, 1986). The EEG effects seen with fluvoxamine are similar to those observed with antidepressants such as imipramine, but suggest less sedative potential (Saletu *et al*, 1983).

Paroxetine
Paroxetine is also well absorbed from the gastrointestinal tract, and develops peak plasma levels two to eight hours following an oral dose. The plasma half-life of paroxetine is approximately 20 hours (Lund *et al*, 1982), allowing once-daily dosage, and the antidepressant is approximately 95% bound to plasma proteins (Kaye *et al*, 1989). Food and antacids do not significantly inhibit absorption (Greb *et al*, 1989), and steady-state plasma levels are achieved within one to two weeks (Kaye *et al*, 1989). Paroxetine is extensively metabolized in the liver, the metabolites being excreted in the urine and bile (Lund *et al*, 1979); none of the metabolites of paroxetine appears to be active. No induction of drug metabolizing enzymes is seen in man (Haddock *et al*, 1989). The dose-effect of paroxetine on the EEG is opposite to that seen with fluoxetine and fluvoxamine: the EEG effects of 30mg of paroxetine resemble those of amitriptyline while a dose of 70mg produces an EEG profile similar to that reported for other SSRIs. This seems to be dissimilar from the effects seen with typical sedative antidepressants, and suggests that the sedative features of paroxetine may be much less marked than those of amitriptyline (McClelland *et al*, 1989).

Elderly subjects may develop significantly higher plasma levels of paroxetine than younger patients given the same dose, although there is considerable overlap (Kaye *et al*, 1989). Twelve patients with histologically confirmed hepatic cirrhosis were given a single dose of 20mg, and no obvious differences were noted in blood concentrations or in pharmacokinetic parameters compared with patients who do not have hepatic impairment (Krastev *et al*, 1989). In another study, patients with severe renal impairment tended to clear a single oral dose of paroxetine more slowly than healthy subjects, but again considerable overlap was observed (Doyle *et al*, 1989). Until data after chronic dosing are available, the investigators in both studies suggest caution in treating these populations.

Sertraline
Sertraline is relatively slowly absorbed from the gastrointestinal tract, peak plasma concentrations occurring six to eight hours after an oral dose (Doogan and Caillard, 1988). Sertraline is very highly (99%) bound to plasma proteins, and the average plasma half-life is 25 hours, rendering once-daily dosing practical.

The primary metabolite, desmethylsertraline, is also an SSRI inhibitor, but is 5-10 times less potent than the parent compound (Doogan and Caillard, 1988; Heym and Koe, 1988). The plasma half-life of desmethylsertraline is approximately 66 hours. The half-life of sertraline is unchanged in the elderly, but the half-life of desmethylsertraline is prolonged.

Sertraline undergoes extensive hepatic metabolism but, at clinically relevant doses, does not appear to induce drug metabolizing enzymes in man. In lower doses, the effect of sertraline on EEG activity is similar to that of activating antidepressants such as desipramine, but in higher doses it produces more sedation. The overall clinical profile is neither stimulant nor sedative (Pfizer, data on file).

Citalopram
Citalopram has a half-life of about 36 hours, and undergoes minimal first-pass metabolism in man. The mono- and di-methylated metabolites of citalopram have the same specificity for serotonin as citalopram, but are less potent by factors of approximately 4 and 13, respectively. The metabolites also enter the brain less readily and are present in lower concentrations. Hence the therapeutic effect of citalopram is essentially due to the parent compound itself. The variability in plasma levels between patients treated with the same dose may be up to seven-fold. A prolonged half-life and reduced metabolism have been noted in elderly patients receiving citalopram, and a lower dose is therefore recommended in this population (Overo *et al*, 1985; Overo, 1989).

Drug interactions

Drug-drug interactions are an important area in the evaluation of any new compound or class of compounds. The SSRIs have fewer clinically meaningful interactions than earlier antidepressants. For example, they do not potentiate the effects of alcohol or other sedatives (Cooper *et al*, 1989; Shillingford *et al*, 1989): in a representative study Cooper and colleagues (1989) tested a single, 30mg dose of paroxetine in healthy subjects and found no impairment of objective psychomotor measures and no potentiation of the sedative effects of haloperidol, amylobarbitone, oxazepam, or alcohol.

Several single-dose interaction studies have been performed with commonly prescribed drugs such as digoxin, cimetidine, and warfarin. However, not all of the SSRIs have been tested with all of the above drugs, and hence generalizations are difficult. Co-administration of paroxetine or fluvoxamine with warfarin may increase bleeding tendency (Bannister *et al*, 1989; Kali Duphar, data on file), and cimetidine may impair the first-pass metabolism of the SSRIs which may lead to build-up of higher drug levels, although the clinical significance of SSRI blood levels is unknown (Bannister *et al*, 1989). Patients who are taking insulin or oral hypoglycaemic agents may occasionally need to have their SSRI dose adjusted, a recommendation that comes from the observation of hypoglycaemia with fluoxetine, which occurred in less than 1% of patients in clinical trials.

Paroxetine and fluoxetine do not appear to have clinically important interactions with diazepam (Lemberger *et al*, 1988; Bannister *et al*, 1989). In one study Lemberger and colleagues (1988) administered single oral doses of 10mg diazepam to six healthy subjects, either alone or in combination with 60mg of fluoxetine; diazepam was given alone, after a single dose of fluoxetine, and after eight daily doses of fluoxetine. Although psychometric data showed that fluoxetine had no significant effect on the psychomotor responses to diazepam, the pharmacokinetic data showed a change in the disposition of diazepam after the administration of fluoxetine. The half-life of diazepam was longer and the plasma clearance was lower after fluoxetine, suggesting that fluoxetine inhibited the metabolism of diazepam. The authors felt that the clinical implications of this interaction were probably minor because psychomotor responses were unaffected and offsetting changes in the kinetics of diazepam and desmethyldiazepam occurred. However, this is an important issue since a benzodiazepine is occasionally prescribed early in the course of treatment with an SSRI to relieve anxiety quickly or to treat side-effects such as insomnia and agitation (Lemberger *et al*, 1988).

Most of the above interaction studies utilized healthy subjects and either single doses or relatively short-term dosing strategies. This leaves open the question of whether any of these drugs is likely to have significant interactions in depressed patients over the long-term. Our clinical experience suggests that the likelihood of significant drug-drug interactions with commonly prescribed medicines is low, but there are a few exceptions worthy of note.

Interactions with tricyclic antidepressants and phenothiazines
Several reports have appeared on the development of increased tricyclic plasma levels when a tricyclic antidepressant (TCA) is administered with fluoxetine. Indeed, in some cases this has lead to increased tricyclic side-effects and even worsening of the depression. Such clinical deterioration may conceivably occur when the 'therapeutic window' of the TCA is exceeded (Bell and Cole, 1988; Editorial, 1989; Goodnick, 1989; Rudorfer and Potter, 1989).

We have treated a number of patients with combinations of an SSRI and a tricyclic and, although we did not routinely measure plasma levels of the TCA, we have not seen an unusual degree of adverse effects in clinical practice. We have also treated a limited number of patients with the combination of fluoxetine and bupropion and have found this to be well tolerated and sometimes effective in very refractory patients. Combination treatment is discussed in greater detail in chapter 9.

Because of the similarities between tricyclics and phenothiazines a similar interaction might be expected when a phenothiazine is administered with an SSRI. Few such interactions have been reported, perhaps because combined treatment with a phenothiazine and an antidepressant is relatively uncommon. We have seen one case in which a patient had been on a stable dose of chlorpromazine with no side-effects. However, when small amounts of fluoxetine

— 10mg every other day — were added to her regimen she developed a dry mouth and pronounced orthostatic hypotension, which resolved when the fluoxetine was discontinued. Furthermore, Tate (1989) described a 39-year-old patient who developed severe extrapyramidal reactions when receiving the combination of fluoxetine and haloperidol, a butyrophenone, although she was able to tolerate haloperidol alone without significant difficulty. Whether this was due to increased plasma levels of haloperidol or to the effects of fluoxetine on the dopaminergic system is unknown.

Interactions with lithium

There have been reports of significant negative interactions between fluoxetine and lithium, including the development of mania (Committee on the Safety of Medicines (UK), 1989; Hadley and Cason, 1989; Salama and Shafey, 1989). As the occurrence of mania suggests, the combination of fluoxetine and lithium may sometimes exert antidepressant properties that are greater than those of either drug alone (Pope *et al*, 1988) (see chapter 9). We have used the combination of fluoxetine and lithium successfully in a number of patients during the depressive phase of a bipolar illness or in patients with refractory unipolar depression.

Noveske and colleagues (1989) described a 53-year-old woman who developed delirium when treated with the combination of fluoxetine and lithium. Her rectal temperature was 101°F and her white blood cell count 17,300/cc^3. Her lithium plasma levels were within the therapeutic range. She was confused, ataxic, had a coarse tremor, was unable to sit, walk or stand unaided, and could not respond to simple commands. Her symptoms and, interestingly, her depression, resolved over the following several days after the medicines were stopped. These symptoms bear some resemblance to the 'serotonergic syndrome', which we will discuss later.

Interactions with monoamine oxidase inhibitors

A potentially serious drug interaction occurs in animals if they are given an SSRI in combination with a monoamine oxidase inhibitor (MAOI) (Marley and Wozniak, 1984a,b). We have seen a number of patients who have developed a similar 'serotonergic syndrome' with the combination of fluoxetine and an MAOI (Sternbach, 1988; Brasseur, 1989; Feighner *et al*, 1990). The most frequent symptoms in these patients were myoclonus, hypertension, and changes in mental status, especially confusion and hypomanic symptoms such as pressured speech, hyperactivity, irritability, and euphoria. There may also be diarrhoea with abdominal cramping, tremor, tachycardia, hypertension, diaphoresis, and elevated temperature. In a severe state hyperpyrexia, cardiovascular collapse, and death may occur (Table I).

In addition to the patients who were treated concurrently with fluoxetine and an MAOI in our clinic six others were started on an MAOI 10 days or more after stopping fluoxetine. In this case the MAOI was generally better tolerated. However, one patient had a severe reaction which required hospitalization, the signs and symptoms of which included hyperthermia, hypertension and

Gastrointestinal	Psychiatric
Abdominal cramping	Manic-like symptoms
Bloating	Racing thoughts
Diarrhoea	Push of speech
Neurological	Elevated or dysphoric mood
Tremulousness	Confusion
Myoclonus	**Other**
Dysarthria	Diaphoresis
Inco-ordination	Hypertension
Cardiovascular	Death by cardiovascular collapse
Tachycardia	
Hypertension	

Table I. Clinical manifestations of the serotonergic syndrome.

hypotension, headache, tremor, confusion, hyperreflexia, myoclonus, and disorientation. The manufacturer recommends that five weeks should elapse when a patient is changed from fluoxetine to an MAOI.

Studies in animals suggest that this serotonergic syndrome may be more severe with tranylcypromine than with phenelzine (Marley and Wozniak, 1984a,b). However, it is important to emphasize that there is not enough information to rate one MAOI as more or less dangerous in this situation in man. Although the only data in man so far on this interaction involve fluoxetine, a similar syndrome has been reported in rats treated with paroxetine plus phenelzine or nialamide (Koshikawa *et al*, 1985; Buus Lassen, 1989).

It is also important to emphasize that this interaction may occur even when an SSRI and an MAOI are not used simultaneously. All currently available MAOIs work by permanently inactivating MAO, so that significant enzyme inhibition may persist for two weeks or more after the MAOI is discontinued. Newer, reversible MAOIs such as moclobemide may theoretically carry a smaller risk. Among the SSRIs fluoxetine may be the most problematic as the antidepressant and its active metabolite may be present in significant amounts for several weeks after treatment with the drug is withdrawn.

Conclusions

In contrast to fluoxetine, citalopram, and sertraline which are all demethylated to produce active metabolites *in vivo*, none of the metabolites of paroxetine appear to be active.

Although significant drug-drug interactions may occur with the SSRIs, these compounds appear to be free of most of the significant interactions that may occur with the earlier antidepressants. The lack of additive effects with alcohol, sedatives, or anticholinergic and antihistaminic drugs may be the most clinically important improvements offered by the SSRIs in this area. Because each of the

SSRIs is structurally very different there is a potential for some interactions to occur with one drug of this class but not with another. Clinicians should exercise caution in this regard and report their experiences as these drugs come into wider use.

References

Bannister SJ, Houser VP, Hulse JD, *et al* (1989) Evaluation of the potential for interactions of paroxetine with diazepam, cimetidine, warfarin and digoxin. *Acta Psychiatr Scand* **80**, 102-106.

Bell IR and Cole JO (1988) Fluoxetine induces elevation of desipramine level of exacerbation of geriatric nonpsychotic depression. *J Clin Psychopharmacol* **8**, 447-448.

Benfield P, Heel RC and Lewis SP (1986) Fluoxetine: review of its pharmacodynamic and pharmacokinetic properties, and therapeutic efficacy in depressive illness. *Drugs* **32**, 481-508.

Brasseur R (1989) A multicentre open trial of fluoxetine in depressed out-patients in Belgium. *Int Clin Psychopharmacol* **4** (Suppl 1), 107-111.

Buus Lassen J (1989) Nialamide-induced hypermotility in mice treated with inhibitors of monoamine uptake, 5-HT antagonists and lithium. *Psychopharmacology* (Berlin) **98**, 257-261.

Committee on the Safety of Medicines (UK) (1989) Fluvoxamine and fluoxetine — interaction with monoamine oxidase inhibitors, lithium, and tryptophan. *Curr Probl* **26**, 61.

Cooper SM, Jackson D, Loudon JM, *et al* (1989) The psychomotor effects of paroxetine alone and in combination with haloperidol, amylobarbitone, oxazepam, or alcohol. *Acta Psychiatr Scand* **80**, 53-55.

De-Bree H, Van-der-Schoot JB and Post LC (1983) Fluvoxamine maleate. Disposition in man. *Eur J Drug Metab Pharmacokinet* **8**, 175-179.

Doogan DP and Caillard V (1988) Sertraline: A new antidepressant. *J Clin Psychiatry* **49** (8), 46-51.

Doyle GD, Laher M, Kelly JG, *et al* (1989) The pharmacokinetics of paroxetine renal impairment. *Acta Psychiatr Scand* **80**, 89-90.

Editorial (1989) More antidepressant/fluoxetine interactions. *Psychiatry Drug Alerts* **111**, 57-58.

Feighner JP, Boyer WF, Tyler D, *et al* (1990) Fluoxetine and MAOIs: adverse interactions. *J Clin Psychiatry* (in press).

Goodnick PJ (1989) Infuence of fluoxetine on plasma levels of desipramine. *Am J Psychiatry* **146**, 552.

Greb WH, Brett MA, Buscher G, *et al* (1989) Absorption of paroxetine under various dietary conditions and following antacid intake. *Acta Psychiatr Scand* **80**, 99-101.

Haddock RE, Jackson D and Woods FR (1989) Paroxetine: lack of effect on hepatic drug metabolizing enzymes. *Acta Psychiatr Scand* **80**, 93-94.

Hadley A and Cason MP (1989) Mania resulting from lithium-fluoxetine combination [letter]. *Am J Psychiatry* **146**, 1637-1638.

Heym J and Koe BK (1988) Pharmacology of sertraline: A review. *J Clin Psychiatry* **49** (8), 40-45.

Kaye CM, Haddock RE, Langley PF, *et al* (1989) A review of the metabolism and pharmacokinetics of paroxetine in man. *Acta Psychiatr Scand* **80**, 60-75.

Koshikawa F, Koshikawa N and Stephenson JD (1985) Effects of antidepressant drug combinations on cortical 5-HT2 receptors and wet-dog shakes in rats. *Eur J Pharmacol* **118**, 273-281.

Krastev Z, Terziivanov D, Vlahov V, *et al* (1989) The pharmacokinetics of paroxetine in patients with liver cirrhosis. *Acta Psychiatr Scand* **80**, 91-92.

Lemberger L, Rowe H, Bosomworth JC, *et al* (1988) The effect of fluoxetine on the pharmacokinetics and psychomotor responses of diazepam. *Clin Pharmacol Ther* **43**, 412-419.

Lund J, Lomholt B, Fabricius J, *et al* (1979) Paroxetine: pharmacokinetics, tolerance and depletion of blood 5-HT in man. *Acta Pharmacol Toxicol* (Copenh) **44**, 289-295.

Lund J, Thayssen P, Mengel H, *et al* (1982) Paroxetine: pharmacokinetics and cardiovascular effects after oral and intravenous single doses in man. *Acta Pharmacol Toxicol* (Copenh) **51**, 351-357.

Marley E and Wozniak KM (1984a) Interactions of a non-selective monoamine oxidase inhibitor, phenelzine, with inhibitors of 5-hydroxytryptamine, dopamine or noradrenaline re-uptake. *J Psychiatr Res* **18**, 173-189.

Marley E and Wozniak KM (1984b) Interactions of non-selective monoamine oxidase inhibitors, tranylcypromine and nialamide, with inhibitors of 5-hydroxytryptamine, dopamine or noradrenaline re-uptake. *J Psychiatr Res* **18**, 191-203.

McClelland GR, Raptopoulos P and Jackson D (1989) The effect of paroxetine on the quantitative EEG. *Acta Psychiatr Scand* **80**, 50-52.

Noveske FG, Hahn KR and Flynn RJ (1989) Possible toxicity of combined fluoxetine and lithium. *Am J Psychiatry* **146**, 1515.

Overmars H, Scherpenisse PM and Post LC (1983) Fluvoxamine maleate: metabolism in man. *Eur J Drug Metab Pharmacokinet* **8**, 269-280.

Overo KF (1989) The pharmacokinetic and safety evaluation of citalopram from preclinical and clinical data. In: Montgomery SA (ed.) *Citalopram: the New Antidepressant from Lundbeck Research*, pp.22-30. Amsterdam: Excerpta Medica.

Overo KF, Toft B, Christophersen L, *et al* (1985) Kinetics of citalopram in elderly patients. *Psychopharmacology* **86**, 253-257.

Pope HG Jr, McElroy SL and Nixon RA (1988) Possible synergism between fluoxetine and lithium in refractory depression. *Am J Psychiatry* **145**, 1292-1294.

Rudorfer MV and Potter WZ (1989) Combined fluoxetine and tricyclic antidepressants. *Am J Psychiatry* **146**, 562-564.

Salama AA and Shafey M (1989) A case of lithium toxicity induced by combined fluoxetine and lithium carbonate. *Am J Psychiatry* **146**, 278.

Saletu B and Grunberger J (1985) Classification and determination of cerebral bioavailability of fluoxetine: pharmacokinetic, pharmaco-EEG, and psychometric analyses. *J Clin Psychiatry* **46** (3), 45-52.

Saletu B, Grunberger J and Rajna P (1983). Pharmaco-EEG profiles of antidepressants. Pharmacodynamic studies with fluvoxamine. *Br J Clin Pharmacol* **15** (Suppl 3), 369S-383S.

Shillingford J, Hindmarch I, Baksi A, *et al* (1989) The effects of sertraline on psychomotor performance in healthy elderly volunteers. In: Stefanis CN, Soldatos CR and Rabavilas AD (eds.) *Psychiatry Today: VIII World Congress of Psychiatry Abstracts*, p.711. New York: Elsevier.

Sternbach H (1988) Danger of MAOI therapy after fluoxetine withdrawal. *Lancet* **II**, 850-851.

Tate JL (1989) Extrapyramidal symptoms in a patient taking haloperidol and fluoxetine. *Am J Psychiatry* **146**, 399-400.

Wheeler SC, Vlasses PH, Dobinska MR, *et al* (1985) Plasma fluvoxamine levels in fasted and fed subjects. *J Clin Pharmacol* **25**, 463.

5

The efficacy of selective serotonin re-uptake inhibitors in depression

W. F. Boyer and J. P. Feighner

Acute treatment for depression

The primary issue for any antidepressant is its efficacy compared with placebo and standard agents in the acute treatment of depressive illness. While there is little doubt that the selective serotonin re-uptake inhibitors (SSRIs) are superior to placebo, not all authors agree that they are as effective as the tricyclic antidepressants (TCAs) (van Praag *et al*, 1987; Bech, 1988). Indeed, one reviewer concluded that they were not, based on finding one study in which a TCA was superior to an SSRI and none in which the SSRI was superior (van Praag *et al*, 1987). However, several more studies published since this review have shown statistical superiority of an SSRI over a TCA (Bremner, 1984; Feighner and Boyer, 1989; Feighner *et al*, 1989b). The published controlled, comparative trials of the SSRIs to date are summarized in tables I-V. Results obtained with the Hamilton Depression Rating scale (HAMD) and the Clinical Global Impression (CGI) scale were used in compiling these tables, since these instruments were common to all studies. In some of the reports either the SSRI or the tricyclic may have been superior on another measure, but there was no consistent pattern favouring either the tricyclic or the SSRI.

Not all of the efficacy data have yet been published. For example, sertraline has been studied in six double-blind, placebo-controlled trials ranging from 6 to 44 weeks in the USA, Canada, and Europe. A total of 1544 patients were included, of whom 825 received sertraline, 288 amitriptyline, and 431 placebo. The results showed that sertraline is as effective as amitriptyline and significantly superior to placebo (Shaw GL, personal communication).

The results of three studies conducted at the Feighner Research Institute to examine the efficacy of paroxetine, fluoxetine, and fluvoxamine are illustrated in Figures 1-3 (Feighner and Boyer, 1989; Feighner *et al*, 1989a, b). These figures

Study	Comparison drug	Outcome
Bremner, 1984		Fluoxetine significantly superior
Cohn and Wilcox, 1985	Imipramine	No significant differences
Stark and Hardison, 1985		
Levine *et al*, 1987		
Byerly *et al*, 1988		
Bressa *et al*, 1989		
Feighner *et al*, 1989a		
Chouinard, 1985	Amitriptyline	
Fawcett *et al*, 1989		
Feighner, 1985		
Masco and Sheetz, 1985		
Montgomery *et al*, 1987a		
Young *et al*, 1987		
Manna *et al*, 1989		
Altamura *et al*, 1989		
South Wales Antidepressant Group, 1988	Dothiepin	
Corne and Hall, 1989		
Feighner and Cohn, 1985	Doxepin	
Tamminen and Lehtinen, 1989		
Holm *et al*, 1987	Maprotiline	
Poeldinger and Haber, 1987		
Muijen *et al*, 1988	Mianserin	
Twomey and Whitehead, 1989		
Perry *et al*, 1989	Trazodone	
Ferreri, 1989	Amineptine	Fluoxetine significantly superior

Table I. Comparative studies of fluoxetine in major depression.

Study	Comparison drug	Outcome
Klok *et al*, 1981	Clomipramine	No significant differences
De-Wilde *et al*, 1983		
Dick and Ferrero, 1983		
Mullin *et al*, 1988	Dothiepin	
Phanjoo *et al*, 1989	Mianserin	
Szulecka and Whitehead, 1989	Amitriptyline	
Guelfi *et al*, 1983	Imipramine	
Itil *et al*, 1983		
Guy *et al*, 1984		
Norton *et al*, 1984		
Dominguez *et al*, 1985		
Lapierre *et al*, 1987		
Bramanti *et al*, 1988		
Lydiard *et al*, 1989		
Feighner and Boyer, 1989		Fluvoxamine significantly superior
Hamilton *et al*, 1989	Flupenthixol	Flupenthixol significantly superior

Table II. Comparative studies of fluvoxamine in major depression.

show the last observable data carried forward, which means that if the patient does not complete the study his or her last valid data are included in the averages for each of the successive weeks. Because the early dropouts include a number of non-responders, the average HAMD scores are relatively high at the end of each study. It is worthwhile examining these studies in greater detail.

Paroxetine
All subjects in the paroxetine study were outpatients with moderate to severe DSM-III major depression of at least one month in duration. They were at least 18 years of age and had a minimum score of 18 on the 17-item HAMD scale.

Study	Comparison drug	Outcome
Laursen et al, 1985	Amitriptyline	No significant differences
Battegay et al, 1985		
Bascara, 1989		
Gagiano et al, 1989		
Kuhs and Rudolf, 1989		
Guillibert et al, 1989	Clomipramine	
Mertens and Pintens, 1988	Mianserin	
Feighner and Boyer, 1989	Imipramine	Paroxetine significantly superior
Peselow et al, 1989a		Imipramine significantly superior

Table III. Comparative studies of paroxetine in major depression.

Following a 4-14 day single-blind, placebo washout phase 120 patients were randomly assigned to six-weeks of double-blind treatment with paroxetine, imipramine, or placebo. The dosage could be increased to a maximum of 50mg paroxetine or 275mg imipramine per day depending on the response and side-effects. Outcome measures included the HAMD scale, the Montgomery-Asberg Depression Rating Scale (MADRS), the CGI scale, the Raskin Depression scale, the Covi Anxiety scale, and the 56-item symptom checklist (SCL-56). The treatment groups were comparable with respect to age, sex, psychiatric history, and baseline scores.

Five of the six outcome measures showed significant differences between the treatment groups, the one measure showing no treatment effects being the SCL-56. Paroxetine was significantly superior to placebo on the above five measures, and a consistent pattern of results was observed in which paroxetine was superior to placebo and imipramine had an intermediate effect. On the total HAMD score the difference between paroxetine and placebo was significant ($p < 0.05$) from week 1 onwards, but the difference between imipramine and placebo was not significant until week 6.

Fluoxetine
Our fluoxetine study followed a similar design. Hence, it was a randomized, double-blind, parallel study of outpatients with DSM-III major depression. The study design also included a 4-14 day single-blind, placebo washout phase followed by six weeks of double-blind treatment with fluoxetine, imipramine,

Study	Comparison drug	Outcome
De-Wilde *et al*, 1985	Mianserin	Citalopram significantly superior
Ahlfors *et al*, 1988*		No significant differences
Mertens, 1989		
Bouchard *et al*, 1987	Maprotiline	
Timmerman *et al*, 1987		
Danish University Antidepressant Group, 1986	Clomipramine	Clomipramine significantly superior
Shaw *et al*, 1986	Amitriptyline	No significant differences
Gravem *et al*, 1987		

Table IV. Comparative studies of citalopram in major depression.
*Mianserin superior in non-endogenous patients.

Study	Comparison drug	Outcome
Fabre, 1989	Amitriptyline	Amitriptyline significantly superior in intention to treat group
Reimherr *et al*, 1988		No significant differences
Peselow *et al*, 1986	Oxaprotiline	

Table V. Comparative studies of sertraline in major depression.

or placebo.

One hundred and ninety-eight patients were enrolled in the study, of whom 178 entered the double-blind treatment phase and 145 completed at least two weeks of treatment. Fifty-one patients were treated with fluoxetine, 46 with imipramine, and 48 with placebo. There were no statistically significant differences between these patients in terms of age, sex, or any of the outcome measures at baseline.

Endpoint analysis demonstrated significant differences between treatment groups on three CGI measures, the patient's rating of global improvement, and two HAMD scale factors — psychomotor retardation and sleep disturbance. Similar trends were seen on the total HAMD score ($p = .07$) and the Raskin Depression scale ($p = .08$). Pairwise t-tests showed that both fluoxetine and

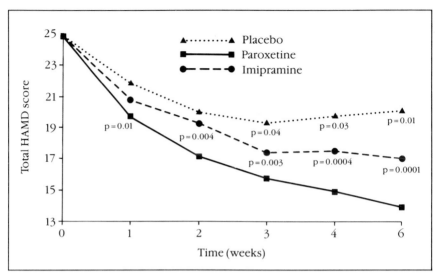

Figure 1. Weekly total HAMD scores during treatment with paroxetine (n = 39), imipramine (n = 40), or placebo (n = 37) (last observable data carried forward).

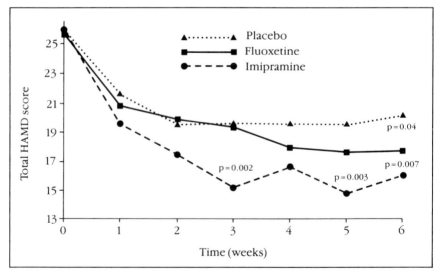

Figure 2. Weekly total HAMD scores during treatment with fluoxetine (n = 52), imipramine (n = 45), or placebo (n = 48) (last observable data carried forward).

imipramine were significantly superior to placebo on all measures, except the HAMD sleep disturbance factor. Imipramine was significantly superior to both placebo and fluoxetine on this variable. None of the other fluoxetine-imipramine differences were statistically significant, although there was a trend towards imipramine on several items.

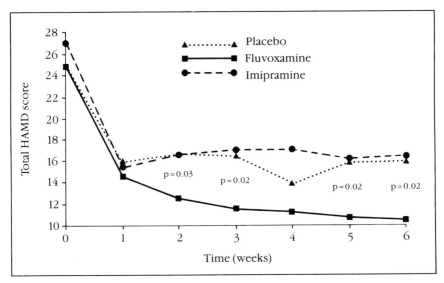

Figure 3. Weekly total HAMD scores during treatment with fluvoxamine (n = 21), imipramine (n = 27), or placebo (n = 12) (last observable data carried forward).

Fluvoxamine

The fluvoxamine study was a six-week, double-blind, placebo-controlled study of inpatients with DSM-III major depression. Thirty-one patients were randomized to fluvoxamine treatment, 36 to imipramine, and 19 to placebo. All patients met DSM-III criteria for major depression and all but one also qualified for the melancholic subtype. Sixty patients completed at least two weeks of treatment following the washout phase and were included in the efficacy analysis; 12 of these were on placebo, 21 on fluvoxamine, and 27 on imipramine.

The statistical analyses showed significant (p<0.05) differences between active drug and placebo on two major measures: the CGI severity of illness and Brief Psychiatric Rating Scale total scores. In addition, there was a trend (p = 0.08) towards differences on the HAMD scale. Pairwise analyses showed that fluvoxamine was significantly superior to both placebo and imipramine on all three measures, while imipramine was not significantly superior to placebo on any of the measures. Further analyses suggested that the relatively poor performance of imipramine was not due to underdosing, but may have been related to the patients having already failed outpatient treatment, which usually included a TCA.

Discussion

The results of these studies, when combined with those shown in Tables I-V, show that the SSRIs are as effective as the TCAs in the treatment of major depression. As Montgomery (1989a) has noted, the HAMD scale, which we used for the comparisons, is heavily weighted with items relating to insomnia, gastrointestinal disturbance, and anxiety. Since all three of these may initially be adversely affected by SSRIs (Oswald and Adam, 1986; Mertens and Pintens, 1988; Shaw and Crimmins, 1989) it is noteworthy that the studies still show approximately equal efficacy to that of the TCAs. While it is true that symptoms such as sleep disturbance may improve more quickly with sedating antidepressants, such as trazodone or amitriptyline, it is important to emphasize that their mood elevating properties are not significantly greater (Gravem et al, 1987; Debus et al, 1988). A patient with significant insomnia who is treated with an SSRI might temporarily be prescribed a sedative-hypnotic until the depression starts to lift and sleep disturbance remits.

One area in which the SSRIs are probably not better is the latency of onset to therapeutic response. Some studies showed significant differences from placebo as early as one or two weeks (De-Wilde et al, 1985; Fabre and Crismon, 1985). However, in other studies the SSRI was not statistically superior to placebo or equivalent to the reference antidepressant until six weeks or more (Brup et al, 1982; Reimherr et al, 1988; Beck, 1989; Feighner et al, 1989b; Kuhs and Rudolf, 1989; Perry et al, 1989; Szulecka and Whitehead, 1989).

A three-week trial of therapy is certainly not long enough. Schweizer and colleagues (1990) published the results of an open study in which 108 patients with major depression were treated with fluoxetine (20mg/day) for three weeks. Non-responders were then assigned to fluoxetine (20 or 60mg/day) for five weeks. Both groups demonstrated an equal and significant decrease in depression scores over this time, which strongly suggests that non-responders at three weeks may respond if allowed to continue medication.

Elderly versus younger patients

Most of the research with SSRIs to date has been limited to adults aged between 18 and 65 years. However, a number of studies have involved elderly patients with major depression, who are often difficult to treat because of increased susceptibility to adverse effects and drug interactions. The results of these studies have been very positive, both in terms of antidepressant effect and patient acceptance (Feighner and Cohn, 1985; Feighner et al, 1988; Altamura et al, 1989; Fabre, 1989; Houillon and Douge, 1989; Lundmark et al, 1989; Phanjoo et al, 1989).

Guillibert and colleagues (1989) investigated 79 patients over 60 years of age with DSM-III major depression in a six-week, double-blind comparison of paroxetine (30mg/day) and clomipramine (75mg/day). The investigators found that although more clomipramine patients were withdrawn due to adverse effects, there were no significant differences in efficacy between the two treatments.

In another study, fluoxetine was compared with doxepin in 157 outpatients aged 65 years or over who suffered from major depressive illness. At the end of this six-week, double-blind study, the mean endpoint scores for all rating scales were significantly improved in both treatment groups. A subsequent 48-week, open-label study showed that both drugs were also effective as maintenance therapy. Fluoxetine was well tolerated by most patients and was associated with fewer side-effects in total than doxepin (Feighner and Cohn, 1985).

Fluoxetine is also prescribed for some younger patients with clinical depression, although much less systematic data are available in this population. In one of the few studies reported so far Simeon and colleagues (1989) treated 30 depressed adolescents with either fluoxetine (40-60mg/day), or placebo in an eight-week, double-blind study. Fluoxetine was demonstrated to be significantly superior to placebo on all measures except sleep disturbance. A statistically significant weight loss was also seen in the fluoxetine group, which may not be desirable for some adolescents. In general, however, side-effects were mild and transient.

Long-term efficacy

Efficacy during maintenance treatment of depression is a further crucial issue for new compounds. As these studies take longer to perform and are more difficult to conduct, fewer have been reported. However the published data, as well as our clinical experience, show that the SSRIs retain efficacy in long-term treatment (Dufour, 1987; Wernicke *et al*, 1987; Montgomery *et al*, 1988; Danion, 1989; Ferrey *et al*, 1989).

Most of the published studies of maintenance or prophylactic treatment have involved fluoxetine. The largest to date examined fluoxetine responders who were symptom free for at least 4.5 months prior to entering the study. These subjects had recently recovered from DSM-III major depression, but were at high risk of recurrence because another entrance requirement was a history of at least two episodes of major depression in the past five years. Of the 222 patients who entered this one-year study, 182 completed it or had a recurrence within the study period. Twenty-three out of 88 patients (26%) had a recurrence while on fluoxetine opposed to 54 out of 94 patients (57%) in the placebo group (p<0.0001).

While this study provides strong evidence for the efficacy of fluoxetine over placebo, it does not address its effectiveness in comparison to the TCAs during long-term treatment.

Fewer patients have been studied in this sort of experiment: Wernicke and colleagues (1987) presented data from 71 patients treated with fluoxetine for 24 weeks compared with 49 on imipramine. The relapse rates were 14% for fluoxetine and 19% for imipramine.

A relatively small amount of data have been published suggesting that the other SSRIs are also effective as maintenance or prophylactic treatment. In one, 39 patients continued double-blind treatment with either imipramine (n = 22) or fluvoxamine (n = 17) for up to 48 weeks following a double-blind multicentre trial. By the end of the study 41% of patients on imipramine compared with 29%

of those treated with fluvoxamine were considered to have relapsed or to be non-responders (Guelfi *et al*, 1987). Feldmann and Denber (1982) reported the results of a one-year, open study of fluvoxamine in 31 depressed male and female patients with a history of various types of chronic or recurrent depression. Two-thirds of these patients were considered to be very much or much improved.

A small open study of citalopram has also been published. Fourteen patients were given maintenance citalopram treatment for 8-113 weeks. One patient developed depression when the dose was reduced from 60 to 40mg while, after cessation of medication seven patients underwent a depressive relapse and six of these who were then treated once more with citalopram responded completely (Pedersen *et al*, 1982).

Not all of the long-term studies of SSRIs have been positive, which is similar to the findings in short-term studies. Wood and colleagues (1983) conducted a study in which they compared prophylactic treatment with lithium and fluvoxamine. The trial had to be discontinued prematurely in some patients due to apparent lack of efficacy, unwanted effects, or a combination of both in fluvoxamine-treated patients. The authors felt that low plasma levels of fluvoxamine may have contributed to the drug's apparent lack of prophylactic efficacy.

Peselow and colleagues (1989b) described 65 patients who responded to paroxetine or imipramine and continued to receive their medication for up to one year. A significantly greater number of relapses was observed in the paroxetine (26%) and placebo (31%) groups than in patients taking imipramine (0%). Patients on imipramine had significantly lower depression scores on the rating scales at the beginning of maintenance treatment, which may have made them less prone to relapse.

Other investigators have also examined the effects of continuation of treatment with paroxetine or imipramine for up to one year. Interim results indicate sustained efficacy in both groups of patients, with a lower rate of relapse in patients on active treatment than placebo (paroxetine = 14%, imipramine = 12%, placebo = 23%). The mean time to relapse with paroxetine was 343 days compared with 157 for imipramine and 122 for placebo. The results of several other long-term studies have not yet been published. Paroxetine, for example, has also been compared with amitriptyline and clomipramine in maintenance therapy. The results of these studies support the therapeutic equivalence of paroxetine and TCAs (data on file, SmithKline Beecham Pharmaceuticals). The balance of data for the other SSRIs is likely to support similar conclusions.

Treatment-resistant depression

The SSRIs are often useful in patients with severe, long-lasting or treatment-refractory depression (Ofsti, 1982; Reimherr *et al*, 1984; Tyrer *et al*, 1987; Delgado *et al*, 1988; Gagiano *et al*, 1989). In one of these studies (Tyrer *et al*, 1987) paroxetine was given to 24 patients with resistant depression, defined as a failure to improve after at least four weeks of conventional antidepressant treatment. The study was further strengthened by the requirement that these patients undergo a period of single-blind placebo administration prior to starting active treatment. Twenty patients completed the study, and paroxetine was seen to produce a statistically significant improvement.

In another study, fluvoxamine was evaluated in 38 depressed inpatients who were considered refractory to standard antidepressants. Twenty-eight patients completed a single-blind protocol involving at least two weeks of placebo and four to six weeks of fluvoxamine treatment. Eight patients (29%) responded to fluvoxamine alone, eight to lithium augmentation of fluvoxamine, and two (7%) to a combination of fluvoxamine, lithium, and perphenazine (Delgado *et al*, 1988).

In a third study, fluoxetine was added to the regimen of 30 patients who had not responded to non-monoamine oxidase inhibitor (MAOI) antidepressants. Twenty-six (86.7%) of these responded. Eight of the responders relapsed when the other antidepressant was withdrawn but improved when it was added again (Weilburg *et al*, 1989).

Although the available evidence is somewhat limited, it indicates that the SSRIs are frequently helpful in patients who have not responded to treatment with other antidepressants. Whether this is due to more potent serotonin re-uptake inhibition than is available with standard agents or to other factors awaits clarification.

Dose-response relationships

An important unsettled issue is the relationship between efficacy and dose. Early studies with fluoxetine commonly used doses of 60 to 80mg/day, but more recent studies indicate that 20mg/day show equal or superior efficacy and cause fewer side-effects (Altamura *et al*, 1988). Increasing the dose is not helpful in the average patient (Dornseif *et al*, 1989), while some research also indicates that doses of fluoxetine as low as 5mg/day may be effective (Wernicke *et al*, 1988). Similarly, doses of more than 50mg/day of sertraline are not associated with significantly superior results (Amin *et al*, 1989). Higher doses of sertraline (200-400mg/day) may actually produce a poorer antidepressant response (Guy *et al*, 1986). In contrast, there is some evidence that a small proportion of patients may benefit from receiving higher doses of paroxetine such as 40 and 50mg per day (Hebenstreit *et al*, 1989).

Use of higher doses may still have a limited place in clinical practice. For example, we have seen a small number of patients with long-standing, refractory depression in whom very high doses of fluoxetine — 80mg/day or more, have been very effective.

A possible dose-response relationship raises the question of whether there may be an association between plasma levels and response. This is a difficult area in which to find significant relationships, as it depends on the diagnostic subtype and severity of depression, as well as on the definition of improvement and statistical techniques (Boyer and Lake, 1987).

Several investigators have looked for a relationship between the plasma levels of an SSRI and response. These studies have generally produced negative results (Brup *et al*, 1982; De-Wilde and Doogan, 1982; Pedersen *et al*, 1982; Bjerkenstedt, 1985; Laursen *et al*, 1985; Dufour *et al*, 1987; Timmerman *et al*, 1987; Hebenstreit *et al*, 1989; Kelly *et al*, 1989; Tasker *et al*, 1989). There is also no suggestion of a relationship between inhibition of serotonin uptake in platelets and response, although the number of studies in this area is smaller (Marsden *et al*, 1987).

Both of the above issues remain unsettled. Bjerkenstedt and colleagues (1985) found an apparent lower limit of 100ng/ml for citalopram in endogenous depression. Patients with non-endogenous depression who fared best had the lowest plasma levels, which suggests a negative correlation.

Relative indications for the SSRIs

Another important issue is whether there are particular subgroups of patients who respond best to the SSRIs. One line of reasoning is that patients with a 'serotonergic' depression would profit most from one of these drugs. However, the very existence of such a subgroup is controversial (Davis *et al*, 1988; Westenberg and Verhoeven, 1988).

Biological measures have generally been unsuccessful in predicting differential response to the SSRIs. One exception is a study by Aberg-Wistedt and colleagues (1981) who reported that depressed patients with low levels of 5-HIAA in the cerebrospinal fluid responded better to zimeldine than those with higher levels. However the major metabolite of zimeldine, norzimeldine, is a highly selective noradrenaline re-uptake inhibitor, and thus specificity cannot be concluded. Studies with more selective compounds have not confirmed the predictive value of pretreatment cerebrospinal fluid measures (Dahl *et al*, 1982; Timmerman *et al*, 1987). Similarly, the dexamethasone test and measurements of monoamine metabolites in the cerebrospinal fluid have not been useful in selecting patients who will respond preferentially to the SSRIs (Benkelfat *et al*, 1987).

Kasper and Yieira (1989) studied the predictive value of changes in serum cortisol and prolactin levels after challenge with fenfluramine. They found a significant negative correlation between the increase in prolactin and the antidepressant response to fluvoxamine, but not maprotiline. Hence, patients with a blunted prolactin response tended to fare better on fluvoxamine than those without. In a somewhat similar study, Mueller-Oerlinghausen and colleagues (1989) studied the predictive value of the melatonin response to fluvoxamine challenge. They also found a significant negative correlation between the increase in melatonin and the antidepressant response.

The predictive value of the thyrotrophin releasing hormone stimulation test was examined in one study in which the test was performed on 100 depressed inpatients (Vanelle *et al*, 1990). Although the authors felt that the results had limited clinical utility, their data showed that patients treated with a serotonergic antidepressant (citalopram or indalpine) were significantly (p<0.05) more likely to improve if they had a blunted thyroid stimulating hormone response. There was no relationship between the results of this test and the clinical response to an adrenergic antidepressant.

Another approach to the question of whether certain patients respond best to SSRIs is to compare results with selective serotonin and noradrenaline re-uptake inhibitors. There have been several such controlled studies in major depression, and the results show no consistent evidence that SSRIs are more effective than noradrenergic compounds in particular subgroups of major depression (Montgomery *et al*, 1981; Peselow *et al*, 1986; Benkelfat *et al*, 1987; Bouchard *et al*, 1987; Holm *et al*, 1987; Montgomery *et al*, 1987b; Nystrom and Hallstrom, 1987; Timmerman *et al*, 1987; Poeldinger and Haber, 1989).

Despite these results there are some clues about possible relative indications for SSRIs. Montgomery (1989b) recently presented data from a meta-analysis of several fluoxetine studies which suggest that this SSRI may be especially useful in patients with anxiety and psychomotor agitation. Moreover, Jouvent and colleagues (1989) found that fluoxetine was more effective than placebo in anxious-impulsive patients than in those with a blunted affect. These are noteworthy findings since 'common sense' suggests that agitated depression should not be treated with fluoxetine because of its activating effects.

There is suggestive evidence that other SSRIs may be especially helpful in anxious depression. Two studies compared fluvoxamine with benzodiazepines in the treatment of patients with mixed anxiety and depression. In both studies the two drugs were equally effective in alleviating anxiety as well as depression (Chabannes and Douge, 1989; Laws *et al*, 1990). In a meta-analysis of six studies, paroxetine had a significantly earlier effect on anxiety symptoms associated with depression when compared with imipramine (Dunbar, 1990).

Atypical features, which include hypersomnia, hyperphagia, and anxiety symptoms, may be an important concept. Reimherr *et al* (1984) found that patients with atypical features may be especially responsive to fluoxetine. Again the evidence with the other SSRIs is suggestive. In one large study citalopram was as effective as clomipramine in patients suffering from non-endogenous depression, but was less effective in the endogenous group (Danish University Antidepressant Group, 1986).

In chapter 6 we discuss the evidence that the SSRIs are effective in other anxiety conditions such as panic disorder and obsessive-compulsive disorder. There is also suggestive evidence of their efficacy in substance abuse disorders, eating disorders, aggression, and some personality disorders (chapter 7). Therefore, a member of this group should be considered for depressed patients with one or more of these associated features. It should be clearly stated, however, that this reasoning makes an assumption about such associated features. It assumes, for example, that a patient with depression plus panic attacks will respond in a similar fashion to a patient with 'pure' panic disorder — in which the SSRIs are superior to the TCAs — than a patient with 'pure' depression, in which the SSRIs are equal to the TCAs in efficacy.

Conclusions

The SSRIs have been compared with the TCAs in a large number of controlled trials. In the majority of these there were no significant differences between the two treatments, while in a few studies either the tricyclic or the SSRI was significantly superior.

Although there may have been subtle differences in patient population or methods which explain these differences, they may also be due to random variation. If two hypothetical treatments are equally effective and one employs a critical probability value of 0.05, one would expect significant differences between treatments in every twentieth trial on a random basis.

Studies of the relationship between clinical response and factors such as dosage, plasma levels, the dexamethasone suppression test, and monoamine measurements in the cerebrospinal fluid have generally been disappointing. Studies comparing selective serotonin and noradrenaline re-uptake inhibitors in major depression have also been inconclusive. Preliminary results with serotonergic challenge strategies, such as the prolactin or melatonin response to fluvoxamine, have been somewhat more encouraging. There is also some evidence that SSRIs may be useful in atypical depression or in depression with other prominent symptoms, such as panic disorder, eating disorders, or obsessive-compulsive disorder. The use of SSRIs in these related conditions is discussed in later chapters.

References

Aberg-Wistedt A, Jostell KG, Ross SB, et al (1981) Effects of zimeldine and desipramine on serotonin and noradrenaline uptake mechanisms in relation to plasma concentrations and to therapeutic effects during treatment of depression. Psychopharmacology 74, 297-305.

Ahlfors UG, Elovaara S, Harma P, et al (1988) Clinical multicentre study of citalopram compared double-blindly with mianserin in depressed patients in Finland. Nord Psykiatr Tidsskr 42, 201-210.

Altamura AC, Montgomery SA and Wernicke JF (1988) The evidence for 20mg a day of fluoxetine as the optimal dose in the treatment of depression. Br J Psychiatry 153, 109-112.

Altamura AC, Percudani M, Guercetti G, et al (1989) Efficacy and tolerability of fluoxetine in the elderly: a double-blind study versus amitriptyline. Int Clin Psychopharmacol 4 (Suppl 1), 103-106.

Amin M, Lehmann H and Mirmiran J (1989) A double-blind, placebo-controlled, dose-finding study with sertraline. Psychopharmacol Bull 25 (2), 164-167.

Bascara L (1989) A double-blind study to compare the effectiveness and tolerability of paroxetine and amitriptyline in depressed patients. Acta Psychiatr Scand 80, 141-142.

Battegay R, Hager M and Rauchfleisch U (1985) Double-blind comparative study of paroxetine and amitriptyline in depressed patients of a university psychiatric outpatient clinic (pilot study). *Neuropsychobiology* **13**, 31-37.

Bech P (1988) A review of the antidepressant properties of serotonin reuptake inhibitors. In: Gastpar M and Wakelin JS (eds.) *Selective 5-HT reuptake inhibitors: Novel or Commonplace agents?*, pp.58-69. Basel: Karger.

Beck P (1989) Clinical properties of citalopram in comparison with other antidepressants: a quantitative metanalysis. In: Montgomery SA (ed.) *Citalopram: the New Antidepressant from Lundbeck Research*, pp.56-58. Amsterdam: Excerpta Medica.

Benkelfat C, Poirier MF, Leouffre P, *et al* (1987) Dexamethasone suppression test and the response to antidepressant depending on their central monoaminergic action in major depression. *Can J Psychiatry* **32**, 175-178.

Bjerkenstedt L, Flyckt L, Overo KF, *et al* (1985) Relationship between clinical effects, serum drug concentration and serotonin uptake inhibition in depressed patients treated with citalopram. A double-blind comparison of three dose levels. *Eur J Clin Pharmacol* **28**, 553-557.

Bouchard JM, Delaunay J, Delisle JP, *et al* (1987) Citalopram versus maprotiline: a controlled, clinical multicentre trial in depressed patients. *Acta Psychiatr Scand* **76**, 583-592.

Boyer WF and Lake CR (1987) Initial severity and diagnosis influence the relationship of tricyclic plasma levels to response. *J Clin Psychopharmacol* **7**, 67-71.

Bramanti P, Ricci RM, Roncari R, *et al* (1988) An Italian multicenter experience with fluvoxamine, a new antidepressant drug, versus imipramine. *Curr Ther Res Clin Exp* **43**, 718-725.

Bremner JD (1984) Fluoxetine in depressed patients: a comparison with imipramine. *J Clin Psychiatry* **45**, 414-419

Bressa GM, Brugnoli R and Pancheri P (1989) A double-blind study of fluoxetine and imipramine in major depression. *Int Clin Psychopharmacol* **4** (Suppl 1), 69-73.

Brup C, Meidahl B, Petersen IM, *et al* (1982) An early clinical phase II evaluation of paroxetine, a new potent and selective 5HT-uptake inhibitor in patients with depressive illness. *Pharmacopsychiatry* **15**, 183-186.

Byerley WF, Reimherr FW, Wood DR, *et al* (1988) Fluoxetine, a selective serotonin uptake inhibitor, for the treatment of outpatients with major depression. *J Clin Psychopharmacol* **8**, 112-115.

Chabannes JP and Douge R (1989) Efficacy on anxiety of fluvoxamine versus prazepam, diazepam with anxiodepressed patients. In: Stefanis CN, Soldatos CR and Rabavilas AD (eds.) *Psychiatry Today: VIII World Congress of Psychiatry Abstracts*, p.282. New York: Elsevier.

Chouinard G (1985) A double-blind controlled clinical trial of fluoxetine and amitriptyline in the treatment of outpatients with major depressive disorder. *J Clin Psychiatry* **46** (3), 32-37.

Cohn JB and Wilcox C (1985) A comparison of fluoxetine, imipramine, and placebo in patients with major depressive disorder. *J Clin Psychiatry* **46** (3), 26-31.

Corne SJ and Hall JR (1989) A double-blind comparative study of fluoxetine and dothiepin in the treatment of depression in general practice. *Int Clin Psychopharmacol* **4**, 245-254.

Dahl LE, Lundin L, le-Fevre-Honore P, *et al* (1982) Antidepressant effect of femoxetine and desipramine and relationship to the concentration of amine metabolites in cerebrospinal fluid. A double-blind evaluation. *Acta Psychiatr Scand* **66**, 9-17.

Danion JM (1989) The effectiveness of fluoxetine in acute studies and long-term treatment. In: Stefanis CN, Soldatos CR and Rabavilas AD (eds.) *Psychiatry Today: VIII World Congress of Psychiatry Abstracts*, p.334. New York: Elsevier.

Danish University Antidepressant Group (1986) Citalopram: clinical effect profile in comparison with clomipramine. A controlled multicenter study. *Psychopharmacology* **90**, 131-138.

Davis JM, Koslow SH, Gibbons RD, *et al* (1988) Cerebrospinal fluid and urinary biogenic amines in depressed patients and healthy controls. *Arch Gen Psychiatry* **45**, 705-717.

Debus JR, Rush AJ, Himmel C, *et al* (1988) Fluoxetine versus trazodone in the treatment of outpatients with major depression. *J Clin Psychiatry* **49**, 422-426.

Delgado PL, Price LH, Charney DS, *et al* (1988) Efficacy of fluvoxamine in treatment-refractory depression. *J Affective Disord* **15**, 55-60.

Dencker SJ and Petersen HE (1989) Side-effect profile of citalopram and reference antidepressants in depression. In: Montgomery SA (ed.) *Citalopram: the New Antidepressant from Lundbeck Research*, pp.31-42. Amsterdam: Excerpta Medica.

De-Wilde J, Mertens C, Over KF, *et al* (1985) Citalopram versus mianserin. A controlled, double-blind trial in depressed patients. *Acta Psychiatr Scand* 72, 89-96.

De-Wilde JE and Doogan DP (1982) Fluvoxamine and chlorimipramine in endogenous depression. *J Affective Disord* 4, 249-259.

De-Wilde JE, Mertens C and Wakelin JS (1983) Clinical trials of fluvoxamine vs chlorimipramine with single and three times daily dosing. *Br J Clin Pharmacol* 15 (Suppl 3), 427S-431S.

Dick P and Ferrero E (1983) A double-blind comparative study of the clinical efficacy of fluvoxamine and chlorimipramine. *Br J Clin Pharmacol* 15 (Suppl 3), 419S-425S.

Dominguez RA, Goldstein BJ, Jacobson AF, *et al* (1985) A double-blind placebo-controlled study of fluvoxamine and imipramine in depression. *J Clin Psychiatry* 46, 84-87.

Dornseif BE, Dunlop SR, Potvin JH, *et al* (1989) Effect of dose escalation after low-dose fluoxetine therapy. *Psychopharmacol Bull* 25 (1), 71-79.

Dufour H (1987) Fluoxetine: Long term treatment and prophylaxis in depression. Presented at the *International Fluoxetine Symposium*, Tyrol, Austria, October 13-17.

Dufour H, Bouchacourt M, Thermoz P, *et al* (1987) Citalopram — a highly selective 5-HT uptake inhibitor — in the treatment of depressed patients. *Int Clin Psychopharmacol* 2, 225-237.

Dunbar GC (1990) The efficacy profile of paroxetine, a new antidepressant, compared with imipramine and placebo. *17th CINP Congress Abstracts* 1, 17.

Fabre L (1989) Sertraline treatment of geriatric major depression compared with amitriptyline. In: Stefanis CN, Soldatos CR and Rabavilas AD (eds.) *Psychiatry Today: VIII World Congress of Psychiatry Abstracts*, p.711. New York: Elsevier.

Fabre LF and Crismon L (1985) Efficacy of fluoxetine in outpatients with major depression. *Curr Ther Res Clin Exp* 37, 115-123.

Fawcett J, Zajecka JM, Kravitz HM, *et al* (1989) Fluoxetine versus amitriptyline in adult outpatients with major depression. *Curr Ther Res Clin Exp* 45, 821-832.

Feighner JP (1985) A comparative trial of fluoxetine and amitriptyline in patients with major depressive disorder. *J Clin Psychiatry* 46, 369-372.

Feighner JP and Boyer WF (1989) Paroxetine in the treatment of major depression. *Acta Psychiatr Scand* 80, 125-129.

Feighner JP, Boyer WF, Meredith CH, *et al* (1988) An overview of fluoxetine in geriatric depression. *Br J Psychiatry* 153, 105-108.

Feighner JP, Boyer WF, Meredith CH, *et al* (1989a) A double-blind comparison of fluoxetine, imipramine and placebo in outpatients with major depression. *Int Clin Psychopharmacol* 4, 127-134.

Feighner JP, Boyer WF, Meredith CH, *et al* (1989b) A placebo-controlled inpatient comparison of fluvoxamine maleate and imipramine in major depression. *Int Clin Psychopharmacol* 4, 239-244.

Feighner JP and Cohn JB (1985) Double-blind comparative trials of fluoxetine and doxepin in geriatric patients with major depressive disorder. *J Clin Psychiatry* 46 (3), 20-25.

Feldmann HS and Denber HC (1982) Long-term study of fluvoxamine: a new rapid-acting antidepressant. *Int Pharmacopsychiatry* 17, 114-122.

Ferreri M (1989) Fluoxetine versus amineptine in the treatment of outpatients with major depressive disorders. *Int Clin Psychopharmacol* 4 (Suppl 1), 97-101.

Ferrey G, Gailledrau J and Beuzen JN (1989) The interest of fluoxetine in prevention of depressive recurrences. In: Stefanis CN, Soldatos CR and Rabavilas AD (eds.) *Psychiatry Today: VIII World Congress of Psychiatry Abstracts*, p.99. New York: Elsevier.

Gagiano CA, Mueller PGM, Fourie J, *et al* (1989) The therapeutic efficacy of paroxetine: (a) an open study in patients with major depression not responding to antidepressants; (b) a double-blind comparison with amitriptyline in depressed outpatients. *Acta Psychiatr Scand* 80, 130-131.

Gravem A, Amthor KF, Astrup C, *et al* (1987) A double-blind comparison of citalopram (Lu 10-171) and amitriptyline in depressed patients. *Acta Psychiatr Scand* 75, 478-486.

Guelfi JD, Dreyfus JF and Pichot P (1983) A double-blind controlled clinical trial comparing fluvoxamine with imipramine. *Br J Clin Pharmacol* **15** (Suppl 3), 411S-417S.

Guelfi JD, Dreyfus JF and Pichot P (1987) Fluvoxamine and imipramine: results of a long-term controlled trial. *Int Clin Psychopharmacol* **2**, 103-109.

Guillibert E, Pelicier Y, Archambault JP, *et al* (1989) A double-blind, multicentre study of paroxetine versus clomipramine in depressed elderly patients. *Acta Psychiatr Scand* **80**, 132-134.

Guy W, Manov G and Wilson WH (1986) Double blind dose determination study of new antidepressant — sertraline. *Drug Dev Res* **9**, 267-272.

Guy W, Wilson WH, Ban TA, *et al* (1984) A double-blind clinical trial of fluvoxamine and imipramine in patients with primary depression. *Psychopharmacol Bull* **20** (1), 73-78.

Hamilton BA, Jones PG, Hoda AN, *et al* (1989) Flupenthixol and fluvoxamine in mild to moderate depression: A comparison in general practice. *Pharmatherapeutica* **5**, 292-297.

Hebenstreit GF, Fellerer K, Zoechling R, *et al* (1989) A pharmacokinetic dose titration study in adult and elderly depressed patients. *Acta Psychiatr Scand* **80**, 81-84.

Holm RM, Heerlein AJ and Diebold K (1987) Fluoxetine versus maprotiline in the treatment of endogenous depression. Presented at the *International Fluoxetine Symposium*, Tyrol, Austria, October 13-17.

Houillon P and Douge R (1989) Treatment by fluvoxamine of elderly patients more than 65 years old, with a major depressive syndrome. *Psychol Med* **21**, 1205-1217.

Itil TM, Shrivastava RK, Mukherjee S, *et al* (1983) A double-blind placebo-controlled study of fluvoxamine and imipramine in out-patients with primary depression. *Br J Clin Pharmacol* **15** (Suppl 3), 433S-438S.

Jouvent R, Baruch P, Ammar S, *et al* (1989) Fluoxetine efficacy in depressives with impulsivity vs blunted affect. In: Stefanis CN, Soldatos CR and Rabavilas AD (eds.) *Psychiatry Today: VIII World Congress of Psychiatry Abstracts*, p.398. New York: Elsevier.

Kasper S and Yieira A (1989) Stimulation with dl-fenfluramine and antidepressive medication in major depressed inpatients. *Pharmacopsychiatry* **22**, 201.

Kelly MW, Perry PJ, Holstad SG, *et al* (1989) Serum fluoxetine and norfluoxetine concentrations and antidepressant response. *Ther Drug Monit* **11**, 165-170.

Klok CJ, Brouwer GJ, van Praag HM, *et al* (1981) Fluvoxamine and clomipramine in depressed patients. A double-blind clinical study. *Acta Psychiatr Scand* **64**, 1-11.

Kuhs H and Rudolf GAE (1989) A double-blind study of the comparative antidepressant effect of paroxetine and amitriptyline. *Acta Psychiatr Scand* **80**, 145-146.

Lapierre YD, Browne M, Horn E, *et al* (1987) Treatment of major affective disorder with fluvoxamine. *J Clin Psychiatry* **48**, 65-68.

Laursen AL, Mikkelsen PL, Rasmussen S, *et al* (1985) Paroxetine in the treatment of depression — a randomized comparison with amitriptyline. *Acta Psychiatr Scand* **71**, 249-255.

Laws D, Ashford JJ and Anstee JA (1990) A multicentre double-blind comparative trial of fluvoxamine versus lorazepam in mixed anxiety and depression treated in general practice. *Acta Psychiatr Scand* **81**, 185-189.

Levine S, Deo R and Mahadevan K (1987) A comparative trial of a new antidepressant, fluoxetine. *Br J Psychiatry* **150**, 653-655.

Lundmark J, Scheel Thomsen I, Fjord-Larsen T, *et al* (1989) Paroxetine: pharmacokinetic and antidepressant effect in the elderly. *Acta Psychiatr Scand* **80**, 76-80.

Lydiard RB, Laird LK, Morton WA Jr, *et al* (1989) Fluvoxamine, imipramine, and placebo in the treatment of depressed outpatients: Effects on depression. *Psychopharmacol Bull* **25** (1), 68-70.

Manna V, Martucci N and Agnoli A (1989) Double-blind controlled study on the clinical efficacy and safety of fluoxetine vs clomipramine in the treatment of major depressive disorders. *Int Clin Psychopharmacol* **4** (Suppl 1), 81-88.

Marsden CA, Tyrer P, Casey P, *et al* (1987) Changes in human whole blood 5-hydroxytryptamine (5-HT) and platelet 5-HT uptake during treatment with paroxetine, a selective 5-HT uptake inhibitor. *J Psychopharmacol* **1**, 244-250.

Masco HL and Sheetz MS (1985) Double-blind comparison of fluoxetine and amitriptyline in the treatment of major depressive illness. *Adv Ther* **2**, 275-284.

Mertens C (1989) Citalopram versus mianserin: a controlled double-blind trial in depressed patients. In: Montgomery SA (ed.) *Citalopram: the New Antidepressant from Lundbeck Research*, pp.50-55. Amsterdam: Excerpta Medica.

Mertens C and Pintens H (1988) Paroxetine in the treatment of depression. A double-blind multicenter study versus mianserin. *Acta Psychiatr Scand* **77**, 683-688.

Montgomery SA (1989a) New antidepressants and 5-HT uptake inhibitors. *Acta Psychiatr Scand* **80** (Suppl 350), 107-116.

Montgomery SA (1989b) Fluoxetine in the treatment of anxiety, agitation and suicidal thoughts. In: Stefanis CN, Soldatos CR and Rabavilas AD (eds.) *Psychiatry Today: VIII World Congress of Psychiatry Abstracts*, p.335. New York: Elsevier.

Montgomery SA, Dufour H, Brion S, *et al* (1988) The prophylactic efficacy of fluoxetine in unipolar depression. *Br J Psychiatry* **153**, 69-76.

Montgomery SA, James D, Hawley C, *et al* (1987a) Plasma level relationship of once weekly or daily fluoxetine in the treatment of depression. Presented at the *International Fluoxetine Symposium*, Tyrol, Austria, October 13-17.

Montgomery SA, James D and Montgomery DB (1987b) Pharmacological specificity is not the same as clinical specificity. In: Dahl SG, Gram LF, Paul SM and Potter WZ (eds.) *Clinical Pharmacology in Psychiatry*, pp.179-183. Springer.

Montgomery SA, Rani SJ, McAuley R, *et al* (1981) The antidepressant efficacy of zimelidine and maprotiline. *Acta Psychiatr Scand* **63**, 219-224.

Mueller-Oerlinghausen B, Rao ML, Stieglitz RD, *et al* (1989) Fluvoxamine challenge test, phototherapy, and successive fluvoxamine treatment in patients with non-seasonal depression. *Pharmacopsychiatry* **22**, 209-210.

Muijen M, Roy D, Silverstone T, *et al* (1988) A comparative clinical trial of fluoxetine, mianserin and placebo in depressed outpatients. *Acta Psychiatr Scand* **78**, 384-390.

Mullin JM, Pandita-Gunawardena VR and Whitehead AM (1988) Double-blind comparison of fluvoxamine and dothiepin in the treatment of major affective disorder. *Br J Clin Pract* **42**, 51-55.

Norton KR, Sireling LI, Bhat AV, *et al* (1984) A double-blind comparison of fluvoxamine, imipramine and placebo in depressed patients. *J Affective Disord* **7**, 297-308.

Nystrom C and Hallstrom T (1987) Comparison between a serotonin and a noradrenaline reuptake blocker in the treatment of depressed outpatients. A cross-over study. *Acta Psychiatr Scand* **75**, 377-382.

Ofsti E (1982) Citalopram — a specific 5-HT-reuptake inhibitor — as an antidepressant drug: a phase II multicentre trial. *Prog Neuropsychopharmacol Biol Psychiatry* **6**, 327-335.

Oswald I and Adam K (1986) Effects of paroxetine on human sleep. *Br J Clin Pharmacol* **22**, 97-99.

Pedersen OL, Kragh-Srensen P, Bjerre M, *et al* (1982) Citalopram, a selective serotonin reuptake inhibitor: clinical antidepressive and long-term effect — a phase II study. *Psychopharmacology* **77**, 199-204.

Perry PJ, Garvey MJ, Kelly MW, *et al* (1989) A comparative trial of fluoxetine versus trazodone in outpatients with major depression. *J Clin Psychiatry* **50**, 290-294.

Peselow ED, Filippi AM, Goodnick P, *et al* (1989a) The short- and long-term efficacy of paroxetine HCl: A. Data from a 6-week double-blind parallel design trial vs. imipramine and placebo. *Psychopharmacol Bull* **25** (2), 267-271.

Peselow ED, Filippi AM, Goodnick P, *et al* (1989b) The short- and long-term efficacy of paroxetine HCl: B. Data from a double-blind crossover study and from a year-long term trial vs. imipramine and placebo. *Psychopharmacol Bull* **25** (2), 272-276.

Peselow ED, Lautin A, Wolkin A, *et al* (1986) The dexamethasone suppression test and response to placebo. *J Clin Psychopharmacol* **6**, 286-291.

Phanjoo A, Wonnacott S, Hodgson A, *et al* (1989) A study of fluvoxamine versus mianserin in elderly depressed patients. In: Stefanis CN, Soldatos CR and Rabavilas AD (eds.) *Psychiatry Today: VIII World Congress of Psychiatry Abstracts*, p.276. New York: Elsevier.

Poeldinger W and Haber H (1987) Fluoxetine 40mg vs maprotiline 75 mg in the treatment of out-patients with depressive disorders. Presented at the *International Fluoxetine Symposium*, Tyrol, Austria, October 13-17.

Poeldinger W and Haber H (1989) Fluoxetine 40mg vs maprotiline 75mg in the treatment of out-patients with depressive disorders. *Int Clin Psychopharmacol* **4** (Suppl 1), 47-50.

van Praag HM, Kahn R, Asnis GM, *et al* (1987) Therapeutic indications for serotonin-potentiating compounds: a hypothesis. *Biol Psychiatry* **22**, 205-212.

Reimherr FW, Byerley WF, Ward MF, *et al* (1988) Sertraline, a selective inhibitor of serotonin uptake, for the treatment of outpatients with major depressive disorder. *Psychopharmacol Bull* **24** (1), 200-205.

Reimherr FW, Wood DR, Byerley B, *et al* (1984) Characteristics of responders to fluoxetine. *Psychopharmacol Bull* **20** (1), 70-72.

Schweizer E, Rickels K, Amsterdam JD, *et al* (1990) What constitutes an adequate antidepressant trial for fluoxetine? *J Clin Psychiatry* **51**, 8-11.

Shaw DM and Crimmins R (1989) A multicentre trial of citalopram and amitriptyline in major depressive illness. In: Montgomery SA (ed.) *Citalopram: the New Antidepressant from Lundbeck Research*, pp.43-49. Amsterdam: Excerpta Medica.

Shaw DM, Thomas DR, Briscoe MH, *et al* (1986) A comparison of the antidepressant action of citalopram and amitriptyline. *Br J Psychiatry* **149**, 515-517.

Simeon JG, Ferguson HB, Copping W, *et al* (1989) Fluoxetine effects in adolescent depression. In: Stefanis CD, Soldatos CR and Rabavilas AD (eds.) *Psychiatry Today: VIII World Congress of Psychiatry Abstracts*, p.748. New York: Elsevier.

South Wales Antidepressant Drug Trial Group (1988) A double-blind multi-centre trial of fluoxetine and dothiepin in major depressive illness. *Int Clin Psychopharmacol* **3**, 75-81.

Stark P and Hardison CD (1985). A review of multicenter controlled studies of fluoxetine vs. imipramine and placebo in outpatients with major depressive disorder. *J Clin Psychiatry* **46** (3), 53-58.

Szulecka TK and Whitehead AM (1989) Fluvoxamine versus amitriptyline in the treatment of depressed patients. In: Stefanis CN, Soldatos CR and Rabavilas AD (eds.) *Psychiatry Today: VIII World Congress of Psychiatry Abstracts*, p.268. New York: Elsevier.

Tamminen TT and Lehtinen VV (1989) A double-blind parallel study to compare fluoxetine with doxepin in the treatment of major depressive disorders. *Int Clin Psychopharmacol* **4** (Suppl 1), 51-56.

Tasker TCG, Kaye CM, Zussman BD, *et al* (1989) Paroxetine plasma levels: lack of correlation with efficacy or adverse events. *Acta Psychiatr Scand* **80**, 152-155.

Timmerman L, de-Beurs P, Tan BK, *et al* (1987) A double-blind comparative clinical trial of citalopram vs maprotiline in hospitalized depressed patients. *Int Clin Psychopharmacol* **2**, 239-253.

Twomey MKP and Whitehead AM (1989) Fluvoxamine versus mianserin: A double-blind study. In: Stefanis CN, Soldatos CR and Rabavilas AD (eds.) *Psychiatry Today: VIII World Congress of Psychiatry Abstracts*, p.268. Amsterdam: Elsevier.

Tyrer P, Marsden CA, Casey P, *et al* (1987) Clinical efficacy of paroxetine in resistant depression. *J Psychopharmacol* **1**, 251-257.

Vanelle JM, Poirier MF, Benkelfat A, *et al* (1990) Diagnostic and therapeutic value of testing stimulation of thyroid-stimulating hormone by thyrotropin-releasing hormone in 100 depressed patients. *Acta Psychiatr Scand* **81**, 156-161.

Weilburg JB, Rosenbaum JF, Biederman J, *et al* (1989) Fluoxetine added to non-MAOI antidepressants converts non-responders to responders: a preliminary report. *J Clin Psychiatry* **50**, 447-449.

Wernicke JF, Bremner JD, Bosomworth J, *et al* (1987) The efficacy and safety of fluoxetine in the long-term treatment of depression. Presented at the *International Fluoxetine Symposium*, Tyrol, Austria, October 13-17.

Wernicke JF, Dunlop SR, Dornseif BE, *et al* (1988) Low-dose fluoxetine therapy for depression. *Psychopharmacol Bull* **24** (1), 183-188.

Westenberg HG and Verhoeven WM (1988) CSF monoamine metabolites in patients and controls: support for a bimodal distribution in major affective disorders. *Acta Psychiatr Scand* **78**, 541-549.

Wood K, Swade C, Abou-Saleh M, *et al* (1983) Drug plasma levels and platelet 5-HT uptake inhibition during long-term treatment with fluvoxamine or lithium in patients with affective disorders. *Br J Clin Pharmacol* **15** (Suppl 3), 365S-368S.

Young JP, Coleman A and Lader MH (1987) A controlled comparison of fluoxetine and amitriptyline in depressed out-patients. *Br J Psychiatry* **151**, 337-340.

6

The efficacy of selective serotonin re-uptake inhibitors in anxiety and obsessive-compulsive disorder

W.F. Boyer, G.A. McFadden, and J.P. Feighner

Introduction

Over the past decade there has been a crescendo of interest in the role of the serotonin system in mediating both anxiety and depressive disorders. Research has provided therapeutic compounds that are selective for re-uptake blockade of the serotonin or noradrenergic systems. The effectiveness of these selective compounds has spurred speculation that the anxiety and depressive disorders may result from dysfunctions of these systems, either alone or in tandem.

The initial excitement regarding the selective serotonin re-uptake inhibitors (SSRIs) was focused on their antidepressant effects plus a superior side-effect profile compared with other antidepressant classes. However there has, more recently, been equal enthusiasm for their potential efficacy in the anxiety disorders.

Epidemiology of anxiety disorders

The epidemiological catchment area study (ECA), supervised by the US National Institute of Mental Health, estimated the frequency of DSM-III diagnosable anxiety disorders at 8.3% of the general population, or 13.1 million people (Figure 1). The prevalence of anxiety disorders exceeded that for mood disorders, which were diagnosed in 6% of the general population. Only 23% of those with anxiety disorders were receiving treatment.

The most common anxiety disorder for which individuals sought help was panic disorder, most probably because of its dramatic and frightening symptoms.

While the estimate of the prevalence of anxiety disorders may have been inflated by the inclusion of simple phobia, the ECA study clearly underlined the high prevalence of untreated anxiety disorders.

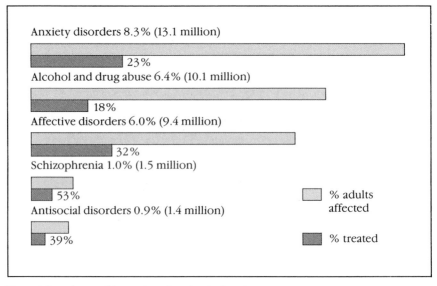

Figure 1. Prevalence of the anxiety disorders in the USA.

Neurobiology of anxiety disorders

The origin of high levels of anxiety or panic has generally been associated with the central noradrenergic system, the major focus of interest being the locus coeruleus, a relatively homogeneous nucleus in the rostral pons which houses approximately 50-70% of the brain's noradrenaline-containing bodies. The locus coeruleus projects widely through the brain but, of perhaps greatest interest, sends major efferent pathways to limbic areas, especially the amygdala and perihippocampal structures. The locus coeruleus is also richly innervated by an inhibitory input of GABA neurones.

These neuro-anatomical and neurophysiological observations have, as mentioned above, led to the concept that anxiety is mediated primarily via the noradrenergic system, which is hyperresponsive and volatile. It also suggests that antidepressants with significant inhibitory effects on the noradrenaline pathway may decrease anxiety by dampening this hyperresponsiveness through modulation of postsynaptic ß-receptors and presynaptic α_2-receptors (Figure 2). This hypothesis is also consistent with the role of benzodiazepine enhancement of the inhibitory GABA input to the locus coeruleus.

This schema of noradrenergic hyperexcitability in anxiety states is also supported by the positron emission tomographic studies carried out by Reiman and associates (1989). These studies have shown the major projections of the locus

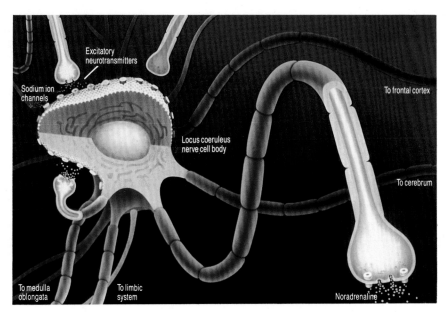

Figure 2. The above neuronal interaction depicts areas of potential down-regulation of postsynaptic ß-receptors, up-regulation of inhibitory presynaptic α_2-receptors, and the modulation of excitation in this neurone by the inhibitory GABA input of the axon entering the right side of the neuronal cell body. See text for further explanation.

coeruleus as markedly hypermetabolic when anxiety symptoms are intense (Figure 3).

The recent reports of decreased symptoms of panic disorder during treatment with an SSRI are not consistent with a simple model of exclusive noradrenergic control. Further neurophysiological studies will be required to clarify the role of the noradrenaline and serotonin systems, in isolation or in combination, in explaining these findings.

Studies of the SSRIs in anxiety disorders

Few double-blind studies of the SSRIs in panic disorder have been carried out. However, Gorman and associates (1987) examined the therapeutic effect of fluoxetine in 16 patients with panic disorder by means of an open-label pilot study. Seven patients (44%) were effectively treated with fluoxetine alone and had minimal side-effects. However, eight of the nine non-responders were unable to tolerate fluoxetine because of side-effects. This study focused attention on the possibility that serotonin might be important in the pathophysiology of panic disorder, and also revealed the initial agitation in patients with panic disorder who received fluoxetine, which may contribute to intolerance during treatment.

Schneier and associates (1990) treated 25 patients suffering from panic

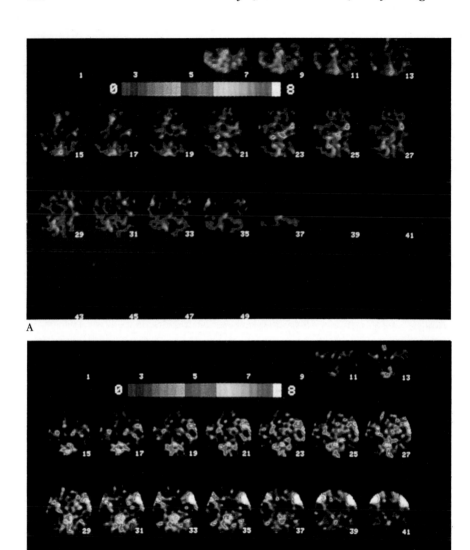

Figure 3. Serial positron emission tomography composite scans of the human brain showing the distribution in intensity of glucose metabolism in healthy subjects injected with sodium lactate. Panel A represents the scans of subjects without panic disorder who exhibited no symptoms of anxiety and no positron emission tomography scan deviations from a normal metabolic profile. Panel B shows patients with panic disorder, who display the highly characteristic abnormality of extremely high glucose metabolism at the frontal poles of both temporal lobes in the area of the amygdala and perihippocampal structures (Reiman *et al*, 1989).

disorder with fluoxetine. In this study the initial dosage was titrated upwards from 5mg/day to minimize side-effects, and the results suggested some advantage to this more cautious approach. Nineteen patients (76%) showed a moderate to marked improvement in their panic attacks, only 4 of the 25 being unable to tolerate fluoxetine because of side-effects.

Other SSRIs have also been shown to improve the symptoms of panic disorder. den-Boer and associates (1987) found that fluvoxamine was as effective as clomipramine in reducing symptoms of anxiety in a double-blind, comparative study of 50 patients. Westenberg and den-Boer (1988) later published the results of a double-blind, comparative study of fluvoxamine and maprotiline, a specific inhibitor of noradrenaline re-uptake. The results showed fluvoxamine to be significantly superior in controlling panic attacks, maprotiline being essentially ineffective.

Humble and associates (1989) treated 20 patients suffering from panic disorder with citalopram in an eight-week open study. The results suggested that citalopram was effective in relieving symptoms of anxiety and was well tolerated. Citalopram also appeared to have beneficial effects on social phobic symptoms. However, some patients reported an initial increase in anxiety, as with the other SSRIs.

These provocative findings clearly call for a rethinking of the pathophysiological mechanisms of anxiety. They also call for an aggressive evaluation of the SSRIs in panic disorder. This is perhaps even more important when one considers their generally superior side-effect profile (see chapter 8).

Studies of the SSRIs in obsessive-compulsive disorder

Obsessive-compulsive disorder (OCD) has traditionally been the bane of the clinician who treats anxiety disorders.

A high level of activity is characteristically seen in the prefrontal lobe of OCD patients on positron emission tomography scans. Figure 4, drawn from the work of Baxter and associates (1989), shows the abnormally high level of metabolic activity, presumptively correlating with the stereotypic activity seen in OCD. The SSRIs are felt by many to provide significant inhibitory input to this dysfunctional prefrontal lobe activity.

It is only recently that specific pharmacotherapeutic agents have created enthusiasm for the potential control of this syndrome. These agents include the SSRIs as well as the tricyclic antidepressant clomipramine, which is a partially selective inhibitor of serotonin re-uptake. Indeed, the superior efficacy of clomipramine in OCD compared with the tricyclic antidepressants has stimulated most of the work regarding the role of serotonin in this disorder (Benkelfat *et al*, 1989). These therapeutic compounds have clearly established their role in the primary treatment of OCD.

Goodman and associates (1989b) conducted an eight-week, double-blind, placebo-controlled trial of fluvoxamine in 42 patients with primary OCD, of

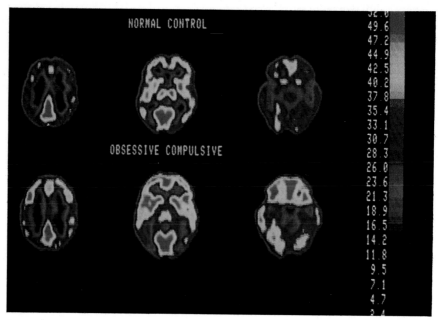

Figure 4. Hypermetabolic prefrontal lobes in the glucose positron emission tomography scan from an OCD patient compared with the same scan in a person without OCD (Baxter *et al*, 1989).

whom approximately one-half also had symptoms of major depression. Nine out of 21 patients responded to fluvoxamine compared with no patients on placebo. Fluvoxamine was effective in patients with OCD both in the presence and absence of secondary depression.

In another study of patients suffering from OCD, the same group compared the efficacy of fluvoxamine with that of desipramine, a relatively specific inhibitor of noradrenaline re-uptake. Thirty-eight patients with a primary diagnosis of DSM-IIIR OCD were randomly assigned to eight weeks of treatment with either fluvoxamine or desipramine. Only 2 out of 19 patients in the desipramine group were responders versus 10 out of 19 in the fluvoxamine group (p = 0.005). A reduction in obsessive-compulsive scores did not correlate significantly with baseline depression (Goodman *et al*, 1989a).

Perse and colleagues (1987) studied sixteen outpatients who met DSM-III criteria for OCD. This was a 20-week, double-blind, crossover trial with fluvoxamine and placebo. Thirteen (81%) improved with fluvoxamine, but only three (19%) improved with placebo. The improvement seen in depressed patients correlated with the improvement in OCD symptom measures, but non-depressed patients also improved on measures of OCD symptoms.

The effects of fluoxetine in OCD have been studied in a number of single-blind and open trials, and the results indicate that fluoxetine is effective in reducing the symptoms of OCD in adults and adolescents. These results also appear to be independent of the drug's antidepressant effect (Fontaine and Chouinard, 1985; Turner *et al*, 1985; Jenike *et al*, 1989; Levine *et al*, 1989; Liebowitz *et al*, 1990; Riddle *et al*, 1990).

The literature suggests that the therapeutic effects are maintained during chronic treatment. Levine and colleagues (1989) studied a group of 75 outpatients suffering from OCD, who were treated with fluoxetine in an open clinical setting. The group showed a significant improvement on all measures, which continued and was progressive over a five-month period.

Fewer data have been published on the use of other SSRIs in OCD and double-blind studies using fluoxetine have not been reported in the literature. Bick and Hackett (1989) treated 87 non-depressed OCD patients with sertraline or placebo in an eight-week, double-blind study, the results indicating that sertraline was significantly superior to placebo.

While these studies suggest that drugs with serotonin re-uptake blocking properties are effective in OCD, they do not bear on which of these drugs may be more effective or better tolerated. Although no such comparative trials have been published, Jenike and associates (1990) indirectly compared fluoxetine with clomipramine in OCD symptoms in a recent meta-analysis. The data came from two separate open studies of each compound in OCD, and the special statistical techniques used suggested that clomipramine had a slightly superior therapeutic effect. Fluoxetine, however, was considerably better tolerated.

Studies in mixed anxiety and depression

Patients often present with a mixture of anxious and depressive features. Although this is not a formally recognized diagnostic category, such patients are commonly seen. Montgomery (1989) recently presented a meta-analysis of several studies of fluoxetine which suggested that this SSRI may be particularly useful in patients with anxiety and psychomotor agitation. Jouvent and colleagues (1989) found that fluoxetine was more effective than placebo in anxious-impulsive patients than in those with a blunted affect. The effect of paroxetine on anxiety symptoms associated with depression was considered in a pooled analysis of data from six centres. Paroxetine had a significantly earlier effect on these symptoms when compared with imipramine (Dunbar, 1990).

Other studies have suggested similar characteristics for other SSRIs. Shaw and Crimmins (1989) compared citalopram and amitriptyline in a six-week trial of 59 in- and outpatients suffering from major depression. No differences in antidepressant effectiveness were observed, and the drugs were equally effective in reducing anxiety despite the greater sedative action of amitriptyline.

Fluvoxamine has been compared with the benzodiazepines in two studies of patients with mixed anxiety and depression. Chabannes and Douge (1989) treated 60 outpatients with 'low mood and anxiety' with either fluvoxamine or diazepam for six weeks, and found that the two treatments had equal effects on the Hamilton anxiety scale.

Laws and colleagues (1990) compared fluvoxamine and lorazepam in 112 patients with mixed anxiety and depression in a six-week study. No significant differences were seen at any point except that anxiety improved more rapidly, but not more completely, in elderly patients given lorazepam. The improvement continued throughout the six-week duration of the study.

Conclusions

In summary, the SSRIs have demonstrated their efficacy in the treatment of panic disorder, OCD, and mixed anxiety and depression. Their usefulness has emphasized the importance of the serotonin system in the aetiology of these disorders.

The SSRIs offer the clinical advantage of providing symptomatic relief for these indications without the anticholinergic, antihistaminic, and cardiovascular side-effects or weight gain associated with tricyclic antidepressants. Fluoxetine, like the tricyclics and the monoamine oxidase inhibitors, is liable to increase anxiety initially in patients suffering from panic disorder. The extent to which this constitutes a problem with other SSRIs is unknown. The efficacy of SSRIs versus those of the tricyclic antidepressants and the monoamine oxidase inhibitors for these indications is also unstudied. Further research is required fully to assess the place of the SSRIs in the treatment and understanding of anxiety disorders.

References

Baxter LR Jr, Schwartz JM, Phelps ME, et al (1989) Reduction of prefrontal cortex glucose metabolism common to three types of depression. Arch Gen Psychiatry 46, 243-250.

Benkelfat C, Murphy DL, Zohar J, et al (1989) Clomipramine in obsessive-compulsive disorder. Further evidence for a serotonergic mechanism of action. Arch Gen Psychiatry 46, 23-28.

Bick PA and Hackett E (1989) Sertraline is effective in obsessive-compulsive disorder. In: Stefanis CN, Soldatos CR and Rabavilas AD (eds.) Psychiatry Today: VIII World Congress of Psychiatry Abstracts, p.152. New York: Elsevier.

den-Boer JA, Westenberg HG, Kamerbeek WD, et al (1987) Effect of serotonin uptake inhibitors in anxiety disorders; a double-blind comparison of clomipramine and fluvoxamine. Int Clin Psychopharmacol 2, 21-32.

Chabannes JP and Douge R (1989) Efficacy on anxiety of fluvoxamine versus prazepam, diazepam with anxiodepressed patients. In: Stefanis CN, Soldatos CR and Rabavilas AD (eds.) Psychiatry Today: VIII World Congress of Psychiatry Abstracts, p.282. New York: Elsevier.

Dunbar GC (1990) The efficacy profile of paroxetine, a new antidepressant, compared with imipramine and placebo. 17th CINP Congress Abstracts 1, 17.

Fontaine R and Chouinard G (1985) Fluoxetine in the treatment of obsessive compulsive disorder. Prog Neuropsychopharmacol Biol Psychiatry 9, 605-608.

Goodman WK, Delgado PL, Price LH, et al (1989a) Fluvoxamine versus desipramine in OCD. New Research Program and Abstracts, American Psychiatry Association 142nd Annual Meeting, p.186.

Goodman WK, Price LH, Rasmussen SA, *et al* (1989b) Efficacy of fluvoxamine in obsessive-compulsive disorder. A double-blind comparison with placebo. *Arch Gen Psychiatry* **46**, 36-44.

Gorman JM, Liebowitz MR, Fyer AJ, *et al* (1987) An open trial of fluoxetine in the treatment of panic attacks [published erratum appears in *J Clin Psychopharmacol* Feb 1988 **8** (1), 13]. *J Clin Psychopharmacol* **7**, 329-332.

Humble M, Koczkas C and Wistedt B (1989) Serotonin and anxiety: an open study of citalopram in panic disorder. In: Stefanis CN, Soldatos CR and Rabavilas AD (eds.) *Psychiatry Today: VIII World Congress of Psychiatry Abstracts*, p.151. New York: Elsevier.

Jenike MA, Baer L and Greist JH (1990) Clomipramine versus fluoxetine in obsessive-compulsive disorder: A retrospective comparison of side effects and efficacy. *J Clin Psychopharmacol* **10**, 122-124.

Jenike MA, Buttolph L, Baer L, *et al* (1989) Open trial of fluoxetine in obsessive-compulsive disorder. *Am J Psychiatry* **146**, 909-911.

Jouvent R, Baruch P, Ammar S, *et al* (1989) Fluoxetine efficacy in depressives with impulsivity vs blunted affect. In: Stefanis CN, Soldatos CR and Rabavilas AD (eds.) *Psychiatry Today: VIII World Congress of Psychiatry Abstracts*, p.398. New York: Elsevier.

Laws D, Ashford JJ and Anstee JA (1990) A multicentre double-blind comparative trial of fluvoxamine versus lorazepam in mixed anxiety and depression treated in general practice. *Acta Psychiatr Scand* **81**, 185-189.

Levine R, Hoffman JS, Knepple ED, *et al* (1989) Long-term fluoxetine treatment of a large number of obsessive-compulsive patients. *J Clin Psychopharmacol* **9**, 281-283.

Liebowitz MR, Hollander E, Fairbanks J, *et al* (1990) Fluoxetine for adolescents with obsessive-compulsive disorder. *Am J Psychiatry* **147**, 370-371.

Montgomery SA (1989) Fluoxetine in the treatment of anxiety, agitation and suicidal thoughts. In: Stefanis CN, Soldatos CR and Rabavilas AD (eds.) *Psychiatry Today: VIII World Congress of Psychiatry Abstracts*, p.335. New York: Elsevier.

Perse TL, Greist JH, Jefferson JW, *et al* (1987) Fluvoxamine treatment of obsessive-compulsive disorder. *Am J Psychiatry* **144**, 1543-1548.

Reiman EM, Raichle ME, Robins E, *et al* (1989) Neuroanatomical correlates of a lactate-induced anxiety attack. *Arch Gen Psychiatry* **46**, 493-500.

Riddle MA, Hardin MT, King R, *et al* (1990) Fluoxetine treatment of children and adolescents with Tourette's and obsessive-compulsive disorders: preliminary clinical experience. *J Am Acad Child Adolesc Psychiatry* **29**, 45-48.

Schneier FR, Liebowitz MR, Davies SO, *et al* (1990) Fluoxetine in panic disorder. *J Clin Psychopharmacol* **10**, 119-121.

Shaw DM and Crimmins R (1989) A multicentre trial of citalopram and amitriptyline in major depressive illness. In: Montgomery SA (ed.) *Citalopram: the New Antidepressant from Lundbeck Research*, pp.43-49. Amsterdam: Excerpta Medica.

Turner SM, Jacob RG, Beidel DC, *et al* (1985) Fluoxetine treatment of obsessive-compulsive disorder. *J Clin Psychopharmacol* **5**, 207-212.

Westenberg HJM and den-Boer JA (1988) Clinical and biochemical effects of selective serotonin-uptake inhibitors in anxiety disorders. In: Gastpar M and Wakelin JS (eds.) *Selective 5-HT reuptake inhibitors: Novel or Commonplace agents?* pp.84-99. Basel: Karger.

7

Other potential indications for selective serotonin re-uptake inhibitors

W.F. Boyer and J.P. Feighner

Suicidal ideation

One of the most exciting aspects of the selective serotonin re-uptake inhibitors (SSRIs) is their potentially broad range of indications. This chapter will review the evidence for the efficacy of SSRIs in conditions other than depression and anxiety disorders. We will first briefly review the connections between serotonin function and each of these target areas and then summarize the available data in man.

A large number of studies have indicated that suicidal ideation, as well as suicide attempts, are linked to serotonin dysfunction. Suicide attempters, especially those who use violent means, have lower concentrations of 5-hydroxyindoleacetic acid (5-HIAA) in the cerebrospinal fluid than do depressed control patients (Traskman *et al*, 1981; Banki and Arato, 1983; Ninan *et al*, 1984; Banki *et al*, 1986; Edman *et al*, 1986). In addition, suicidal patients exhibit a blunted prolactin response to fenfluramine, a serotonin releaser (Coccaro *et al*, 1989b). Suicide victims also have increased 5-HT$_2$ binding sites in the frontal cortex (Stanley and Mann, 1983), which may reflect compensation for decreased availability of serotonin. Although there are a large number of potentially confounding factors in these studies the consistency of results pointing to dysfunction is remarkable.

Several studies have found fluoxetine, fluvoxamine, and citalopram to be more effective than a comparison tricyclic in reducing suicidal ideation (Muijen *et al*, 1988; Mullin *et al*, 1988; Wakelin, 1988; Gaszner, 1989; Montgomery, 1989). Conversely, drugs that inhibit the re-uptake of noradrenaline may be associated with an increased risk of suicide compared with placebo (Montgomery *et al*,

1989). These findings are important, especially since patients with high levels of suicidal ideation are excluded from most clinical trials, which should make it harder to detect significant differences. Because the SSRIs have a beneficial effect on suicidal ideation and are safer than the tricyclics in overdose (Pedersen *et al*, 1982; Banerjee, 1988; Cooper, 1988; Finnegan and Gabiola, 1988; Riddle *et al*, 1989), clinicians should seriously consider the advantages of prescribing a drug of this class for depressed patients with suicidal ideation.

However, this discussion must be tempered by a report from Teicher and colleagues (1990) of six patients suffering from depression and other psychiatric conditions who developed intense, intrusive, and violent suicidal ideation after two to seven weeks of treatment with fluoxetine and who had not experienced a similar state with other psychotropic medications. It is possible that these patients experienced a paradoxical reaction, and the true incidence of this sort of reaction and its clinical significance remain to be determined (see also page 145).

Substance abuse disorder

Alcoholism may also be tied to dysfunction of the serotonergic system (Borg *et al*, 1985), the evidence for this coming from several sources. Serotonin depletion enhances alcohol use in animals (Tollefson, 1989) and recent studies of 5-HT_{1A} agonists, such as buspirone, suggest efficacy in reducing a craving for alcohol (Bruno, 1989). Lithium, which may work through serotonergic mechanisms (Muller-Oerlinghausen, 1985), has also been reported to aid abstinence in alcoholics (Kline *et al*, 1974; Merry *et al*, 1976; McMillan, 1981; Himmelhoch *et al*, 1983; Fawcet *et al*, 1984).

Several studies have shown that the SSRIs reduce alcohol consumption in animals and in man (Gill *et al*, 1985, 1988a,b; Murphy *et al*, 1985; Naranjo *et al*, 1986, 1987; Li *et al*, 1987; Grupp *et al*, 1988; McBride *et al*, 1988; Murphy *et al*, 1988; Weintraub and Evans, 1988; Gill and Amit, 1989; Gorelick, 1989; Naranjo and Sellers, 1989). Much of the evidence from animal studies comes from rats selectively bred to prefer alcohol, one major difference between these alcohol-preferring and non-alcohol-preferring rats being a lowered content of serotonin in the brains of the 'alcoholic' variety (Li *et al*, 1987). Murphy and coworkers (1988) reported that the SSRIs fluoxetine and fluvoxamine significantly reduced ethanol intake in these rats.

The mechanism by which the SSRIs alter ethanol preference remains unclear (Murphy *et al*, 1985). Pretreatment with antagonists for 5-HT_1 and 5-HT_2, as well as the alpha- and beta-noradrenergic, receptor systems does not reverse the attenuation of ethanol intake. One possible mechanism is that the alcohol-reducing effect is a byproduct of the reduction in appetite associated with the SSRIs (Gill and Amit, 1989). It may also be mediated at least in part by the renin-angiotensin system: in one study injection of an angiotensin converting enzyme inhibitor, enalapril, partially reversed the reduction in alcohol intake produced by fluoxetine (Grupp *et al*, 1988).

The inhibition of alcohol consumption begins within an hour of drug administration and lasts several days after discontinuation, but tolerance may develop. The immediate onset and occasional loss of effect after a few days suggests that the effect is separate from the antidepressant property of the drug, which follows the opposite time course. Human alcoholics may also return to their baseline level of drinking after the first week, but heavy social drinkers and early problem drinkers did not develop tolerance to this effect within the three- to four-week duration of most studies (Gorelick, 1989).

In one of these trials in man Naranjo and colleagues (1987) tested citalopram in 39 non-depressed male subjects who were early problem drinkers. Subjects were randomly assigned to receive one of two doses of citalopram — 20 or 40mg/day — or placebo in a double-blind, crossover trial. Ethanol intake was assessed both by self-report and objectively. At a dose of 20mg/day, citalopram did not show any effect on alcohol consumption. However, at a dose of 40mg/day, citalopram decreased the number of drinks consumed and increased the number of abstinent days.

The same investigators found similar results with the SSRIs zimeldine, fluoxetine, and viqualine: treatment with one of these drugs decreased the total number of drinks consumed by early problem drinkers by an average of 20-30%. However, the investigators also observed marked interindividual variations in response to the SSRIs and were unable to predict which individuals would respond (Naranjo and Sellers, 1989).

As discussed in chapter 4, the SSRIs do not generally potentiate the effects of alcohol on measures of sedation or psychomotor performance (Lemberger *et al*, 1985, 1988; McClelland and Raptopoulos, 1985; Tartara *et al*, 1985; Schaffler, 1986; Moskowitz and Burns, 1988; Allen and Lader, 1989). Hence a drug of this class could be considered for a depressed patient prone to alcohol abuse.

Data from animal studies suggest that fluoxetine may also be helpful in the treatment of stimulant abuse (Yu, *et al*, 1986). Rats trained to self-administer intravenous dextroamphetamine administer significantly less of the stimulant following chronic treatment with fluoxetine, while animals trained to self-administer intravenous saline show no such decrease. However, this effect may not apply to all stimulants; for example, Porrino and colleagues (1989) found that fluoxetine decreased behaviour reinforced by amphetamine but not that reinforced by cocaine.

Ritz and Kuhar (1989) investigated the receptors associated with the reinforcing properties of amphetamine and related phenylethylamines and compared the potencies of these compounds in reinforcing behaviour with their binding potencies at monoaminergic uptake and neurotransmitter receptor sites. Their findings implicated the serotonin transport system. Specifically, the self-administration of amphetamine and related compounds was inversely related to the inhibition of binding of radioactively labelled paroxetine to the serotonin transporter, suggesting that inhibition of serotonin uptake may oppose the reinforcing effects of amphetamine. Studies of the effects of SSRIs on stimulant abuse in man have not yet been published.

Research is also being conducted into the efficacy of the SSRIs in patients exhibiting addiction to nicotine. There is considerable interest in this indication but little has been published to date. One study showed that fluoxetine had a 'remarkable' and almost immediate effect in alleviating withdrawal from nicotine (Hapworth and Hapworth, 1989), while another study demonstrated that neither citalopram nor zimeldine reduced the number of cigarettes smoked (Sellers *et al*, 1987). The second study differed from the first in that the patients studied were exclusively heavy drinkers and it was not a specific study of smoking cessation. This suggests that the expectancies in the experimental situation may influence the study results or that this may be another indication in which the SSRIs are not equally effective.

Eating disorders

Eating disorders bear some similarities to substance abuse disorders and serotonin may also be involved here. Serotonin regulates satiety (Carruba *et al*, 1986), and thus low serotonin activity can cause overeating in animals (Breisch *et al*, 1976) and may be linked to obesity in man (Donders *et al*, 1985). Donders and colleagues (1985) found that the thyroid stimulating hormone response to thyrotrophin releasing hormone was significantly elevated in obese subjects and the prolactin response was comparatively blunted. This was taken as an indication of low serotonin activity because serotonin stimulates prolactin release and inhibits thyroid stimulating hormone in man.

Anorexia is associated with an increase in the function of serotonin (Samanin *et al*, 1980; von-Meyenfeldt *et al*, 1982; Nichols *et al*, 1983; Fanelli *et al*, 1986). For example, Fanelli and colleagues (1986) studied 45 patients with various types of cancer and compared them with 13 control subjects. The patients were unaware of their malignancy at the time of the study and had not received any antineoplastic treatment. The results demonstrated that free tryptophan in the plasma was significantly increased in cancer patients with anorexia.

Clinical use of the SSRIs may be associated with loss of appetite and of weight. This effect is generally proportional to their potency in blocking re-uptake of serotonin (Angel *et al*, 1988). But this is not absolute, since paroxetine is a more potent SSRI than fluoxetine and yet seems to have less effect on weight. Dosage may be a factor, however, since paroxetine was used in the range 20-50mg while that for fluoxetine was 20-80mg. Several of the SSRIs have therefore been examined for weight-reducing effects in depressed and non-depressed obese subjects. The results demonstrated them to be superior to placebo in promoting weight loss (Abell *et al*, 1986; Ferguson and Feighner, 1987; Levine *et al*, 1987; Clark and Rosenblatt, 1989; Feighner and Rosenblatt, 1989); they were also generally well tolerated (Zerbe, 1987). The above studies are summarized in Table I.

Weight loss does not depend on whether the patient experiences nausea, but appears instead to be related to whether the patient has carbohydrate craving

Study	SSRI	Comparison group	Subjects	Duration	Outcome
Abell *et al*, 1986	Fluvoxamine, 100-200mg/day	Placebo	40 patients with 'refractory obesity'	12 weeks	Non-significant greater weight loss with fluvoxamine
Ferguson and Feighner, 1987	Fluoxetine, 20-80mg/day	Benzphetamine, placebo	150 non-depressed, obese subjects		Fluoxetine produced significantly greater weight loss than placebo, non-significantly greater weight loss than benzphetamine
Levine *et al*, 1987	Fluoxetine, 10, 20, 40, or 60 mg/day		120 otherwise healthy, obese subjects	8 weeks	Higher doses of fluoxetine were associated with greater weight loss
Clark and Rosenblatt, 1989	Sertraline, 150mg/day	Placebo	80 non-depressed, obese, diabetic inpatients		Sertraline produced significantly greater weight loss
Feighner and Rosenblatt, 1989	Sertraline, 50-200mg/day		158 non-depressed, obese subjects		

Table I. Results of controlled trials of the SSRIs in weight loss.

(Ferguson and Feighner, 1987), which itself may be a sign of serotonergic dysfunction (Wurtman and Wurtman, 1986; Wurtman, 1988). An important question for future research relates to how well this weight loss is maintained.

Bulimia may also be related to serotonin dysfunction (Kaye *et al*, 1984, 1988; Marazziti *et al*, 1988; Jimerson *et al*, 1989). Kaye and colleagues (1988) have published an interesting paper in this regard, in which they suggest that bingeing and vomiting may change the ratios of plasma amino acids which in turn enhances serotonin-mediated satiety in the brain and/or may result in improved mood. This hypothesis was based on data showing that the intake of dietary carbohydrates increases the brain uptake of tryptophan by increasing the plasma ratio of tryptophan to the other amino acids that compete for uptake into the brain. They found that bulimic subjects who developed an increased plasma tryptophan ratio during bingeing and vomiting had fewer binge-purge cycles and a greater increase in plasma prolactin than subjects who did not develop an increased tryptophan ratio.

In addition, other evidence points to an alteration of serotonin function in bulimia. For example, the severity of bulimic symptoms correlates with the lowering of 5-HIAA in the cerebrospinal fluid (Jimerson, et al, 1989), while weight-recovered bulimic patients also have lower levels of 5-HIAA in the cerebrospinal fluid than weight-recovered anorexic patients (Kaye et al, 1984).

Published data concerning SSRIs in the treatment of bulimia have so far been limited to fluoxetine. In one open study 10 bulimic patients were treated with 60 to 80mg of fluoxetine daily. Seven of these subjects stopped their bulimic behaviour completely, two improved, and one was unchanged (Freeman and Hampson, 1987). In a larger, placebo-controlled study Enas and colleagues (1989) compared two doses of fluoxetine in 382 bulimic women outpatients. At a dose of 60mg/day fluoxetine was significantly superior to placebo in decreasing the frequency of binge-eating and vomiting episodes. At a dose of 20mg/day an intermediate effect was seen. Many symptoms associated with bulimia nervosa, such as depression and pathological eating attitudes and behaviour, as well as carbohydrate craving, improved significantly with fluoxetine. Walsh (1989) has recently summarized the studies conducted with fluoxetine in bulimia.

Fluoxetine may be effective in bulimia when a patient has failed a trial with a tricyclic antidepressant (Mitchell et al, 1989). Mitchell and colleagues (1989) conducted open-label antidepressant trials in a series of bulimic patients who had had an inadequate response to an initial trial of imipramine and found that a significant percentage of these subjects responded to a second trial of an alternative agent. Overall, 47% showed a complete remission of symptoms, usually with fluoxetine or with a monoamine oxidase inhibitor (MAOI).

Personality disorders

Serotonin activity correlates with some aspects of personality. Lowered serotonin function, reflected by low levels of 5-HIAA in the cerebrospinal fluid and by low MAO activity in the platelets, correlates with impulsivity, anger, anxiety, and poor tolerance to anxiety (Rydin et al, 1982; Kent et al, 1988; Schalling, 1989). In one study blind ratings of Rorschach variables were compared between depressed patients with low and normal levels of 5-HIAA in the cerebrospinal fluid using 14 patient pairs matched for sex, age, height, and interview-based ratings of the severity of depression. Subjects with low levels of 5-HIAA displayed significantly more anxiety and hostility in the Rorschach ratings. Their anxiety tolerance was lower, and they were significantly less efficient in their handling of conflict (Rydin et al, 1982). In another study, the authors examined 15 male outpatients with frequent loss of self control and violent acts and found that serotonin uptake into platelets correlated significantly with impulsivity (Kent et al, 1988).

Serotonin dysfunction has been found in patients with personality disorders, especially those with a tendency to impulsive, violent behaviour toward themselves or others (Brown *et al*, 1982; Montgomery, 1987; Coccaro *et al*, 1989a,b). One study investigated 16 patients with various DSM-III personality disorders. Blunting of the prolactin response to the serotonin probes fenfluramine and m-CPP correlated significantly with ratings of impulsive aggression (Coccaro *et al*, 1989a). In another paper Brown, Goodwin, and Bunney (1982) summarized two studies of 28 US navy inpatients on active duty. In both studies the lowering of 5-HIAA levels in the cerebrospinal fluid correlated significantly with current measures and history of aggression.

The relationship between serotonin and impulsive violence may also have prognostic value. Virkunnen and colleagues (1989) found that recidivism in a cohort of violent offenders and impulsive fire setters was more common among those with lower levels of 5-HIAA in the cerebrospinal fluid. Furthermore, violent outbursts are reduced by tryptophan, lithium, and propranolol (Linnoila, 1988), all of which may work through enhancement of serotonergic transmission (Muhlbauer and Muller-Oerlinghausen, 1985; Muller-Oerlinghausen, 1985; Price *et al*, 1989).

The characteristics of impulsivity, anger, anxiety, poor anxiety tolerance, and violent dyscontrol are most closely associated with cluster 'B' of the DSM-III personality disorders — the so-called 'dramatic-emotional-erratic' cluster. This group includes patients with borderline, histrionic, narcissistic, and antisocial personality disorders. There is also a frequent overlap of these disorders with other conditions that respond to SSRIs, such as panic disorder, alcoholism, bulimia, and impulsive suicidal behaviour.

Data on the use of SSRIs in patients with personality disorders are therefore interesting. Cornelius and coworkers (1989) reported significant improvement in impulse control and depression in an open study of five inpatients with borderline personality disorder who were treated with fluoxetine. In another open trial Norden (1989) reported that 8 out of 12 patients with borderline personality disorder improved to a significant degree with fluoxetine. Other data are more indirect. Primeau and Fontaine (1987) described two cases of obsessive-compulsive disorder in which compulsive self-mutilation, a common feature of some patients with personality disorders, responded to serotonergic antidepressants. In another small study of fluoxetine Jouvent and colleagues (1989) found that fluoxetine was more effective in patients characterized as 'anxious-impulsive' than in those with a blunted affect.

Cluster 'C' of the DSM-III personality disorders is also known as the 'anxious-fearful' cluster because anxiety is a common feature of these disorders. Because of the beneficial effects of the SSRIs in axis I anxiety disorders patients with one of these related axis II disorders may also improve. Deltito and Stam (1989) reported positive results with fluoxetine or an MAOI in the treatment of a small series of patients with avoidant personality disorder, but the response was often delayed. It is unclear whether this was due to a slower onset of action with the SSRIs, the ingrained nature of the disorder, or both. The authors recommended two- to three-month trials of medication.

Uses in neurology

The SSRIs may be employed in neurology for the treatment of several disorders, some of which lie in the borderland between psychiatry and neurology. For example, Seliger and Hornstein (1989) reported that fluoxetine was helpful in the treatment of one patient with pseudobulbar crying spells following a stroke. A number of other treatments had been ineffective or had not been tolerated (Corne and Hall, 1989).

Cassidy (1989) conducted an open trial with fluoxetine in nine patients suffering from depression following severe head injury, and who were unable to tolerate treatment with standard agents. Five patients showed moderate to marked improvement by six weeks, although side-effects such as sedation and anxiety were noted.

The SSRIs may also be useful in the treatment of some myoclonic syndromes (Magnussen et al, 1982; Van-Woert et al, 1983). Fluoxetine had no beneficial effect by itself in four patients with intention myoclonus. However, in two patients with intention myoclonus responsive to L-5-hydroxytryptophan and carbidopa, fluoxetine reduced the required dose of L-5-hydroxytryptophan to approximately one-third and produced greater antimyoclonic activity and decreased side-effects (Van-Woert et al, 1983). Paroxetine may also have some value in certain of these patients (Magnussen et al, 1982).

In addition, the SSRIs may have some benefit in the treatment of cataplexy (Schachter and Parkes, 1980; Langdon et al, 1986). In one study either fluvoxamine or clomipramine was given to 18 subjects with narcolepsy and cataplexy. Both drugs improved cataplexy but not narcolepsy. Fluvoxamine was less active than clomipramine, but both drugs abolished cataplexy in individual subjects (Schachter and Parkes, 1980).

Beneficial effects of SSRIs on memory function raise the question as to whether they may be useful in the treatment of dementing disorders. Some of this evidence comes from animal research (Flood and Cherkin, 1987): in one study fluoxetine enhanced one-week memory retention in mice when the drug was injected two minutes after training. Fluoxetine also enhanced retention when administered prior to training and increased recall scores when injected one hour before the one-week retention test, indicating an enhancing effect on memory retrieval. Neither the pre-training nor pre-testing effects depended on improved learning. The time course of these effects suggested that the improvement might have been due to a non-specific alerting effect, an issue deservant of further study.

In man both citalopram and fluvoxamine have been helpful in the treatment of alcohol-related and other dementias (Nyth et al, 1987, 1989; Martin et al, 1989). In a four-week, double-blind, crossover study fluvoxamine (100-200mg/day) was found to improve memory in patients with alcoholic amnesic disorder, these improvements being significantly correlated with the reduction in 5-HIAA in the cerebrospinal fluid (Martin et al, 1989). Fluoxetine has also been reported to be effective in the treatment of agitated dementia (Sobin et al, 1989).

In another study the authors treated 98 demented patients with either citalopram or placebo in a four-week, double-blind trial. Citalopram was helpful in decreasing emotional symptoms in patients with senile dementia of the Alzheimer's type, but not in patients with vascular dementia. In this study no significant improvements were seen in cognitive deficits (Nyth *et al*, 1989). Therefore elucidation as to whether the SSRIs improve symptoms other than emotional ones in dementing disorders is awaited.

Pain is another area in which the SSRIs may make a contribution, but relatively few studies have been reported. Fluvoxamine produces analgesic effects in laboratory animals (Gibert-Rahola *et al*, 1989), which may be related to effects on endogenous opioids. In one of these studies fluvoxamine increased plasma levels of beta-endorphin and beta-lipotrophin in male rats (Cella *et al*, 1983).

Theesen and Marsh (1989) described a patient with painful diabetic neuropathy and major depression, both of which responded to fluoxetine. This 31-year-old woman, who had advanced diabetes mellitus with secondary autonomic and peripheral neuropathy was admitted to hospital for treatment of major depression and was given 5mg of fluoxetine daily, which resulted in a decrease of the pain due to the patient's neuropathy. Further increases in fluoxetine dosage resulted in improvement of her depression and increased pain relief with no exacerbation of her orthostatic hypotension.

Fluoxetine may also have some use in the treatment of headache (Diamond and Freitag, 1989) and fibrositis (Geller, 1989). Geller (1989) reported the case of a 29-year-old white female with fibrositis diagnosed by two independent rheumatologists. Treatment with amitriptyline, non-steroidal anti-inflammatory drugs, and transcutaneous electrical stimulation was ineffective. Treatment was then started with fluoxetine at a dose of 20mg/day, which was increased to 40mg/day. The patient experienced complete relief of symptoms over one month and no recurrence of symptoms was seen over a six-month follow-up period.

Summary

The SSRIs are likely to possess indications beyond major depression, obsessive-compulsive disorder, and anxiety disorders. In this chapter we have reviewed evidence both from the laboratory and from the clinic concerning some of these indications. It is likely that future research will support the efficacy of the SSRIs in some, but not all, of these areas. It is also likely that other potential indications for the SSRIs will unfold as more clinical experience is gained with these compounds.

Goff and colleagues (1990) recently published a case series which may open a whole new area of exploration for the SSRIs. They conducted a trial of adjunctive fluoxetine in treatment-resistant schizophrenia and found that ratings of depression, as well as positive and negative symptoms, significantly improved in nine patients who completed this six-week open trial in which fluoxetine was added to neuroleptic treatment. Responders were younger and had a shorter duration of illness than non-responders. Newer antipsychotic agents such as risperidone differ from earlier agents by combining dopamine receptor blockade with an action on the serotonin system (Janssen *et al*, 1988; Leysen *et al*, 1988). Whether the improvement noted in this trial is due to this or to an antidepressant effect is unclear. However, this is only one of many possible future indications for the SSRIs, and the whole area will be a very exciting one to watch.

References

Abell CA, Farquhar DL, Galloway SM, *et al* (1986) Placebo controlled double-blind trial of fluvoxamine maleate in the obese. *J Psychosom Res* **30**, 143-146.

Allen D and Lader M (1989) Interactions of alcohol with amitriptyline, fluoxetine and placebo in normal subjects. *Int Clin Psychopharmacol* **4** (Suppl 1), 7-14.

Angel I, Taranger MA, Claustre Y, *et al* (1988) Anorectic activities of serotonin uptake inhibitors: correlation with their potencies at inhibiting serotonin uptake in vivo and 3H-mazindol binding in vitro. *Life Sci* **43**, 651-658.

Banerjee AK (1988) Recovery from prolonged cerebral depression after fluvoxamine overdose. *Br Med J* **296**, 1774.

Banki CM and Arato M (1983) Amine metabolites and neuroendocrine responses related to depression and suicide. *J Affective Disord* **5**, 223-232.

Banki CM, Arato M and Kilts CD (1986) Aminergic studies and cerebrospinal fluid cations in suicide. *Ann NY Acad Sci* **487**, 221-230.

Borg S, Kvande H, Liljeberg P, *et al* (1985) 5-hydroxyindoleacetic acid in cerebrospinal fluid in alcoholic patients under different clinical conditions. *Alcohol* **2**, 415-418.

Breisch ST, Zemlan FP and Hoebel BG (1976) Hyperphagia and obesity following serotonin depletion by intraventricular p-chlorophenylalanine. *Science* **192**, 382-385.

Brown GL, Goodwin FK and Bunney WE (1982) Human aggression and suicide: Their relationship to neuropsychiatric diagnoses and serotonin metabolism. In: Ho BT, Schoolar JC and Usdin E (eds.) *Serotonin in Biological Psychiatry*, pp.287-307. New York: Raven Press.

Bruno F (1989) Buspirone in the treatment of alcoholic patients. *Psychopathology* **22**, 49-59.

Carruba MO, Mantegazza P, Memo M, *et al* (1986) Peripheral and central mechanisms of action of serotoninergic anorectic drugs. *Appetite* **7** (Suppl), 105-113.

Cassidy JW (1989) Fluoxetine: a new serotonergically active antidepressant. Special issue: visual system dysfunction. *Journal of Head Trauma Rehabilitation* **4**, 67-69.

Cella S, Penalva A, Locatelli V, *et al* (1983) Neuroendocrine studies with fluvoxamine: animal data. *Br J Clin Pharmacol* **15** (Suppl 3), 357S-364S.

Clark C and Rosenblatt S (1989) A multicenter study of sertraline in the treatment of diabetic obesity. Paper presented at *Progress in the Treatment of Simple and Complicated Obesity*, Lisbon, 19 September.

Coccaro EF, Siever LJ, Kavoussi R, *et al* (1989a) Impulsive aggression in personality disorder: evidence for involvement in 5-HT-1 receptors. *Biol Psychiatry* **25** (Suppl 7A), 86A.

Coccaro EF, Siever LJ, Klar HM, *et al* (1989b) Serotonergic studies in patients with affective and personality disorders: Correlates with suicidal and impulsive aggressive behavior. *Arch Gen Psychiatry* **46**, 587-599.

Cooper GL (1988) The safety of fluoxetine — An update. *Br J Psychiatry* **153**, 77-86.

Corne SJ and Hall JR (1989) A double-blind comparative study of fluoxetine and dothiepin in the treatment of depression in general practice. *Int Clin Psychopharmacol* **4**, 245-254.

Cornelius JR, Soloff PH, Perel JM, *et al* (1989) Fluoxetine trial in borderline personality. *New Research Program and Abstracts, American Psychiatric Association 142nd Annual Meeting*, p.192.

Deltito JA and Stam M (1989) Psychopharmacological treatment of avoidant personality disorder. *Compr Psychiatry* **30**, 498-504.

Diamond S and Freitag FG (1989) The use of fluoxetine in the treatment of headache. *Clin J Pain* **5**, 200-201.

Donders SH, Pieters GF, Heevel JG, *et al* (1985) Disparity of thyrotropin (TSH) and prolactin responses to TSH-releasing hormone in obesity. *J Clin Endocrinol Metab* **61**, 56-59.

Edman G, Asberg M, Levander S, *et al* (1986) Skin conductance habituation and cerebrospinal fluid 5-hydroxyindoleacetic acid in suicidal patients. *Arch Gen Psychiatry* **43**, 586-592.

Enas GG, Pope HG and Vevine LR (1989) Fluoxetine in bulimia nervosa: Double-blind study. *New Research Program and Abstracts, American Psychiatric Association 142nd Annual Meeting*, p.204.

Fanelli FR, Cangiano C, Cecil F, *et al* (1986) Plasma tryptophan and anorexia in human cancer. *Eur J Cancer Clin Oncol* **22**, 89-95.

Fawcet J, Clark DC, Gibbons RD, *et al* (1984) Evaluation of lithium therapy for alcoholism. *J Clin Psychiatry* **45**, 494-499.

Feighner JP and Rosenblatt S (1989) A double-blind placebo-controlled study of sertraline in the treatment of obesity. Paper presented at *Progress in the Treatment of Simple and Complicated Obesity*, Lisbon, 19 September.

Ferguson JM and Feighner JP (1987) Fluoxetine-induced weight loss in overweight non-depressed humans. *Int J Obes* **11** (Suppl 3), 163-170.

Finnegan KT and Gabiola JM (1988) Fluoxetine overdose. *Am J Psychiatry* **145**, 1604.

Flood JF and Cherkin A (1987) Fluoxetine enhances memory processing in mice. *Psychopharmacology* **93**, 36-43.

Freeman CPL and Hampson M (1987) Fluoxetine as a treatment for bulimia nervosa. *Int J Obesity* **11**, 171-177.

Gaszner P (1989) Fluvoxamine therapy for depressed patients. In: Stefanis CN, Soldatos CR and Rabavilas AD (eds.) *Psychiatry Today: VIII World Congress of Psychiatry Abstracts*, p.55. New York: Elsevier.

Geller SA (1989) Treatment of fibrositis with fluoxetine hydrochloride (Prozac). *Am J Med* **87**, 594-595.

Gibert-Rahola J, Elorza J and Casas J (1989) Analgesic effects of the antidepressants fluvoxamine and clovoxamine. In: Stefanis CN, Soldatos CR and Rabavilas AD (eds.) *Psychiatry Today: VIII World Congress of Psychiatry Abstracts*, p.269. New York: Elsevier.

Gill K and Amit Z (1989) Serotonin uptake blockers and voluntary alcohol consumption. A review of recent studies. *Recent Dev Alcohol* **7**, 225-248.

Gill K, Amit Z and Koe BK (1988a) Treatment with sertraline, a new serotonin uptake inhibitor, reduces voluntary ethanol consumption in rats. *Alcohol* **5**, 349-354.

Gill K, Amit Z and Ogren SO (1985) The effects of zimeldine on voluntary ethanol consumption: studies on the mechanism of action. *Alcohol* **2**, 343-347.

Gill K, Fillon Y and Amit Z (1988b) Further examination of the effects of sertraline on voluntary ethanol consumption. *Alcohol* **5**, 355-358.

Goff DC, Brotman AW, Waites M, *et al* (1990) Trial of fluoxetine added to neuroleptics for treatment-resistant schizophrenic patients. *Am J Psychiatry* **147** (4), 492-494.

Gorelick DA (1989) Serotonin uptake blockers and the treatment of alcoholism. *Recent Dev Alcohol* **7**, 267-281.

Grupp LA, Perlanski E and Stewart RB (1988) Attenuation of alcohol intake by a serotonin uptake inhibitor: evidence for mediation through the renin-angiotensin system. *Pharmacol Biochem Behav* **30**, 823-827.

Hapworth WE and Hapworth M (1989) Nicotine withdrawal cessation by fluoxetine. *New Research Program and Abstracts, American Psychiatric Association 142nd Annual Meeting*, p.197.

Himmelhoch JM, Hill S, Steinberg B, *et al* (1983) Lithium, alcoholism and psychiatric diagnosis. *Journal of Psychiatric Treatment and Diagnosis* **5**, 83-88.

Janssen PA, Niemegeers CJ, Awouters F, *et al* (1988) Pharmacology of risperidone (R 64 766), a new antipsychotic with serotonin-S2 and dopamine-D2 antagonistic properties. *J Pharmacol Exp Ther* **244**, 685-693.

Jimerson DC, Lesem MD, Kaye WH, *et al* (1989) Serotonin and symptom severity in eating disorders. *Biol Psychiatry* **25** (Suppl 7A), 143A.

Jouvent R, Baruch P, Ammar S, *et al* (1989) Fluoxetine efficacy in depressives with impulsivity vs blunted affect. In: Stefanis CN, Soldatos CR and Rabavilas AD (eds.) *Psychiatry Today: VIII World Congress of Psychiatry Abstracts*, p.398. New York: Elsevier.

Kaye WH, Ebert MH, Gwirtsman HE, *et al* (1984) Differences in brain serotonergic metabolism between nonbulimic and bulimic patients with anorexia nervosa. *Am J Psychiatry* **141**, 1598-1601.

Kaye WH, Gwirtsman HE, Brewerton TD, *et al* (1988) Bingeing behavior and plasma amino acids: a possible involvement of brain serotonin in bulimia nervosa. *Psychiatry Res* **23**, 31-43.

Kent TA, Brown CS, Bryant SG, *et al* (1988) Blood platelet uptake of serotonin in episodic aggression: Correlation with red blood cell proton T1 and impulsivity. *Psychopharmacol Bull* **24** (3), 454-457.

Kline NS, Wren JC, Cooper TB, *et al* (1974) Evaluation of lithium therapy in chronic and periodic alcoholism. *Am J Med Sci* **268**, 15-22.

Langdon N, Shindler J, Parkes JD, *et al* (1986) Fluoxetine in the treatment of cataplexy. *Sleep* **9**, 371-373.

Lemberger L, Rowe H, Bergstrom RF, *et al* (1985) Effect of fluoxetine on psychomotor performance, physiologic response, and kinetics of ethanol. *Clin Pharmacol Ther* **37**, 658-664.

Lemberger L, Rowe H, Bosomworth JC, *et al* (1988) The effect of fluoxetine on the pharmacokinetics and psychomotor responses of diazepam. *Clin Pharmacol Ther* **43**, 412-419.

Levine LR, Rosenblatt S and Bosomworth J (1987) Use of a serotonin re-uptake inhibitor, fluoxetine, in the treatment of obesity. *Int J Obes* **11** (Suppl 3), 185-190.

Leysen JE, Gommeren W, Eens A, *et al* (1988) Biochemical profile of risperidone, a new antipsychotic. *J Pharmacol Exp Ther* **247**, 661-670.

Li TK, Lumeng L, McBride WJ, *et al* (1987) Alcoholism: is it a model for the study of disorders of mood and consummatory behavior? *Ann NY Acad Sci* **499**, 239-249.

Linnoila M (1988) Serotonin uptake inhibitors in other clinical conditions. In: Gastpar M and Wakelin JS (eds.) *Selective 5-HT reuptake inhibitors: Novel or Commonplace agents?*, pp.100-104. Basel: Karger.

Magnussen I, Mondrup K, Engbaek F, *et al* (1982) Treatment of myoclonic syndromes with paroxetine alone or combined with 5-HTP. *Acta Neurol Scand* **66**, 276-282.

Marazziti D, Macchi E, Rotondo A, *et al* (1988) Involvement of serotonin system in bulimia. *Life Sci* **43**, 2123-2126.

Martin PR, Adinoff B, Eckardt MJ, *et al* (1989) Effective pharmacotherapy of alcoholic amnestic disorder with fluvoxamine. *Arch Gen Psychiatry* **46**, 617-624.

McBride WJ, Murphy JM, Lumeng L, *et al* (1988) Effects of Ro 15-4513, fluoxetine and desipramine on the intake of ethanol, water and food by the alcohol-preferring (P) and -nonpreferring (NP) lines of rats. *Pharmacol Biochem Behav* **30**, 1045-1050.

McClelland GR and Raptopoulos P (1985) Psychomotor effects of paroxetine and amitriptyline, alone and in combination with ethanol. *Br J Clin Pharmacol* **19**, 578.

McMillan TM (1981) Lithium and the treatment of alcoholism: A critical review. *Br J Addict* **76**, 245-248.

Merry J, Reynolds CM and Coppen A (1976) Prophylactic treatment of alcoholism by lithium carbonate (a controlled study). *Lancet* **II**, 481-482.

von-Meyenfeldt M, Chance WT and Fischer JE (1982) Correlation of changes in brain indoleamine metabolism with onset of anorexia in rats. *Am J Surg* **143**, 133-138.

Mitchell JE, Pyle RL, Eckert ED, *et al* (1989) Response to alternative antidepressants in imipramine nonresponders with bulimia nervosa. *J Clin Psychopharmacol* **9**, 291-293.

Montgomery SA (1987). The psychopharmacology of borderline personality disorders. *Acta Psychiatr Belg* **87**, 260-266.

Montgomery SA (1989) 5-HT reuptake inhibitors in the treatment of depression. In: Montgomery SA (ed.) *Citalopram: the New Antidepressant from Lundbeck Research*, pp.1-10. Amsterdam: Excerpta Medica.

Montgomery SA, Baldwin D and Green M (1989) Why do amitriptyline and dothiepin appear to be so dangerous in overdose? *Acta Psychiatr Scand* **80**, 47-54.

Moskowitz H and Burns M (1988) The effects on performance of two antidepressants, alone and in combination with diazepam. *Prog Neuropsychopharmacol Biol Psychiatry* **12**, 783-792.

Muhlbauer HD and Muller-Oerlinghausen B (1985) Fenfluramine stimulation of serum cortisol in patients with major affective disorders and healthy controls: further evidence for a central serotonergic action of lithium in man. *J Neural Transm* **61**, 81-94.

Muijen M, Roy D, Silverstone T, *et al* (1988) A comparative clinical trial of fluoxetine, mianserin and placebo in depressed outpatients. *Acta Psychiatr Scand* **78**, 384-390.

Muller-Oerlinghausen B (1985) Lithium long-term treatment — does it act via serotonin? *Pharmacopsychiatry* **18**, 214-217.

Mullin JM, Pandita-Gunawardena VR and Whitehead AM (1988) A double-blind comparison of fluvoxamine and dothiepin in the treatment of major affective disorder. *Br J Clin Pract* **42**, 51-55.

Murphy JM, Waller MB, Gatto GJ, *et al* (1985) Monoamine uptake inhibitors attenuate ethanol intake in alcohol-preferring (P) rats. *Alcohol* **2**, 349-352.

Murphy JM, Waller MB, Gatto GJ, *et al* (1988) Effects of fluoxetine on the intragastric self-administration of ethanol in the alcohol preferring P line of rats. *Alcohol* **5**, 283-286.

Naranjo CA and Sellers EM (1989) Serotonin uptake inhibitors attenuate ethanol intake in problem drinkers. *Recent Dev Alcohol* **7**, 255-266.

Naranjo CA, Sellers EM and Lawrin MO (1986) Modulation of ethanol intake by serotonin uptake inhibitors. *J Clin Psychiatry* **47** (Suppl), 16-22.

Naranjo CA, Sellers EM, Sullivan JT, *et al* (1987) The serotonin uptake inhibitor citalopram attenuates ethanol intake. *Clin Pharmacol Ther* **41**, 266-274.

Nichols M, Maickel RP and Yim GK (1983) Increased central serotonergic activity associated with nocturnal anorexia induced by Walker 256 carcinoma. *Life Sci* **32**, 1819-1825.

Ninan PT, van-Kammen DP, Scheinin M, *et al* (1984) CSF 5-hydroxyindoleacetic acid levels in suicidal schizophrenic patients. *Am J Psychiatry* **141**, 566-569.

Norden MJ (1989) Fluoxetine in borderline personality disorder. *Prog Neuropsychopharmacol Biol Psychiatry* **13**, 885-893.

Nyth AL, Balidin J, Elgen K, *et al* (1987) Treatment with citalopram in dementia. Normalization of dexamethasone suppression test. *Nord Psykiatr Tidsskr* **41**, 423-429.

Nyth AL, Gottfries CG, Elgen K, *et al* (1989) The clinical efficacy of citalopram in treatment of emotional disturbances in dementia disorders. In: Stefanis CN, Soldatos CR and Rabavilas AD (eds.) *Psychiatry Today: VIII World Congress of Psychiatry Abstracts*, p.503. New York: Elsevier.

Pedersen OL, Kragh-Sorensen P, Bjerre M, *et al* (1982) Citalopram, a selective serotonin reuptake inhibitor: clinical antidepressive and long-term effect — a phase II study. *Psychopharmacology* **77**, 199-204.

Porrino LJ, Ritz MC, Goodman NL, *et al* (1989) Differential effects of the pharmacological manipulation of serotonin systems on cocaine and amphetamine self-administration in the rat. *Life Sci* **45**, 1529-1535.

Price LH, Charney DS, Delgado PL, *et al* (1989) Lithium treatment and serotoninergic function. Neuroendocrine and behavioral response to intravenous tryptophan in affective disorder. *Arch Gen Psychiatry* **46**, 13-19.

Primeau F and Fontaine R (1987) Obsessive disorder with self-mutilation: a subgroup responsive to pharmacotherapy. *Can J Psychiatry* **32**, 699-701.

Riddle MA, Brown N, Dzubinski D, *et al* (1989) Fluoxetine overdose in an adolescent. *J Am Acad Child Adolesc Psychiatry* **28**, 587-588.

Ritz MC and Kuhar MJ (1989) Relationship between self-administration of amphetamine and monoamine receptors in brain: comparison with cocaine. *J Pharmacol Exp Ther* **248**, 1010-1017.

Rydin E, Schalling D and Asberg M (1982) Rorschach ratings in depressed and suicidal patients with low levels of 5-hydroxyindoleacetic acid in cerebrospinal fluid. *Psychiatry Res* **7**, 229-243.

Samanin R, Mennini T and Garattini S (1980) Evidence that it is possible to cause anorexia by increasing release and/or directly stimulating postsynaptic serotonin receptors in the brain. *Prog Neuropsychopharmacol Biol Psychiatry* **4**, 363-369.

Schachter M and Parkes JD (1980) Fluvoxamine and clomipramine in the treatment of cataplexy. *J Neurol Neurosurg Psychiatry* **43**, 171-174.

Schaffler K (1986) Study on performance and alcohol interaction with the antidepressant fluoxetine — a selective serotonin reuptake inhibitor — using computer assisted psychophysiological methodology. *Br J Clin Pract* **40**, 28-33.

Schalling D (1989) Biochemical correlates of temperament dimensions. *Biol Psychiatry* **25** (Suppl 7A), 139A-140A.

Seliger GM and Hornstein A (1989) Serotonin, fluoxetine, and pseudobulbar affect. *Neurology* **39** (10), 1400.

Sellers EM, Naranjo CA and Kadlec K (1987) Do serotonin uptake inhibitors decrease smoking? Observations in a group of heavy drinkers. *J Clin Psychopharmacol* **7**, 417-420.

Sobin P, Schneider L and McDermot H (1989) Fluoxetine in the treatment of agitated dementia. *Am J Psychiatry* **146**, 1636.

Stanley M and Mann JJ (1983) Increased serotonin-2 binding sites in frontal cortex of suicide victims. *Lancet* **II**, 214-216.

Tartara A, Formigli L, Crema F, *et al* (1985) Alcohol interactions with typical and atypical antidepressants. *Neurobehav Toxicol Teratol* **7**, 139-141.

Teicher MH, Glod C and Cole JO (1990) Emergence of intense suicidal preoccupation during fluoxetine treatment. *Am J Psychiatry* **147**, 207-210.

Theesen KA and Marsh WR (1989) Relief of diabetic neuropathy with fluoxetine. *DICP* **23**, 572-574.

Tollefson GD (1989) Serotonin and alcohol: interrelationships. 16th collegium internationale neuropsychopharmacologicum congress satellite conference: new findings with anxiolytic drugs (1988, Munich, Federal Republic of Germany). *Psychopathology* **22**, 37-48.

Traskman L, Asberg M, Bertilsson L, *et al* (1981) Monoamine metabolites in CSF and suicidal behavior. *Arch Gen Psychiatry* **38**, 631-636.

Van-Woert MH, Magnussen I, Rosenbaum D, *et al* (1983) Fluoxetine in the treatment of intention myoclonus. *Clin Neuropharmacol* **6**, 49-54.

Virkunnen M, De Jong J, Bartko J, *et al* (1989) Relationship of psychobiological variables to recidivism in violent offenders and impulsive fire setters. *Arch Gen Psychiatry* **46**, 600-603.

Wakelin JS (1988) The role of serotonin in depression and suicide: Do serotonin reuptake inhibitors provide a key? In: Gastpar M and Wakelin JS (eds.) *Selective 5-HT reuptake inhibitors: Novel or Commonplace agents?*, pp.70-83. Basel: Karger.

Walsh TB (1989) Review of clinical studies of fluoxetine in bulimia. In: Stefanis CN, Soldatos CR and Rabavilas AD (eds.) *Psychiatry Today: VIII World Congress of Psychiatry Abstracts*, p.519. New York: Elsevier.

Weintraub M and Evans P (1988) Citalopram: 5-HT reuptake blocker with possible usefulness in the treatment of alcoholism. *Hosp Formul* **23**, 141-145.

Wurtman JJ (1988) Carbohydrate craving, mood changes, and obesity. *J Clin Psychiatry* **49** (Suppl), 37-39.

Wurtman RJ and Wurtman JJ (1986) Carbohydrate craving, obesity, and brain serotonin. *Appetite* **7** (Suppl), 99-103.

Yu DS, Smith FL, Smith DG, *et al* (1986) Fluoxetine-induced attenuation of amphetamine self-administration in rats. *Life Sci* **39**, 1383-1388.

Zerbe RL (1987) Safety of fluoxetine in the treatment of obesity. *Int J Obes* **11** (Suppl 3), 191-199.

8

Side-effects of the selective serotonin re-uptake inhibitors

W.F. Boyer and J.P. Feighner

Withdrawals from clinical studies

Side-effect profile is perhaps the most important area in which the selective serotonin re-uptake inhibitors (SSRIs) differ from earlier antidepressants. One meaningful global measure of how well medications are tolerated is the number of patients who have dropped out of double-blind trials because of adverse effects. Most double-blind studies of SSRIs have had more such dropouts among patients treated with the reference antidepressant (Tables I-IV). In the majority of these studies the reference drug was a tertiary amine tricyclic, such as imipramine, amitriptyline, clomipramine, or doxepin.

The SSRIs have also been compared with maprotiline, mianserin, and dothiepin in a smaller number of trials, but the differences in dropout rates were less clear in these studies, probably due in part to the smaller number of studies involved, but perhaps also as a reflection of a lower incidence of adverse effects for these other antidepressants.

While the number of dropouts provides useful information, this variable is also important for the examination of specific side-effects. Our own experience comes from three similarly designed studies of paroxetine, fluoxetine, and fluvoxamine, these studies being described in more detail in chapter 5. In the paroxetine study, 120 outpatients with major depression were randomly assigned to six-week, double-blind treatment with paroxetine, imipramine, or placebo. Twelve patients on imipramine (30%) dropped out because of an adverse reaction versus four receiving paroxetine (10%) and no patients on placebo. The difference in the number of dropouts between paroxetine and imipramine was significant (p = 0.024).

The most commonly reported adverse effects are shown in **Figure 1**.

Study	Comparison drug	Outcome
Guelfi *et al*, 1983	Imipramine	Fewer patients on fluvoxamine dropped out because of side-effects
Guy *et al*, 1984		
Lapierre *et al*, 1987		
Bramanti *et al*, 1988		
Feighner *et al*, 1989b		
Itil *et al*, 1983		More patients on fluvoxamine dropped out because of side-effects
Norton *et al*, 1984		
Dominguez *et al*, 1985		
Lydiard *et al*, 1989		
Mullin *et al*, 1988	Dothiepin	
Hamilton *et al*, 1989	Flupenthixol	
Klok *et al*, 1981	Clomipramine	Equal numbers of drop-outs during the study
Dick and Ferrero, 1983		
De-Wilde *et al*, 1983		

Table I. Tolerability of fluvoxamine in controlled, comparative trials.

Paroxetine was most often associated with somnolent (drowsiness and fatigue) and gastrointestinal side-effects (nausea and reduced appetite), while imipramine most commonly produced the classic anticholinergic side-effects of dry mouth, constipation, and urinary retention.

In our fluoxetine study, almost exactly the same percentage (31%) of patients on imipramine withdrew from the study early because of adverse experiences, compared with 13 (21%) on fluoxetine and five (8%) on placebo. Pairwise comparisons showed that the imipramine-placebo difference was highly significant (p = 0.005), but the difference between fluoxetine and placebo was only marginally so (p<0.1). The severity of the side-effects was significantly higher with imipramine than with fluoxetine (p = 0.02). Individual adverse effects with an incidence of over 10% in any treatment group are shown in Figure 2. Imipramine was most frequently associated with six of these nine symptoms, fluoxetine with two, and placebo with one.

In the fluvoxamine study, the rates of premature termination were once again very similar. Thirty-seven per cent of the 35 patients on imipramine, 23% of 31

Study	Comparison drug	Dropouts
Bremner, 1984	Imipramine	Fewer patients on fluoxetine dropped out because of side-effects
Cohn and Wilcox, 1985		
Stark and Hardison, 1985		
Feighner *et al*, 1989a		
Cohn *et al*, 1989		
Chouinard, 1985	Amitriptyline	
Feighner, 1985		
Masco and Sheetz, 1985		
Fawcett *et al*, 1989		
Altamura *et al*, 1989*		
South Wales Antidepressant Drug Trial Group, 1988	Dothiepin	
Ferreri, 1989	Amineptine	
Feighner and Cohn, 1985*	Doxepin	More patients on fluoxetine dropped out because of side-effects
Tamminen and Lehtinen, 1989		
Levine *et al*, 1987	Imipramine	
Young *et al*, 1987	Amitriptyline	
Corne and Hall, 1989	Dothiepin	
Byerley *et al*, 1988	Imipramine	Equal numbers of dropouts in both groups
Muijen *et al*, 1988	Mianserin	
Perry *et al*, 1989	Trazodone	
Bressa *et al*, 1989	Imipramine	No dropouts due to side-effects in either group

Table II. Tolerability of fluoxetine in controlled, comparative trials.
*Study in elderly patients.

Study	Comparison drug	Dropouts
Feighner and Boyer, 1989	Imipramine	Fewer dropouts among paroxetine-treated patients
Guillibert *et al*, 1989*	Clomipramine	
Battegay *et al*, 1985		
Laursen *et al*, 1985		
Bascara, 1989	Amitriptyline	
Gagiano *et al*, 1989		
Kuhs and Rudolf, 1989		More dropouts among paroxetine-treated patients
Peselow *et al*, 1989	Imipramine	
Mertens and Pintens 1988	Mianserin	Equal numbers of dropouts

Table III. Tolerability of paroxetine in controlled, comparative trials.
*Study in elderly patients.

on fluvoxamine, and 5% of 19 on placebo were withdrawn from the study due to adverse effects. Moreover, the number of non-tolerators in the imipramine group was significantly greater than in those receiving placebo ($p<0.05$), but no significant differences were seen between fluvoxamine and placebo in this regard. An average of 3.6 treatment-emergent symptoms per patient was observed in the placebo group, 3.4 with fluvoxamine, and 3.9 in imipramine-treated patients. The most common side-effects with fluvoxamine were nausea and agitation, while dry mouth, syncope, sweating, and constipation were most commonly associated with imipramine (Figure 3).

    In these three studies 30-37% of patients were not able to tolerate the tricyclic antidepressant imipramine, compared with 10-23% of patients treated with an SSRI. The highest dropout rate was associated with fluvoxamine and the lowest with paroxetine.

Dosage and tolerability

The tolerability of fluvoxamine, like that of other SSRIs, may be influenced by several factors, one of these being the dosage schedule. In our study fluvoxamine was given in divided doses. Siddiqui and colleagues (1985) compared the efficacy and side-effects of a single night-time dose of fluvoxamine, a single daytime dose, and a twice-daily regimen. All treatments were equally effective in alleviating depression, but fewer patients receiving the single night-time dose dropped out

Study	Study drug	Comparison drug	Dropouts
Danish University Antidepressant Group, 1986	Citalopram	Clomipramine	Fewer dropouts on citalopram
Shaw *et al*, 1986		Amitriptyline	
Gravem *et al*, 1987			
Bouchard *et al*, 1987		Maprotiline	
Timmerman *et al*, 1987			Equal numbers of dropouts*
De-Wilde *et al*, 1985		Mianserin	One dropout in each group
Ahlfors *et al*, 1988			
Reimherr *et al*, 1988	Sertraline	Amitriptyline	More dropouts on sertraline
Fabre, 1989			Fewer dropouts on sertraline

Table IV. Tolerability of citalopram and sertraline in controlled, comparative trials.
*One patient on maprotiline committed suicide early in treatment.

because of side-effects. Insomnia was not a significant problem with the night-time dose.

The tolerability of the SSRIs may also be related to the total dose. Early clinical testing with fluoxetine used doses of up to 80mg/day. However, it is now apparent that lower doses, of the order of 20mg/day, are adequate (Fabre and Putman, 1987; Altamura *et al*, 1988; Bressa *et al*, 1989; Dornseif *et al*, 1989), and even doses as low as 5mg/day may be effective (Wernicke *et al*, 1988). Higher doses of fluoxetine and sertraline are associated with more side-effects (Guy *et al*, 1986; Fabre and Putman, 1987; Saletu and Grunberger, 1988; Amin *et al*, 1989; Bressa *et al*, 1989).

Little has been published on the relationship between the dosage of paroxetine or citalopram and adverse effects. In a study of 53 elderly patients Hebenstreit and colleagues (1989) found a non-significant decrease in adverse events as the average dose of paroxetine rose from 30 to 50mg/day, while Tasker *et al* (1989) could find no evidence for an association between steady-state plasma levels of paroxetine and either efficacy or adverse events. Bjerkenstedt *et al* (1985) compared the efficacy and tolerability of daily citalopram doses of 5, 25, and 50mg. The two higher doses were associated with significant, and equal,

Organ system	Symptom	Clinical considerations
Gastrointestinal	Nausea	Usually transient and dose related. Possibly more common with fluvoxamine. May respond to dose reduction or to symptomatic measures such as food or antacids
	Loss of appetite	More pronounced in overweight patients and those with carbohydrate craving. May lead to abuse in patients with bulimia or anorexia nervosa. Possibly more common with fluoxetine
	Diarrhoea	Usually transient and dose related
CNS	Increased anxiety and nervousness	Occurs early in treatment, especially in patients with prominent anxiety symptoms. May be handled with support, dose reduction, or concomitant treatment with a benzodiazepine. May be less marked with paroxetine
	Insomnia	
	Tremor	May respond to dose reduction, a beta-blocker, or a benzodiazepine

Table V. Common side-effects of the SSRIs.

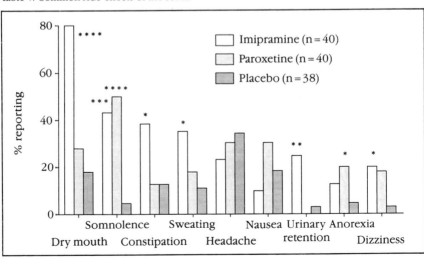

Figure 1. Adverse effects with an incidence of more than 10% in a placebo-controlled comparison of paroxetine and imipramine. *p<0.05; **p<0.01; ***p<0.001; ****p<0.0001 (significantly different from placebo).

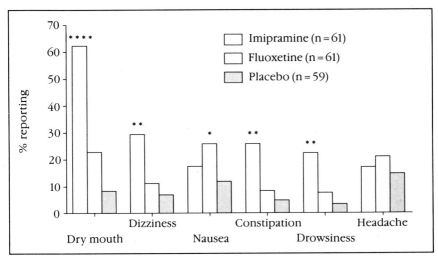

Figure 2. Adverse effects with an incidence of more than 10% in a placebo-controlled comparison of fluoxetine and imipramine. *p<0.05; **p<0.01; ***p<0.0001 (significantly different from placebo).

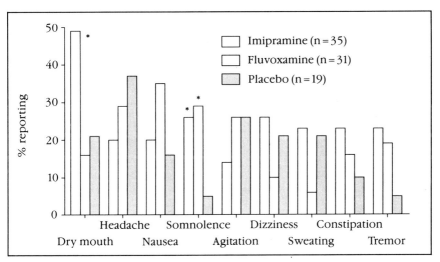

Figure 3. Adverse effects with an incidence of more than 10% in a placebo-controlled comparison of fluvoxamine and imipramine. *p<0.05 (significantly different from placebo).

antidepressant effect, and side-effects did not appear to be related to dose within the range studied.

Cardiovascular effects

Our discussion so far has been concerned with adverse effects in general. However this is, of course, only part of the picture, and some attention should also be given to particular adverse effects. One of the most important of these is the effects of the antidepressant on the cardiovascular system. Tricyclic antidepressants (TCAs) slow cardiac conduction through the His-Purkinje system, and this quinidine-like effect may help to suppress supraventricular arrhythmias in some patients, while leading to the development of heart block in others (Prager *et al*, 1986). The SSRIs do not share this quinidine-like property and thus do not have the same effects on heart rhythm as the TCAs.

Fisch (1985) compared the effects of fluoxetine on the ECG with those of placebo, imipramine, amitriptyline, and doxepin by examining the tracings obtained at the beginning and end of several drug studies without knowledge of which drug was involved. It was found that the TCAs increased heart rate, and there was a small — but statistically significant — decrease in average heart rate in patients receiving fluoxetine. Intraventricular conduction delays were noted in five patients who received imipramine and in one patient who received amitriptyline: four of these patients developed left bundle branch block. No intraventricular conduction delays were noted in fluoxetine-treated patients.

Edwards and colleagues (1989) studied the electrocardiographic effects of paroxetine. High-speed electrocardiograms were recorded from 20 patients with major depression before and after four weeks of treatment with either paroxetine or placebo. None of the patients had a history or clinical evidence of cardiovascular disease, and the ECG measurements were made blind to both patient and treatment. No significant changes in heart rate, or in PR and QTc intervals or T-wave height were found after treatment with either active drug or placebo. A small, but statistically significant, increase in the QRS width was seen in the paroxetine group.

The SSRIs appear to be safer than the TCAs in their effects on cardiac rhythm, but they should not be regarded as completely safe in this respect. Studies with citalopram in cats indicate that it has a tendency to produce the same types of cardiac side-effects as the TCAs, but the doses needed to produce the same effects are considerably higher (Boeck *et al*, 1984). An early clinical report stated that citalopram was 'devoid' of cardiotoxic effects (Hyttel, 1982), but the development of citalopram was temporarily suspended because of cardiotoxic effects in dogs. However, this was eventually determined to be due to a toxic metabolite which achieved high levels in dogs but not in man (Overo, 1989).

Citalopram should not be particularly singled out in this regard. In one of the earliest open-label studies of fluvoxamine Saletu and colleagues (1977) reported that a 54-year-old male experienced a myocardial infarction while participating in gymnastics. This patient had had premature ventricular contractions prior to entering the study. In a later study Klok and colleagues (1981) compared the efficacy and safety of fluvoxamine and clomipramine under double-blind conditions. Two patients in each drug group discontinued treatment early because of the development of disturbances in cardiac rhythm. However, the authors noted that the small sample sizes, 16 patients in each group, precluded any definite conclusions about the cardiac safety of fluvoxamine.

We do not mean to imply from this extended discussion that the SSRIs are more dangerous than the TCAs in terms of heart function. In fact, the opposite is probably true (Fisch, 1985; Upward *et al*, 1988). The SSRIs should be seen as different from the TCAs, probably safer on the whole, but not without the potential to affect cardiac function adversely.

All of the TCAs block adrenergic receptors to some degree, and this property is primarily responsible for the frequent occurrence of orthostatic hypotension. The SSRIs do not block adrenergic receptors and are free of orthostatic hypotension (Pedersen *et al*, 1982; Christensen *et al*, 1985). For example, Laursen and colleagues (1985) found that paroxetine was associated with significantly fewer orthostatic complaints than amitriptyline, while Theesen and Marsh (1989) used fluoxetine effectively in the treatment of a patient with painful diabetic neuropathy who could not tolerate other antidepressants because of orthostatic hypotension.

In general, the SSRIs are much safer from a cardiovascular perspective than the TCAs or MAOIs. This viewpoint is supported by both research and clinical experience. In addition overdose data, although limited, strongly support a significant cardiovascular advantage for SSRIs as compared to TCAs and MAOIs. The only consistent cardiovascular effect of the SSRIs has been a clinically non-significant slowing of pulse rate.

Anticholinergic effects

SSRIs do not have 'true' anticholinergic side-effects. Symptoms such as dry mouth and blurred vision, which occasionally occur with these compounds, are probably caused by mechanisms other than anticholinergic blockade. Blurred vision is probably mediated through serotonergic innervation of the pupil (Moro *et al*, 1981; Saletu *et al*, 1986), while constipation may occur because of effects on the rich serotonergic innervation of the gut.

Dry mouth is occasionally reported with the SSRIs and, in one study with citalopram, was in fact the most common side-effect reported (Mertens, 1989). As the authors point out, this symptom frequently occurs in depression, and may also be mediated by indirect enhancement of noradrenergic innervation of the salivary glands. These 'anticholinergic-like' side-effects rarely have the severe intensity witnessed with the TCAs.

Effects on weight

Weight gain is an all too frequent consequence of TCA treatment. It may expose patients to the medical complications of obesity or, if it leads patients to discontinue treatment, will place them at risk from a relapse of depression. Unlike the TCAs, the SSRIs are not associated with weight gain (Chouinard, 1985; Bernstein 1987, 1988; Harto *et al*, 1988; Altamura *et al*, 1989; Fawcett *et al*, 1989); patients treated with one of these drugs commonly experience a mild to moderate weight loss, especially if they are overweight prior to treatment. As discussed in chapter 7, this property has been used to treat obesity in non-depressed subjects.

Berken and colleagues (1984) evaluated body weight and appetite in 40 depressed outpatients from a private psychiatric clinic who received amitriptyline, nortriptyline, or imipramine for an average of six months. A mean weight increase of 1.3-2.9 pounds per month was observed, which led to an average total weight gain of 3-16 pounds, depending on the drug, dose, and duration. These increases in weight were linear over time and were accompanied by a marked increase in preference for sweets. Ultimately, excessive weight gain was the most common cause for discontinuation of treatment, occurring in half of the patients, and significant weight loss occurred when patients stopped taking the drug. These findings show that chronic administration of low to moderate doses of the TCAs frequently causes considerable weight gain and can significantly interfere with the ability to provide long-term maintenance therapy.

Gastrointestinal effects

Up to now we have discussed the side-effects that do not accompany treatment with the SSRIs. We shall now turn to the adverse effects that are associated with these drugs (Table V). The most common type of adverse effect is gastrointestinal (Dencker and Petersen, 1989; Dunbar, 1989). This is usually experienced as mild nausea, which resolves with continued treatment (Laws *et al*, 1990). Diarrhoea often accompanies treatment with an SSRI. Gastrointestinal distress may occasionally be severe and may be accompanied by vomiting.

CNS effects

It is not uncommon for patients to experience some degree of activating effect, especially early in treatment. This may present as racing thoughts, anxiety, nervousness, tremor, insomnia, or headache. Although some of the SSRIs have activating properties, the potential for abuse is minimal, perhaps because of the rapid development of tolerance to this effect and a lack of associated euphoria. One patient with depression and an undiagnosed eating disorder abused fluoxetine for its anorectic effects (Wilcox, 1987).

The SSRIs may also occasionally produce sedation, especially at higher doses (Saletu and Grunberger, 1985, 1988; Saletu *et al*, 1986; Doogan and Caillard, 1988). Indeed, it may be that some of the SSRIs are more prone to produce sedation than others. In our studies we found a 50% incidence of somnolence with paroxetine compared with an 8.3% incidence of sedation with fluoxetine. On the other hand, nervousness occurred in 9.8% of fluoxetine patients and in none of those receiving paroxetine.

The risk of other, more serious, adverse effects is probably similar with both the SSRIs and the earlier antidepressants. Although EEG studies and early clinical data suggested that the SSRIs are not associated with seizures (Wernicke, 1985; Sedgwick *et al*, 1987; Cooper, 1988), more recent experience has shown that seizures may occur, especially in overdose (Riddle *et al*, 1989; Ware and Stewart, 1989; Weber, 1989). As with other effective antidepressants, these agents may also induce mania (Settle and Settle, 1984; Turner *et al*, 1985; Chouinard and Steiner, 1986; Laporta *et al*, 1987; Lebegue, 1987; Hon and Preskorn, 1989).

Hypersensitivity reactions

Zimeldine, an early SSRI, was withdrawn because of serious hypersensitivity reactions. Fortunately, this does not appear to be a property of SSRIs in general, and has not been reported with other drugs in this class. In fact, several patients who had hypersensitivity reactions to zimeldine have been successfully, and safely, treated with other SSRIs (Chouinard and Jones, 1984; Montgomery *et al*, 1989).

Attempts at overdose

Available data suggest that the SSRIs are considerably safer than the TCAs in overdose (Pedersen *et al*, 1982; Banerjee, 1988; Cooper, 1988; Finnegan and Gagiola, 1988; Riddle *et al*, 1989). For example, no deaths have been attributable to fluoxetine overdose alone (Cooper, 1988). One of these overdoses was a 13-year-old boy with Tourette's syndrome and obsessive-compulsive disorder who ingested a large quantity of fluoxetine. The patient's symptomatic course after the overdose included a grand mal seizure, depressed ST segments on the ECG, nausea, dizziness, and headache. In general, fluoxetine was well tolerated and all the symptoms and signs remitted spontaneously (Riddle *et al*, 1989).

Fluvoxamine has been used in over 40 attempts at overdose, the maximum dose taken being 6.5g. One patient died, but the autopsy showed that the fluvoxamine tablets remained intact in the patient's stomach. The death was attributed to an overdose of propranolol (Banerjee, 1988).

Experience with other SSRIs has been similar to date. Twenty-eight patients have taken an overdose of paroxetine, the largest dose being 850mg. None of the patients died, had convulsions, cardiac complications, or even lost consciousness (data on file, SmithKline Beecham Pharmaceuticals). One patient took an overdose of citalopram, which resulted in plasma levels that were approximately six times the average therapeutic level, but no signs of severe toxicity were observed. In particular, no changes occurred in consciousness, ECG variables or blood pressure (Pedersen *et al*, 1982).

Effects on anxiety

Many clinicians will choose an antidepressant because of presumably beneficial side-effects, and some may be wary of prescribing an SSRI for patients with agitation and insomnia because these are potential side-effects of the SSRIs. However, experimental evidence suggests that these concerns are probably unfounded. An analysis of pooled placebo-controlled, double-blind studies of fluoxetine shows it to be significantly superior to placebo and TCAs in the treatment of patients with marked agitation (Montgomery, 1989b). This is probably also true for other SSRIs. For example, Shaw and Crimmins (1989) published the results of a multicentre study of citalopram versus amitriptyline, which showed that both drugs had significantly positive effects on anxiety despite the greater hypnotic effect of amitriptyline. Likewise, Dunbar (1990) found a significant early effect of paroxetine on anxiety symptoms associated with depression when compared with imipramine.

Effects on the dopaminergic system

Fluoxetine has been reported to produce or exacerbate extrapyramidal reactions in a few individuals, probably by an indirect influence on dopaminergic function (Meltzer *et al*, 1979; Bouchard *et al*, 1989; Tate, 1989). Tate (1989) described a 39-year-old patient who developed severe, intractable extrapyramidal reactions while taking a combination of fluoxetine and haloperidol. She was, however, able to take haloperidol alone without such side-effects both before and after her severe reaction to the combination.

In an early open trial of fluoxetine, Meltzer and colleagues (1979) described the development of a dystonic reaction in one of nine patients receiving the drug. This particular patient also had increased serum prolactin and decreased homovanillic acid in the cerebrospinal fluid, both of these factors suggesting a decrease in dopaminergic activity. Lipinski and colleagues (1989) recently described five patients with what appeared to be akathisia related to fluoxetine, and hypothesized that this may have been due to serotonergically mediated dopamine inhibition. This is supported by the finding that the SSRIs produce oral dyskinesia and exacerbate haloperidol-induced dystonia and parkinsonism in monkeys (Korsgaard *et al*, 1985). In our clinic, one patient on fluoxetine, who had never been exposed to neuroleptic treatment developed an oral-lingual dyskinesia typical of tardive dyskinesia.

The SSRIs are unlikely to inhibit dopamine function in all situations. Indeed, citalopram has been reported to increase the level of homovanillic acid in the cerebrospinal fluid, suggesting an increase in dopamine turnover (Bjerkenstedt *et al*, 1985). Citalopram has even been studied as a possible therapeutic agent in 13 patients with tardive dyskinesia, but was shown to have no positive or negative effect on either this syndrome or on parkinsonian symptoms (Korsgaard *et al*, 1986). Mandalos and Szarek (1990) reported a dose-related paranoid reaction with fluoxetine in one patient, which would not be expected if fluoxetine merely inhibited dopamine function.

Further study is required to evaluate the clinical significance of the interaction between the SSRIs and the dopaminergic system. It is doubtful that the SSRIs have true neuroleptic properties, and none of the current data indicate that psychosis improves with one of these drugs. It should also be remembered that other antidepressants — especially amoxapine, but also amitriptyline, nortriptyline, doxepin, trazodone, phenelzine, and tranylcypromine have been linked with extrapyramidal side-effects (Sedivec *et al*, 1970; Sathananthan and Gershon, 1973; Fann *et al*, 1976; Gabriel *et al*, 1976; Finder *et al*, 1982; Papini *et al*, 1982; Ross *et al*, 1983; Krishnan *et al*, 1984; Luna *et al*, 1984; Teusink *et al*, 1984; Zubenko *et al*, 1987; Lee, 1988; Pande and Max, 1989; Jarecke and Reid, 1990). Whether the SSRIs carry a greater or lesser risk of this type of side-effect remains to be determined.

Uncommon adverse reactions

Teicher and colleagues (1990) reported a potentially serious side-effect of fluoxetine. In their study, six patients suffering from depression and other psychiatric conditions developed intense, intrusive, and violent suicidal obsessions after two to seven weeks of treatment with fluoxetine. Great care must be taken when evaluating an uncontrolled trial such as this. Firstly, it is important to note that patients have also developed suicidal ideation after taking TCAs such as desipramine (Damluji and Ferguson, 1988). Rouillon and colleagues (1989) reported on a trial using maprotiline — a selectively noradrenergic antidepressant — which relates to this issue. In this study 1141 patients, considered to be maprotiline responders, were entered into a one-year study of maprotiline versus placebo. During the study 14 of the 521 patients receiving maprotiline attempted or completed suicide compared with only 1 out of 212 patients on placebo ($p = 0.03$). These findings which must, of course, be replicated, suggest that suicide attempts may be more likely with noradrenergic antidepressants than with placebo. The double-blind data available for fluoxetine and paroxetine, encompassing thousands of patients, show that treatment-emergent suicidal ideation is no more common with SSRI treatment than with a TCA or placebo — possibly even less so (Fava and Rosenbaum, 1990). Controlled studies have also shown that the SSRIs generally reduce pretreatment suicidal ideation more than the TCAs (Muijen *et al*, 1988; Mullin *et al*, 1988; Wakelin, 1988; Gaszner, 1989; Montgomery, 1989a).

Adverse effects on sexual function, primarily anorgasmia, have also been reported (Kline, 1989; Lydiard and George 1989; Modell, 1989). Of the first 60 patients treated with fluoxetine in one clinic, five (8.3%) developed sexual side-effects: either anorgasmia or delayed orgasm. However, three of these five patients had experienced sexual side-effects with previous antidepressants. Kline (1989) and Modell (1989) have reported cases of repeated yawning, clitoral engorgement, and orgasm associated with fluoxetine. However, whether the SSRIs are more prone to cause sexual side-effects than other antidepressants remains to be studied. The reports of delayed ejaculation raise the question as to whether an SSRI may be helpful for some patients with premature ejaculation. Such areas bear watching as they significantly affect the future of these compounds.

During clinical testing of fluoxetine we observed three cases of adverse reactions characterized by arthralgia, rash, and lymphadenopathy. However, extensive medical and laboratory testing showed no abnormalities and these symptoms and signs resolved when fluoxetine was discontinued. Miller and colleagues (1989) recently reported a somewhat similar case in which a 27-year-old man developed a syndrome of fever, arthralgia, rash, and lymphadenopathy three to four weeks after starting to take fluoxetine. It was concluded that this represented a case of serum sickness. This reaction remains to be characterized further.

As the SSRIs come into wider use there will be more reports of uncommon or interesting adverse reactions. For example, fluoxetine has been linked to the syndrome of inappropriate antidiuretic hormone secretion in one patient (Hwang and Magraw, 1989), a 75-year-old male with recurrent depression, who developed a serum sodium of 126nmol/l soon after starting to take fluoxetine. No other cause could be determined for the syndrome, which resolved when fluoxetine was discontinued.

Some of these uncommon side-effects may not actually be side-effects; for example, Forrest (1990) published an interesting case report of a 50-year-old woman whose maintenance medication was changed to fluoxetine. Her psychiatric status improved but her menstrual cycles, which had ceased several years ago, resumed. She underwent extensive medical evaluation, including a dilatation and currettage, for evaluation of this 'side-effect' and the entire evaluation proved negative. It appeared that her previous psychotropic medications had suppressed her menstrual function, which then reappeared when she was switched to fluoxetine.

Conclusions

The SSRIs represent a significant improvement over earlier antidepressants in their side-effect profile. Although most of the published comparative studies have been against amitriptyline and imipramine, which may have biased the side-effect outcome in favour of the SSRIs, it is likely that refinement in dosing regimens, such as once-daily administration and the use of lower doses, will further improve the side-effect profile of these agents. As these drugs are used by greater numbers of patients there will be reports of less common side-effects, some of which may be potentially serious, and these will help to put the SSRIs into their proper clinical perspective.

References

Ahlfors UG, Elovaara S, Harma P, *et al* (1988) Clinical multicentre study of citalopram compared double-blindly with mianserin in depressed patients in Finland. *Nord Psykiatr Tidsskr* **42**, 201-210.

Altamura AC, Montgomery SA and Wernicke JF (1988) The evidence for 20mg a day of fluoxetine as the optimal dose in the treatment of depression. *Br J Psychiatry* **153**, 109-112.

Altamura AC, Percudani M, Guercetti G, *et al* (1989) Efficacy and tolerability of fluoxetine in the elderly: a double-blind study versus amitriptyline. *Int Clin Psychopharmacol* **4** (Suppl 1), 103-106.

Amin M, Lehmann H and Mirmiran J (1989) A double-blind, placebo-controlled, dose-finding study with sertraline. *Psychopharmacol Bull* **25** (2), 164-167.

Banerjee AK (1988) Recovery from prolonged cerebral depression after fluvoxamine overdose. *Br Med J* **296**, 1774.

Bascara L (1989) A double-blind study to compare the effectiveness and tolerability of paroxetine and amitriptyline in depressed patients. *Acta Psychiatr Scand* **80**, 141-142.

Battegay R, Hager M and Rauchfleisch U (1985) Double-blind comparative study of paroxetine and amitriptyline in depressed patients of a university psychiatric outpatient clinic (pilot study). *Neuropsychobiology* **13**, 31-37.

Berken GH, Weinstein DO and Stern WC (1984) Weight gain: A side effect of tricyclic antidepressants. *J Affective Disord* **7**, 133-138.

Bernstein JG (1987) Induction of obesity by psychotropic drugs. *Ann NY Acad Sci* **499**, 203-215.

Bernstein JG (1988) Psychotropic drug induced weight gain: mechanisms and management. *Clin Neuropharmacol* **11** (Suppl 1), S194-S206.

Bjerkenstedt L, Edman G, Flyckt L, *et al* (1985) Clinical and biochemical effects of citalopram, a selective 5-HT reuptake inhibitor — a dose-response study in depressed patients. *Psychopharmacology* **87**, 253-259.

Boeck V, Jrgensen A and Overo KF (1984) Comparative animal studies on cardiovascular toxicity of tri- and tetracyclic antidepressants and citalopram; relation to drug plasma levels. *Psychopharmacology* **82**, 275-281.

Bouchard JM, Delaunay J, Delisle JP, *et al* (1987) Citalopram versus maprotiline: a controlled, clinical multicentre trial in depressed patients. *Acta Psychiatr Scand* **76**, 583-592.

Bouchard RH, Pourcher E and Vincent P (1989) Fluoxetine and extrapyramidal side effects [letter]. *Am J Psychiatry* **146**, 1352-1353.

Bramanti P, Ricci RM, Roncari R, *et al* (1988) An Italian multicenter experience with fluvoxamine, a new antidepressant drug, versus imipramine. *Curr Ther Res Clin Exp* **43**, 718-725.

Bremner JD (1984) Fluoxetine in depressed patients: a comparison with imipramine. *J Clin Psychiatry* **45** 414-419.

Bressa GM, Brugnoli R and Pancheri P (1989) A double-blind study of fluoxetine and imipramine in major depression. *Int Clin Psychopharmacol* **4** (Suppl 1), 69-73.

Byerley WF, Reimherr FW, Wood DR, *et al* (1988) Fluoxetine, a selective serotonin uptake inhibitor, for the treatment of outpatients with major depression. *J Clin Psychopharmacol* **8**, 112-115.

Chouinard G (1985) A double-blind controlled clinical trial of fluoxetine and amitriptyline in the treatment of outpatients with major depressive disorder. *J Clin Psychiatry* **46** (3), 32-37.

Chouinard G and Jones B (1984) No crossover of hypersensitivity between zimelidine and fluoxetine. *Can Med Assoc J* **131**, 1190.

Chouinard G and Steiner W (1986) A case of mania induced by high-dose fluoxetine treatment. *Am J Psychiatry* **143**, 686.

Christensen P, Thomsen HY, Pedersen OL, *et al* (1985) Orthostatic side effects of clomipramine and citalopram during treatment for depression. *Psychopharmacology* **86**, 383-385.

Cohn JB, Collins G, Ashbrook E, *et al* (1989) A comparison of fluoxetine, imipramine and placebo in patients with bipolar depressive disorder. *Int Clin Psychopharmacol* **4**, 313-322.

Cohn JB and Wilcox C (1985) A comparison of fluoxetine, imipramine, and placebo in patients with major depressive disorder. *J Clin Psychiatry* **46** (3), 26-31.

Cooper GL (1988) The safety of fluoxetine — An update. *Br J Psychiatry* **153**, 77-86.

Corne SJ and Hall JR (1989) A double-blind comparative study of fluoxetine and dothiepin in the treatment of depression in general practice. *Int Clin Psychopharmacol* **4**, 245-254.

Damluji NF and Ferguson JM (1988) Paradoxical worsening of depressive symptomatology caused by antidepressants. *J Clin Psychopharmacol* **8**, 347-349.

Danish University Antidepressant Group (1986) Citalopram: clinical effect profile in comparison with clomipramine. A controlled multicenter study. *Psychopharmacology* **90**, 131-138.

Dencker SJ and Petersen HE (1989) Side-effect profile of citalopram and reference antidepressants in depression. In: Montgomery SA (ed.) *Citalopram: the New Antidepressant from Lundbeck Research*, pp.31-42. Amsterdam: Excerpta Medica.

De-Wilde J, Mertens C, Overo KF, *et al* (1985) Citalopram versus mianserin. A controlled, double-blind trial in depressed patients. *Acta Psychiatr Scand* **72**, 89-96.

De-Wilde JE, Mertens C and Wakelin JS (1983) Clinical trials of fluvoxamine vs chlorimipramine with single and three times daily dosing. *Br J Clin Pharmacol* **15** (Suppl 3), 427S-431S.

Dick P and Ferrero E (1983) A double-blind comparative study of the clinical efficacy of fluvoxamine and chlorimipramine. *Br J Clin Pharmacol* **15** (Suppl 3), 419S-425S.

Dominguez RA, Goldstein BJ, Jacobson AF, *et al* (1985) A double-blind placebo-controlled study of fluvoxamine and imipramine in depression. *J Clin Psychiatry* **46**, 84-87.

Doogan DP and Caillard V (1988) Sertraline: A new antidepressant. *J Clin Psychiatry* **49** (8), 46-51.

Dornseif BE, Dunlop SR, Potvin JH, *et al* (1989) Effect of dose escalation after low-dose fluoxetine therapy. *Psychopharmacol Bull* **25** (1), 71-79.

Dunbar GC (1989) An interim overview of the safety and tolerability of paroxetine. *Acta Psychiatr Scand* **80**, 135-137.

Dunbar GC (1990) The efficacy profile of paroxetine, a new antidepressant, compared with imipramine and placebo. *17th CINP Congress Abstracts* **1**, 17.

Edwards JG, Goldie A and Papayanni-Papasthatis S (1989) Effect of paroxetine on the electro-cardiogram. *Psychopharmacology* **97**, 96-98.

Fabre L (1989) Sertraline treatment of geriatric major depression compared with amitriptyline. In: Stefanis CN, Soldatos CR and Rabavilas AD (eds.) *Psychiatry Today: VIII World Congress of Psychiatry Abstracts,* p.711. New York: Elsevier.

Fabre LF and Putman HP (1987) A fixed-dose clinical trial of fluoxetine in outpatients with major depression. *J Clin Psychiatry* **48**, 406-408.

Fann WE, Sullivan JL and Richman BW (1976) Dyskinesias associated with tricyclic antidepressants. *Br J Psychiatry* **128**, 490-493.

Fava M and Rosenbaum JF (1990) Suicidality and fluoxetine, is there a relationship? New Abstract **475**. Presented at the *Annual Meeting of the American Psychiatric Association*, New York, May.

Fawcett J, Zajecka JM, Kravitz HM, *et al* (1989) Fluoxetine versus amitriptyline in adult outpatients with major depression. *Curr Ther Res Clin Exp* **45**, 821-832.

Feighner JP (1985) A comparative trial of fluoxetine and amitriptyline in patients with major depressive disorder. *J Clin Psychiatry* **46**, 369-372.

Feighner JP and Boyer WF (1989) Paroxetine in the treatment of major depression. *Acta Psychiatr Scand* **80**, 125-129.

Feighner JP, Boyer WF, Meredith CH, *et al* (1989a) A double-blind comparison of fluoxetine, imipramine and placebo in outpatients with major depression. *Int Clin Psychopharmacol* **4**, 127-134.

Feighner JP, Boyer WF, Meredith CH, *et al* (1989b) A placebo-controlled inpatient comparison of fluvoxamine maleate and imipramine in major depression. *Int Clin Psychopharmacol* **4**, 239-244.

Feighner JP and Cohn JB (1985) Double-blind comparative trials of fluoxetine and doxepin in geriatric patients with major depressive disorder. *J Clin Psychiatry* **46** (3), 20-25.

Ferreri M (1989) Fluoxetine versus amineptine in the treatment of outpatients with major depressive disorders. *Int Clin Psychopharmacol* **4** (Suppl 1), 97-101.

Finder E, Lin KM and Ananth J (1982) Dystonic reaction to amitriptyline [letter]. *Am J Psychiatry* **139**, 1220.

Finnegan KT and Gagiola JM (1988) Fluoxetine overdose. *Am J Psychiatry* **145**, 1604.

Fisch C (1985) Effect of fluoxetine on the electrocardiogram. *J Clin Psychiatry* **46** (3), 42-44.

Forrest DV (1990) Reappearance of menses in a patient taking fluoxetine. *Am J Psychiatry* **147**, 257.

Gabriel E, Karobath M and Lenz G (1976) The extrapyramidal symptoms in the combination of long-term lithium therapy with nortriptyline. A case report on the formation of a pathogenesis hypothesis. *Nervenarzt* **47**, 46-48.

Gagiano CA, Mueller PGM, Fourie J, *et al* (1989) The therapeutic efficacy of paroxetine: (a) an open study in patients with major depression not responding to antidepressants; (b) a double-blind comparison with amitriptyline in depressed outpatients. *Acta Psychiatr Scand* **80**, 130-131.

Gaszner P (1989) In: Stefanis CN, Soldatos CR and Rabavilas AD (eds.) *Psychiatry Today: VIII World Congress of Psychiatry Abstracts*, p.55. New York: Elsevier.

Gravem A, Amthor KF, Astrup C, *et al* (1987) A double-blind comparison of citalopram (Lu 10-171) and amitriptyline in depressed patients. *Acta Psychiatr Scand* **75**, 478-486.

Guelfi JD, Dreyfus JF and Pichot P (1983) A double-blind controlled clinical trial comparing fluvoxamine with imipramine. *Br J Clin Pharmacol* **15** (Suppl 3), 411S-417S.

Guillibert E, Pelicier Y, Archambault JP, *et al* (1989) A double-blind, multicentre study of paroxetine versus clomipramine in depressed elderly patients. *Acta Psychiatr Scand* **80**, 132-134.

Guy W, Manov G and Wilson WH (1986) Double blind dose determination study of new antidepressant — sertraline. *Drug Dev Res* **9**, 267-272.

Guy W, Wilson WH, Ban TA, *et al* (1984) A double-blind clinical trial of fluvoxamine and imipramine in patients with primary depression. *Psychopharmacol Bull* **20** (1), 73-78.

Hamilton BA, Jones PG, Hoda AN, *et al* (1989) Flupenthixol and fluvoxamine in mild to moderate depression: A comparison in general practice. *Pharmatherapeutica* **5**, 292-297.

Harto NE, Spera KF and Branconnier RJ (1988) Fluoxetine-induced reduction of body mass in patients with major depressive disorder. *Psychopharmacol Bull* **24** (2), 220-223.

Hebenstreit GF, Fellerer K, Zoechling R, *et al* (1989) A pharmacokinetic dose titration study in adult and elderly depressed patients. *Acta Psychiatr Scand* **80**, 81-84.

Hon DE and Preskorn SH (1989) Mania during fluoxetine treatment for recurrent depression. *Am J Psychiatry* **146**, 1638-1639.

Hwang AS and Magraw RM (1989) Syndrome of inappropriate secretion of antidiuretic hormone due to fluoxetine. *Am J Psychiatry* **146**, 399.

Hyttel J (1982) Citalopram — pharmacological profile of a specific serotonin uptake inhibitor with antidepressant activity. *Prog Neuropsychopharmacol Biol Psychiatry* **6**, 277-295.

Itil TM, Shrivastava RK, Mukherjee S, *et al* (1983) Double blind placebo controlled study of fluvoxamine and imipramine in outpatients with primary depression. *Br J Clin Pharmacol* **15**, 433S-438S.

Jarecke CR and Reid PJ (1990) Acute dystonic reaction induced by a monoamine oxidase inhibitor. *J Clin Psychopharmacol* **10**, 144-145.

Jouvent R, Baruch P, Ammar S, *et al* (1989) Fluoxetine efficacy in depressives with impulsivity vs blunted affect. In: Stefanis CN, Soldatos CR, Rabavilas AD (eds.) *Psychiatry Today: VIII World Congress of Psychiatry Abstracts*, p. 398. New York: Elsevier.

Kline MD (1989) Fluoxetine and anorgasmia. *Am J Psychiatry* **146**, 804-805.

Klok CJ, Brouwer GJ, van-Praag HM, *et al* (1981) Fluvoxamine and clomipramine in depressed patients. A double-blind clinical study. *Acta Psychiatr Scand* **64**, 1-11.

Korsgaard S, Gerlach J and Christensson E (1985) Behavioral aspects of serotonin-dopamine interaction in the monkey. *Eur J Pharmacol* **118**, 245-252.

Korsgaard S, Noring U, Povlsen UJ, *et al* (1986) Effects of citalopram, a specific serotonin uptake inhibitor, in tardive dyskinesia and parkinsonism. *Clin Neuropharmacol* **9**, 52-57.

Krishnan KR, France RD and Ellinwood EH Jr (1984) Tricyclic-induced akathisia in patients taking conjugated estrogens. *Am J Psychiatry* **141**, 696-697.

Kuhs H and Rudolf GAE (1989) A double-blind study of the comparative antidepressant effect of paroxetine and amitriptyline. *Acta Psychiatr Scand* **80**, 145-146.

Lapierre YD, Browne M, Horn E, *et al* (1987) Treatment of major affective disorder with fluvoxamine. *J Clin Psychiatry* **48**, 65-68.

Laporta M, Chouinard G, Goldbloom D, et al (1987) Hypomania induced by sertraline, a new serotonin reuptake inhibitor. Am J Psychiatry **144**, 1513-1514.

Laursen AL, Mikkelsen PL, Rasmussen S, et al (1985) Paroxetine in the treatment of depression — a randomized comparison with amitriptyline. Acta Psychiatr Scand **71**, 249-255.

Laws D, Ashford JJ and Anstee JA (1990) A multicentre double-blind comparative trial of fluvoxamine versus lorazepam in mixed anxiety and depression treated in general practice. Acta Psychiatr Scand **81**, 185-189.

Lebegue B (1987) Mania precipitated by fluoxetine. Am J Psychiatry **144**, 1620.

Lee HK (1988) Dystonic reactions to amitriptyline and doxepin [letter]. Am J Psychiatry **145**, 649.

Levine S, Deo R and Mahadevan K (1987) A comparative trial of a new antidepressant, fluoxetine. Br J Psychiatry **150**, 653-655.

Lipinski JF Jr, Mallya G, Zimmerman P, et al (1989) Fluoxetine-induced akathisia: clinical and theoretical implications. J Clin Psychiatry **50**, 339-342.

Luna OC, Jayatilaka A and Walker V (1984) Amoxapine and extrapyramidal symptoms [letter]. J Clin Psychiatry **45**, 407.

Lydiard RB and George MS (1989). Fluoxetine-related anorgasmy [letter] South Med J **82**, 933-934.

Lydiard RB, Laird LK, Morton WA Jr, et al (1989) Fluvoxamine, imipramine, and placebo in the treatment of depressed outpatients: Effects on depression. Psychopharmacol Bull **25** (1), 68-70.

Mandalos GE and Szarek BL (1990) Dose-related paranoid reaction associated with fluoxetine. J Nerv Ment Dis **178**, 57-58.

Masco HL and Sheetz MS (1985) Double-blind comparison of fluoxetine and amitriptyline in the treatment of major depressive illness. Adv Ther **2**, 275-284.

Meltzer HY, Young, M, Metz, J, et al (1979) Extrapyramidal side effects and increased serum prolactin following fluoxetine, a new antidepressant. J Neural Transm **45**, 165-175.

Mertens C (1989) Citalopram versus mianserin: a controlled double-blind trial in depressed patients. In: Montgomery SA (ed.) Citalopram: the New Antidepressant from Lundbeck Research, pp.50-55. Amsterdam: Excerpta Medica

Mertens C and Pintens H (1988) Paroxetine in the treatment of depression. A double-blind multicenter study versus mianserin. Acta Psychiatr Scand **77**, 683-688.

Miller LG, Bowman RC, Mann D, et al (1989) A case of fluoxetine-induced serum sickness. Am J Psychiatry **146**, 1616-1617.

Modell JG (1989) Repeated observations of yawning, clitoral engorgement, and orgasm associated with fluoxetine administration. J Clin Psychopharmacol **9**, 63-65.

Montgomery SA (1989a) 5-HT reuptake inhibitors in the treatment of depression. In: Montgomery SA (ed.) Citalopram: the New Antidepressant from Lundbeck Research, pp.1-10. Amsterdam: Excerpta Medica.

Montgomery SA (1989b) Fluoxetine in the treatment of anxiety, agitation and suicidal thoughts. In: Stefanis CN, Soldatos CR and Rabavilas AD (eds.) Psychiatry Today: VIII World Congress of Psychiatry Abstracts, p.335. New York: Elsevier.

Montgomery SA, Gabriel R, James D, et al (1989) Hypersensitivity to zimeldine without cross reactivity to fluoxetine. Int Clin Psychopharmacol **4** (Suppl 1), 27-29.

Moro F, Scapagnini U, Scaletta S, et al (1981) Serotonin nerve endings and regulation of pupillary diameter. Ann Opthalmol **13**, 487-490.

Muijen M, Roy D, Silverstone T, et al (1988) A comparative clinical trial of fluoxetine, mianserin and placebo in depressed outpatients. Acta Psychiatr Scand **78**, 384-390.

Mullin JM, Pandita-Gunawardena VR and Whitehead AM (1988) Double-blind comparison of fluvoxamine and dothiepin in the treatment of major affective disorder. Br J Clin Pract **42**, 51-55.

Norton KR, Sireling LI, Bhat AV, et al (1984) A double-blind comparison of fluvoxamine, imipramine and placebo in depressed patients. J Affective Disord **7**, 297-308.

Overo KF (1989) The pharmacokinetic and safety evaluation of citalopram from preclinical and clinical data. In: Montgomery SA (ed.) Citalopram: the New Antidepressant from Lundbeck Research, pp.22-30. Amsterdam: Excerpta Medica.

Pande AC and Max P (1989) A dystonic reaction occurring during treatment with tranylcypromine. *J Clin Psychopharmacol* **9**, 229-230.

Papini M, Martinetti MG and Pasquinelli A (1982) Trazodone symptomatic extrapyramidal disorders of infancy and childhood. *Ital J Neurol Sci* **3**, 161-162.

Pederson OL, Kragh-Srensen P, Bjerre M, *et al* (1982) Citalopram, a selective serotonin reuptake inhibitor: clinical antidepressive and long-term effect — a phase II study. *Psychopharmacology* **77**, 199-204.

Perry PJ, Garvey MJ, Kelly MW, *et al* (1989) A comparative trial of fluoxetine versus trazodone in outpatients with major depression. *J Clin Psychiatry* **50**, 290-294.

Peselow ED, Filippi AM, Goodnick P, *et al* (1989) The short- and long-term efficacy of paroxetine HCl: A. Data from a 6-week double-blind parallel design trial vs. imipramine and placebo. *Psychopharmacol Bull* **25** (2), 267-271.

Prager G, Cimander K, Wagner W, *et al* (1986) The cardiotropic effect of antidepressants: A comparison with fluvoxamine. *Adv Pharmacother* **2**, 133-150.

Reimherr FW, Byerley WF, Ward MF, *et al* (1988) Sertraline, a selective inhibitor of serotonin uptake, for the treatment of outpatients with major depressive disorder. *Psychopharmacol Bull* **24** (1), 200-205.

Riddle MA, Brown N, Dzubinski D, *et al* (1989) Fluoxetine overdose in an adolescent. *J Am Acad Child Adolesc Psychiatry* **28**, 587-588.

Ross DR, Walker JI and Peterson J (1983) Akathisia induced by amoxapine. *Am J Psychiatry* **140**, 115-116.

Rouillon F, Phillips R, Surrier D, *et al* (1989) Rechutes de depression unipolaire et efficacite del la maprotiline. *L'Encephale* **15**, 527-534.

Saletu B and Grunberger J (1985) Classification and determination of cerebral bioavailability of fluoxetine: pharmacokinetic, pharmaco-EEG, and psychometric analyses. *J Clin Psychiatry* **46** (3), 45-52.

Saletu B and Grunberger J (1988) Drug profiling by computed electroencephalography and brain maps, with special consideration of sertraline and its psychometric effects. *J Clin Psychiatry* **49** (8), 59-71.

Saletu B, Grunberger J and Linzmayer L (1986) On central effects of serotonin re-uptake inhibitors: quantitative EEG and psychometric studies with sertraline and zimelidine. *J Neural Transm* **67**, 241-266.

Saletu B, Schjerve M, Grunberger J, *et al* (1977) Fluvoxamine — a new serotonin re-uptake inhibitor: first clinical and psychometric experiences in depressed patients. *J Neural Transm* **41**, 17-36.

Sathananthan GL and Gershon S (1973) Imipramine withdrawal: an akathisia-like syndrome. *Am J Psychiatry* **130**, 1286-1287.

Sedgwick EM, Cilasun J and Edwards JG (1987) Paroxetine and the electroencephalogram. *J Psychopharmacol* **1**, 31-34.

Sedivec V, Valenova Z and Paceltova L (1970) Persistent extrapyramidal oral dyskinesias following treatment with thymoleptics. *Act Nerv Super (Praha)* **12**, 67-68.

Settle EC Jr and Settle GP (1984) A case of mania associated with fluoxetine. *Am J Psychiatry* **141**, 280-281.

Shaw DM and Crimmins RA (1989) A multicentre trial of citalopram and amitriptyline in major depressive illness. In: Montgomery SA (ed.) *Citalopram: the New Antidepressant from Lundbeck Research*, pp.43-49. Amsterdam: Excerpta Medica.

Shaw DM, Thomas DR, Briscoe MH, *et al* (1986) A comparison of the antidepressant action of citalopram and amitriptyline. *Br J Psychiatry* **149**, 515-517.

Siddiqui UA, Chakravarti SK and Jesinger DK (1985) The tolerance and antidepressive activity of fluvoxamine as a single dose compared to a twice daily dose. *Curr Med Res Opin* **9**, 681-690.

South Wales Antidepressant Drug Trial Group (1988) A double-blind multi-centre trial of fluoxetine and dothiepin in major depressive illness. *Int Clin Psychopharmacol* **3**, 75-81.

Stark P and Hardison CD (1985) A review of multicenter controlled studies of fluoxetine vs. imipramine and placebo in outpatients with major depressive disorder. *J Clin Psychiatry* **46** (3), 53-58.

Tamminen TT and Lehtinen VV (1989) A double-blind parallel study to compare fluoxetine with doxepin in the treatment of major depressive disorders. *Int Clin Psychopharmacol* **4** (Suppl 1), 51-56.

Tasker TCG, Kaye CM, Zussman BD, *et al* (1989) Paroxetine plasma levels: lack of correlation with efficacy or adverse events. *Acta Psychiatr Scand* **80**, 152-155.

Tate JL (1989) Extrapyramidal symptoms in a patient taking haloperidol and fluoxetine. *Am J Psychiatry* **146**, 399-400.

Teicher MH, Glod C and Col JO (1990) Emergence of intense suicidal preoccupation during fluoxetine treatment. *Am J Psychiatry* **147**, 207-210.

Teusink JP, Alexopoulos GS and Shamoian CA (1984) Parkinsonian side effects induced by a monoamine oxidase inhibitor. *Am J Psychiatry* **141**, 118-119.

Theesen KA and Marsh WR (1989) Relief of diabetic neuropathy with fluoxetine. *DICP* **23**, 572-574.

Timmerman L, de-Beurs P, Tan BK, *et al* (1987) A double-blind comparative clinical trial of citalopram vs maprotiline in hospitalized depressed patients. *Int Clin Psychopharmacol* **2**, 239-253.

Turner SM, Jacob RG, Beidel DC, *et al* (1985) A second case of mania associated with fluoxetine. *Am J Psychiatry* **142**, 274-275.

Upward JW, Edwards JG, Goldie A, *et al* (1988) Comparative effects of fluoxetine and amitriptyline on cardiac function. *Br J Clin Pharmacol* **26**, 399-402.

Wakelin JS (1988) The role of serotonin in depression and suicide: Do serotonin reuptake inhibitors provide a key? In: Gastpar M and Wakelin JS (eds.) *Selective 5-HT reuptake inhibitors: Novel or Commonplace agents?,* pp.70-83. Basel: Karger.

Ware MR and Stewart RB (1989) Seizures associated with fluoxetine therapy. *DICP Ann Pharmacother* **23**, 428.

Weber JJ (1989) Seizure activity associated with fluoxetine therapy. *Clin Pharm* **8**, 296-298.

Wernicke JF (1985) The side effect profile and safety of fluoxetine. *J Clin Psychiatry* **46** (3), 59-67.

Wernicke JF, Dunlop SR, Dornseif BE, *et al* (1988) Low-dose fluoxetine therapy for depression. *Psychopharmacol Bull* **24** (1), 183-188.

Wilcox JA (1987) Abuse of fluoxetine by a patient with anorexia nervosa. *Am J Psychiatry* **144**, 1100.

Young JP, Coleman A and Lader MH (1987) A controlled comparison of fluoxetine and amitriptyline in depressed out-patients. *Br J Psychiatry* **151**, 337-340.

Zubenko GS, Cohen BM and Lipinski JF (1987) Antidepressant-related akathisia. *J Clin Psychopharmacol* **7**, 254-257.

9

Clinical use of the selective serotonin re-uptake inhibitors

W.F. Boyer, G.A. McFadden, and J.P. Feighner

Introduction

Most of the currently published information concerning selective serotonin re-uptake inhibitors (SSRIs) comes from randomized, parallel group, placebo-controlled trials of four to eight weeks in duration. While such controlled data are essential, it is also true that clinical practice is anything but controlled. Patients present in a variety of situations, with a diversity of symptoms and an assortment of special concerns and mitigating circumstances. A combination of experience and good judgement is necessary to manage all of these situations. In this chapter, we will address a number of clinical issues that may arise with these drugs.

Weight loss

We discussed the indications for the SSRIs in chapters 5 and 6. However, some situations may still arise which require special consideration. For example, there may be concern about administering an SSRI to a patient who is underweight. Controlled studies and our experience indicate that clinically significant weight loss is usually limited to patients who are overweight initially. Nonetheless, clinicians should exercise caution if the patient has current symptoms of restricting bulimarexia as, in such a situation, the patient may abuse the medication in order to lose more weight (Wilcox, 1987).

Anxiety

Another concern may arise if the patient has significant levels of anxiety, as this may be a side-effect of SSRI treatment. However, the data available suggest that this concern might not be as critical as it may seem at first glance.

For example fluoxetine, imipramine, and placebo were studied in 698 outpatients with major depression. Improvement with fluoxetine and imipramine was not significantly different and was independent of whether the patient initially had psychomotor agitation, retardation, or no psychomotor changes (Beasley *et al*, 1990). We sometimes do find it necessary initially to treat anxiety or insomnia either by dose reduction or concomitant administration of a sedative or hypnotic drug. Benzodiazepines can be used effectively over the short-term to control these symptoms, doses being the same as if the benzodiazepines were being used alone.

Dosage schedule

The dosage schedule may also be manipulated to manage side-effects. Siddiqui and associates (1985) conducted a six-week, double-blind study of fluvoxamine given as a single daily dose or in divided doses. Patients were randomly assigned to receive 100mg of fluvoxamine either as a single daytime dose, a single night-time dose, or as 50mg twice daily. All three dosage regimens produced significant improvements, and no significant differences were observed among the three groups. However, patients receiving a single night-time dose experienced fewer side-effects that led to withdrawal before completion of the study than the other two groups (Siddiqui *et al*, 1985). Although all of the SSRIs have sufficiently long half-lives to allow once-a-day dosing, bedtime administration should not be used if the patient experiences activating effects.

Choice of an SSRI

Currently there are no published studies which compare one SSRI with another, but these are underway. In countries where more than one SSRI is available the choice between them must be made on clinical grounds. One should remember that most practitioners feel that there are significant clinical differences between the tricyclic antidepressants, even though their chemical structures differ very little. The chemical structures of the SSRIs are very different from each other, however, which suggests that there may be even greater differences. Experience with these compounds already points to some meaningful distinctions. The very long half-lives of fluoxetine and its metabolite norfluoxetine make it possible to treat patients every few days (Lemberger *et al*, 1985; Montgomery *et al*, 1987). Although this may be an advantage for patients who are unable to comply with a regular treatment regimen, it may lead to side-effects being more prolonged.

When selecting an antidepressant it is good practice to have an alternative in mind if the first drug is ineffective. If a monoamine oxidase inhibitor is a future option it would be best to choose an SSRI with a relatively short half-life as this will minimize the washout period before a switch is made to the monoamine oxidase inhibitor.

The side-effect profiles of the different SSRIs are likely to differ. Somnolence may be more common with fluvoxamine and paroxetine than with fluoxetine, sertraline, or citalopram. We have also observed a higher frequency of nausea with fluvoxamine and a lower incidence of weight loss with paroxetine. Since minimum effective doses have not been established for most of these drugs it is possible that some of these clinical differences may also be dose dependent.

Changes in tolerance

Occasionally, a patient may present who has a history of chronic or recurrent depression and who has been unable to tolerate fluoxetine in the past. We have treated several of these patients again with fluoxetine and found them to exhibit few or no adverse effects. Why this phenomenon occurs and whether it occurs with the other SSRIs remains to be determined.

Just as fluoxetine may sometimes 'lose' its side-effects it may also stop being effective at times. Diamond, Hamner, and Sunde (1989) reported two cases of major depression, two of obsessive-compulsive disorder (OCD), and a fifth with chronic low back pain in which fluoxetine was initially effective, but subsequently required increasing doses and eventually was no longer effective despite the administration of maximum doses (60-80mg). The true incidence of this tolerance with fluoxetine and the other SSRIs remains to be determined.

Speed of response

An important clinical issue is how to handle patients who do not respond adequately. The first point is when to decide that a patient is a non-responder. Schweizer and colleagues (1990) reported the results of a study in which 108 patients with major depression were treated with fluoxetine at a dose of 20mg/day in open fashion for three weeks. Non-responders were then assigned to fluoxetine at a dose of 20 or 60mg/day for five weeks. Both groups of patients demonstrated an equal and significant decrease in depression scores over this time, suggesting that three weeks was probably not a sufficiently long trial.

Most comparative studies indicate that the SSRIs begin to exert a therapeutic effect at about the same time as the tricyclic antidepressants (Dominguez *et al*, 1985; Dunbar, 1990). However, the response may sometimes be delayed to six weeks or more (Brup *et al*, 1982; Reimherr *et al*, 1988; Beck, 1989; Szulecka and Whitehead, 1989).

Clinicians will sometimes be faced with patients who do not appear to be responding and for whom something else should be done. In these cases combination treatment may be considered (Schraml *et al*, 1989).

Combination treatment

It is not uncommon in our practice to combine fluoxetine with a tricyclic antidepressant, especially when a seriously depressed patient has had a partial response to one or the other. Rather than discontinue the first drug and risk clinical deterioration while waiting for the second to work we administer both drugs together.

There is some published evidence that a combination of an SSRI and a tricyclic antidepressant may be helpful for patients who do not respond to the tricyclic. Weilburg and colleagues (1989) summarized their experience with 30 patients who had not responded to non-monoamine oxidase inhibitor antidepressants. All had fluoxetine added to their regimens, and 26 (86.7%) subsequently responded. Of these, eight relapsed when the other antidepressant was withdrawn but improved when it was restarted. There may be a theoretical basis for this combination since studies in animals indicate that co-administration of desipramine and fluoxetine results in a more rapid down-regulation of beta-adrenergic receptors than either drug alone (Baron *et al*, 1988).

The combination of an SSRI and a tricyclic antidepressant should be used with caution because of reports of serious toxicity. Preskorn and colleagues (1990) presented three such cases in which the reaction appeared to be linked to elevated plasma levels of the tricyclic compound. In two cases the patients experienced a grand mal seizure and in one case the patient experienced delirium.

The adjunctive use of lithium with an SSRI may also be helpful. Pope and colleagues (1988) reported on five depressed patients who had shown no improvement with trials of antidepressants from several chemical families, including fluoxetine. These patients responded when lithium was given in conjunction with fluoxetine.

Delgado and associates (1988) studied 38 consecutively admitted depressed patients who were refractory to standard antidepressant treatments. Twenty-eight patients completed a single-blind protocol involving at least two weeks of placebo and four to six weeks of fluvoxamine treatment. Eight (29%) were judged to be responders to fluvoxamine alone, eight (29%) responded to lithium augmentation of fluvoxamine, and two (7%) responded to fluvoxamine, lithium, and perphenazine.

Patients who take both lithium and fluoxetine should be cautioned about and observed for evidence of a serotonergic syndrome, which may at times be serious (Noveske *et al*, 1989). This is discussed more fully in chapter 4.

Other psychotropic drug combinations with SSRIs may have value when used to treat other conditions. For example, Linet (1989) reported a case of refractory depression treated with a combination of fluoxetine and amphetamine.

The combination of fluoxetine plus thyroid hormone was reported to be effective in one elderly patient with refractory depression (Crowe *et al*, 1990).

Panic disorder

We often use a two-step approach for the control of panic disorder. The first step is the rapid blockade of panic attacks with one of the high-potency benzodiazepines, while the second step provides for long-term prophylaxis by the use of an SSRI or other antidepressant.

The immediate control of panic disorder symptoms may be achieved with standing daily regimens of the high-potency benzodiazepines, which should ideally be initiated during the first week of treatment.

Alprazolam, with a duration of action of four to six hours, may be started in a four times daily regimen to avoid 'breakthrough' panic attacks. It is very important to allow the patient, in conjunction with the clinician, to titrate the dosages at each of these times. At the proper dosage the patient will not experience subtherapeutic effects, such as 'surges' or 'waves' of panic; neither should the patient experience significant sedation or impaired performance.

The same schema may be used for clonazepam. The duration of action of clonazepam is 10-12 hours, so that blockade of panic attacks may be achieved with a twice-daily dosing regimen. These regimens for the high potency benzodiazepines should be maintained for approximately four to six weeks, during which time the long-term prophylactic therapies may become fully effective.

The second step is initiating treatment with an SSRI, tricyclic antidepressant, or monoamine oxidase inhibitor. Often it is most useful to begin such treatment after the panic attacks have been successfully blocked with one of the high-potency benzodiazepines, as this will facilitate patient comfort and compliance with the overall treatment plan. The dosage should be increased slowly, in order to minimize the 'jitteriness syndrome' frequently seen during initial treatment with any of the antidepressant, anti-panic medications.

For example, when using fluoxetine the dosage should ideally begin at 5mg/day with titration over at least a week to the 20mg range. When the antidepressant medication has remained at full dose for two to three weeks the patient should be tapered from the high-potency benzodiazepine. This should be at the rate of approximately 0.5mg/week, or as tolerated, so that anxiety symptoms are not exacerbated.

Giesecke (1990) reported a case which underlines how gradual the dosage titration may sometimes need to be. The patient was a 24-year-old male who was treated with fluoxetine for panic disorder. Following a single, 20mg dose of fluoxetine the patient experienced 18 hours of intense nervousness, headache, inability to concentrate, and increased panic and was unable to tolerate even 5mg doses. He was instructed to dissolve one 20mg capsule in 100ml of water or apple juice and to begin by taking 5ml of the solution, or 1mg of fluoxetine, nightly. The solution was kept refrigerated. Even with the 1mg dose the patient experienced some jitteriness, difficulty concentrating, and an increase in panic, but these problems diminished over the following two weeks. Subsequently, the dose could be increased in 1mg, and then 2mg, increments approximately every two weeks. It took three to four days for the effect of each increase to be fully felt, and the patient reported marked improvement at a dose of 10mg/night. Re-emergence of some symptoms prompted a gradual increase to 20mg/night on which he has fared very well.

Obsessive-compulsive disorder

Combination treatments may also be helpful in OCD. We have found that, ideally, the patient is begun on clomipramine, the dosage increasing to 150-200mg/day if side-effects allow. Electrocardiography is performed routinely after the dosage exceeds 150mg, regardless of the presence of side-effects. If the patient demonstrates a partial response, fluoxetine is added in doses of up to 40mg/day. We have found significant additive effects when both compounds are appropriately combined and particular attention is paid to side-effects.

Combination treatment with other medications may sometimes be helpful. Buspirone, at a dose of up to 30mg/day was added to fluoxetine in 12 patients with OCD who had not fully responded to 10 weeks of fluoxetine treatment alone, and produced a further improvement (Markovitz *et al*, 1989). Swerdlow and Andia (1989) reported that a combination of fluoxetine and trazodone was effective in the treatment of OCD when either drug given alone was not.

McDougle and associates (1989) examined the efficacy of adding a neuroleptic to the regimens of 17 patients with OCD who were refractory to an adequate trial of fluvoxamine alone. In some of these patients lithium had also been used as an adjunct. Nine patients responded to the combination, and it was observed that the existence of comorbid schizotypal features or tic-spectrum disorders predicted a positive response.

Hollander and colleagues (1990) reported on seven patients with DSM-IIIR OCD who had only a partial response to, or were unable to tolerate, fluoxetine, fluvoxamine, or clomipramine. In these patients, open fenfluramine augmentation at doses of 20 to 60mg/day was well tolerated and resulted in a further decrease in obsessions and compulsions in six patients.

Conclusions

The optimum clinical use of the SSRIs is evolving as these drugs come into wider use around the world. During this process it is reasonable to expect a number of reports in the literature of single cases or case series with interesting or unusual observations or outcomes. By combining this with his own increasing experience, the clinician can achieve the maximum benefits for his or her patients with minimal risk.

References

Baron BM, Ogden AM, Siegel BW, *et al* (1988) Rapid down regulation of beta-adrenoceptors by co-administration of desipramine and fluoxetine. *Eur J Pharmacol* **154**, 125-134.

Beasley C, Sayler M and Bosomworth J (1990) Fluoxetine in agitated and retarded depression. *17th CINP Congress Abstracts* **1**, 77.

Beck P (1989) Clinical properties of citalopram in comparison with other antidepressants: a quantitative metanalysis. In: Montgomery SA (ed.) *Citalopram: the New Antidepressant from Lundbeck Research*, pp.56-68. Amsterdam: Excerpta Medica.

Brup C, Meidahl B, Petersen IM, *et al* (1982) An early clinical phase II evaluation of paroxetine, a new potent and selective 5HT-uptake inhibitor in patients with depressive illness. *Pharmacopsychiatria* **15**, 183-186.

Crowe D, Collins JP and Rosse RB (1990) Thyroid hormone supplementation of fluoxetine treatment. *J Clin Psychopharmacol* **10**, 150-151.

Delgado PL, Price LH, Charney DS, *et al* (1988) Efficacy of fluvoxamine in treatment-refractory depression. *J Affective Disord* **15**, 55-60.

Diamond B, Hamner M and Sunde D (1989) Possible tolerance to the antidepressant, anti-obsessive-compulsive, and analgesic effects of fluoxetine. *Biol Psychiatry* **25** (Suppl 7A), 155A.

Dominguez RA, Goldstein BJ, Jacobson AF, *et al* (1985) A double-blind placebo-controlled study of fluvoxamine and imipramine in depression. *J Clin Psychiatry* **46**, 84-87.

Dunbar GC (1990) The efficacy profile of paroxetine, a new antidepressant, compared with imipramine and placebo. *17th CINP Congress Abstracts* **1**, 17.

Giesecke ME (1990) Overcoming hypersensitivity to fluoxetine in a patient with panic disorder. *Am J Psychiatry* **147**, 532-533.

Hollander E, DeCaria CM, Schneier FR, *et al* (1990) Fenfluramine augmentation of serotonin reuptake blockade antiobsessional treatment. *J Clin Psychiatry* **51**, 119-123.

Lemberger L, Bergstrom RF, Wolen RL, *et al* (1985) Fluoxetine: clinical pharmacology and physiologic disposition. *J Clin Psychiatry* **46** (3), 14-19.

Linet LS (1989) Treatment of a refractory depression with a combination of fluoxetine and d-amphetamine. *Am J Psychiatry* **146**, 803-804.

Markovitz PJ, Stagno SJ and Calabrese JR (1989) Buspirone augmentation of fluoxetine in obsessive-compulsive disorder. *Biol Psychiatry* **25** (Suppl 7A), 186A.

McDougle CJ, Goodman WK, Price LH, *et al* (1989) Neuroleptic addition in fluvoxamine-refractory OCD. *New Research Program and Abstracts, American Psychiatric Association 142nd Annual Meeting*, p.189.

Montgomery SA, James D, Hawley C, *et al* (1987) Plasma level relationship of once weekly or daily fluoxetine in the treatment of depression. *International Fluoxetine Symposium*, Tyrol Austria, October 13-17.

Noveske FG, Hahn KR and Flynn RJ (1989) Possible toxicity of combined fluoxetine and lithium. *Am J Psychiatry* **146**, 1515.

Pope HG Jr, McElroy SL and Nixon RA (1988) Possible synergism between fluoxetine and lithium in refractory depression. *Am J Psychiatry* **145**, 1292-1294.

Preskorn SH, Beber JH, Faul JC, *et al* (1990) Serious adverse effects of combining fluoxetine and tricyclic antidepressants. *Am J Psychiatry* **147**, 532.

Reimherr FW, Byerley WF, Ward MF, *et al* (1988) Sertraline, a selective inhibitor of serotonin uptake, for the treatment of outpatients with major depressive disorder. *Psychopharmacol Bull* **24** (1), 200-205.

Schraml F, Benedetti G, Hoyle K, *et al* (1989) Fluoxetine and nortriptyline combination therapy [letter]. *Am J Psychiatry* **146**, 1636-1637.

Schweizer E, Rickels K, Amsterdam JD, *et al* (1990) What constitutes an adequate antidepressant trial for fluoxetine? *J Clin Psychiatry* **51**, 8-11.

Siddiqui UA, Chakravarti SK and Jesinger DK (1985) The tolerance and antidepressive activity of fluvoxamine as a single dose compared to a twice daily dose. *Curr Med Res Opin* **9**, 681-690.

Swerdlow NR and Andia AM (1989) Trazodone-fluoxetine combination for treatment of obsessive-compulsive disorder [letter]. *Am J Psychiatry* **146**, 1637.

Szulecka TK and Whitehead AM (1989) Fluvoxamine versus amitriptyline in the treatment of depressed patients. In: Stefanis CN, Soldatos CR and Rabavilas AD (eds.) *Psychiatry Today: VIII World Congress of Psychiatry Abstracts*, p.268. New York: Elsevier.

Weilburg JB, Rosenbaum JF, Biederman J, *et al* (1989) Fluoxetine added to non-MAOI antidepressants converts non-responders: a preliminary report. *J Clin Psychiatry* **50**, 447-449.

Wilcox JA (1987) Abuse of fluoxetine by a patient with anorexia nervosa. *Am J Psychiatry* **144**, 1100.

Index

The following abbreviations are used in the index:
CNS   Central nervous system
SSRIs   Selective serotonin re-uptake inhibitors